The radical bourgeoisie

The radical bourgeoisie

The Ligue de l'enseignement and the origins of the Third Republic 1866–1885

KATHERINE AUSPITZ

CAMBRIDGE UNIVERSITY PRESS

CAMBRIDGE
LONDON   NEW YORK   NEW ROCHELLE
MELBOURNE   SYDNEY

Published by the Press Syndicate of the University of Cambridge
The Pitt Building, Trumpington Street, Cambridge CB2 1RP
32 East 57th Street, New York, NY 10022, USA
296 Beaconsfield Parade, Middle Park, Melbourne 3206, Australia

First published 1982

Printed in the United States of America

Library of Congress Cataloging in Publication Data
Auspitz, Katherine.
The radical bourgeoisie.
Bibliography: p.
Includes index.
1. France – Politics and government – 1848–
1870. 2. France – Politics and government –
1870–1940. 3. Radicalism – France. 4. Ligue
française de l'enseignement. I. Title.
DC331.A87   944.07   81-15462
ISBN 0 521 23861 7   AACR2

For my parents, John and Marie Holahan,
and in memory of my grandmother,
Catharine Dangler Maute

Contents

Acknowledgments

THIS BOOK DESCRIBES the social and political struggles that culminated, in 1881 and 1882, with the passage of the lois Ferry, laws establishing free, compulsory, secular primary schooling for French children of both sexes. I rejoice in that centenary and in the ideal of democratic community based on common literacy.

My own education delighted and strengthened me. Stanley Hoffmann, as generous as he is lucid, was my tutor at Radcliffe College; and he advised the dissertation with which this book began. David Landes gave the manuscript uncompromising scrutiny and efficacious support. Everyone who seeks to understand France is in Laurence Wylie's debt; and gratitude to one so kind is a special pleasure. Richard Cobb, my Oxford tutor, shared with me his boundless knowledge and love of France. From all my teachers I learned that a historian should acknowledge rather than suppress honest partisanship.

David Riesman has helped me, as he has helped legions, unstintingly. Sarah and Albert Hirschman have been dear and most erudite friends. Betso and Dick Shields gave me precious encouragement. Many friends criticized earlier versions of this book: Suzanne Berger, Stephen Bornstein, Emilie Buck, Duncan Foley, Clara Lovett, Katherine Lynch, Roy MacLeod, Alan Ritter, and my former student Robert Ambaras. Learning as a basis for fellowship does not seem to be a utopian notion in their company. I have been helped immeasurably, on every page, by the political and literary judgment of my husband, Josiah Lee Auspitz.

It is impossible to acknowledge individually all the French historians, archivists, and citizens who contributed to this book. Exceptional thanks are due to: M. E. Gautier, director of the *Service de Documentation* of the *Ligue de l'enseignement*; Maître Boivin, who shared his knowledge of the Seine-Maritime with me; M. C. Hohl, director of the *services d'Archives de l'Yonne*; and M. Hours, municipal archivist of Lyon, who obligingly set aside *fonds* for me to work with during the otherwise paralyzing *fermature annuelle*. Mme L'Henry of La Gravetière, Broye (Saône-et-Loire), made available to my family her agreeable flat in the Eighteenth Arrondissement of Paris. Mme Robert Parly found room for us on her farm at Fleury-la-Vallée in the Yonne.

Lastly, I would like to thank the Radcliffe Graduate Fund and the Center for European Studies at Harvard for financial support and camaraderie.

K.A.

Introduction: bourgeois radicalism after 1848

We are dealing with a people who belong in the marrow
of their bones to the Revolution, who marry, by tradition,
fear of the word with a profound love of the thing.
Jean Macé, *Les Origines de la Ligue de l'enseignement, 1861–1870*[1]

MOST RESPECTED WRITERS AGREE that in 1848 the bourgeois revolutionary ceased to exist. The term became, as "bourgeois gentleman" had once been, a ludicrous oxymoron. Confronted with the violent literalism of the poor, bourgeois radicals abandoned fraternity for repression and enlightened criticism for pious cant. The heirs of 1789, men of the commercial and industrial classes, free professionals, and peasant proprietors, found that talk of liberty and equality threatened their privileged positions; and so, it is argued, they relied upon authoritarian devices – the central administration, the church, and a Bonaparte – to keep order on their behalf. This, of course, was Marx's analysis of the collapse of the Second Republic. Tocqueville, similarly contemptuous, saw republicans as poseurs playing at revolution rather than continuing it; Flaubert's *Sentimental Education* told, unforgettably, the story of their disenchantment and capitulation and of the convergence in the "party of order" of the established and those who aspired to be established. Jules Michelet, describing the bourgeois as "liberal in principle, egoist in application," had even earlier anticipated the caricatured Radical of the Third Republic – with his heart on the left and his wallet on the right.[2]

Modern scholars have tended to concur with nineteenth-century commentators. In his monumental contribution to the *Oxford History of Modern Europe, France 1848–1945*, Theodore Zeldin has gone so far as to say, "It could be argued that after 1848 politics ceased to be a major preoccupation."[3] His view is shared by many, including the American political scientist Nicholas Wahl, who wrote that "in France the workers and the middle classes broke irrevocably in 1848. From then on they became the most violent enemies; consequently all hope was lost for associating the French worker with a 'reasonable' reformist movement led by the liberal bourgeoisie."[4]

The bourgeoisie is said to have turned then to the more mature pleasures of money making, and Emperor Napoleon III so judiciously man-

1

aged a policy of repression, concession, and social-overhead investment that nothing more was said of revolution until an accident, the surrounding of the emperor by the Prussians at Sedan, caused the imperial machine to collapse. Adolphe Thiers hastily substituted republicans at the head of the machine, largely because of the manifest incapacity of the pretender, Henry V; and thus the "accidental republic" was born of an understanding between Thiers and Otto von Bismarck, created by a German victory in 1870, and overthrown by another German invasion in 1940.

Historians have accepted as true this description of France: light-mindedly insurrectionist in revolutionary times, careerist in eras of administrative calm. Political scientists have elevated the narrative into a paradigm of alternating legislative and executive rule, a model of ideological politics unsupported by the aggregation of interests. Anglo-American moralists have found here a deplorable fable of the citizen and the deputy – incapable of voluntary association, powerless before the functionary, mired in *immobilisme*, and ready to welcome the Bonaparte or Bonaparte-surrogate who would deliver them.

That familiar interpretation, plausible as it may seem, remains incomplete and misleading. This book challenges it and asks a question that has, alas, not ceased to be pertinent: What do progressive people do when revolutions fail (as they so often do), or when they succeed most incompletely? Many, of course, do not survive to be perplexed by reaction. Happy, Stendhal said, the heroes dead before 1804, when Napoleon Bonaparte made himself emperor.[5] Some withdraw from politics in despair or revulsion. Others, trimmers or men horrified by the atrocity of civil war, opt for the blessings and emoluments of peace. However, there are – everywhere, perhaps, but certainly in France – people with democratic principles and cheerful dispositions who refuse to accept their defeat as definitive. They find comfort in their most obvious shortcomings: Failure so conspicuous must be corrigible. Jean Macé and those who, in association with him, organized the circles of the Ligue de l'enseignement were just this sort.

Historians who neglect Macé and others like him cannot account for the ceaseless activity of provincial republicans in the 1860s, nor for their success in municipal and departmental elections and in the general elections of 1869. Further, they are unable to explain either the increasingly pronounced radical character of the Third Republic in the seventies or the commitment of generations of French citizens, stalwarts of the Center and of the Left, to free, compulsory, secular education. They cannot bring themselves even to notice the many civic projects voluntarily undertaken in the 1860s and 1870s or, if they do admit them, to acknowledge their significance.

I contend that it was precisely in this period, the last decade of the Second Empire and the first decade of the Third Republic, that politics – reformist and increasingly radical republican politics – assumed national importance. In fact, it can be argued that far from marking the end of the radical persuasion, the events of 1848 initiated its most fruitful period, a period characterized by an extraordinary congruence of thought and action. French democrats, after repeated failure to create a republic, came to understand that success would come only when all citizens – peasants, workers, and women, as well as bourgeois men – believed themselves to be heirs of 1789. They also had the sense to see that propaganda alone would not accomplish this. Republicans had learned from 1848 that seizure of power was empty unless it gave expression to changes in the mores and self-definition of the people.

Those who laid the foundations of the Third Republic in the 1860s and 1870s seemed to work as people can when they look to the past, or a part of their past, for inspiration and to their posterity with hope. More elegant and persuasive statements of radical themes may have come earlier, in the upstart brilliance of the philosophes, or later, assured and definitive, from professors of the republican University like Emile Durkheim, Alain, Georges Lefebvre, and Marc Bloch; but this generation connected the aspirations of the eighteenth century with the institutions of the twentieth. The career of the tawdriest opportunist cannot be understood adequately without sympathetic consideration of the ideals he invoked, the ends with which decent contemporaries credited him or, at any rate, allied with him to accomplish.

It was the revolutionary society – egalitarian, secular, and civic – that radicals struggled throughout the nineteenth century to realize. They remained faithful to the Declaration of the Rights of Man and the Citizen of 1789: Indeed, the promiscuous circulation of this document was one of the improprieties cited by the prefect of the Somme when, in 1873, he dissolved the Ligue de l'enseignement in his department (as described in Chapter 3). Their principles were those upon which an earlier generation had proposed to reconstitute France: "*Men are born and remain free and equal in rights. Social distinctions may be based only on common utility* (Article I)" and "*No body or individual may exercise authority which does not emanate from the nation expressly.*" (Article III)[6]

Radicals understood freedom and equality to be inseparable, logically and constitutionally, from popular sovereignty. They were fiercely anticlerical, not from principled hostility to Catholic doctrine alone, but chiefly because they insisted that legitimate authority could not derive from supernatural, any more than from hereditary, pretensions. *Ni Dieu, ni maître.* They claimed the right of all to participate in governing; and, as heirs of the third estate, they rejected monopolies of public office conferred by birth or sacrament.

Radicalism continued to define itself as the antithesis of feudal Christianity. Radical ideology, as it developed during the nineteenth century, served to emphasize the differences between traditional and modern societies and to vindicate the movement away from one and toward the other as progress. Jules Michelet, the great republican historian and polemicist, pitted the old regime, which was based upon Arbitrary Grace – ascriptive hierarchies reigning according to *bon plaisir* – against a new society grounded in Necessary Justice.[7] Michelet's antinomies resemble others that are perhaps more familiar to English-speaking readers, such as Tönnies's *Gemeinschaft-Gesellschaft*, Sir Henry Maine's status-contract, or the American abolitionists' irrepressible conflict between slave-holding and free nations, and anticipate later French typologies created by republican scholars as engaged in the politics of their day as Michelet was in his own. Emile Durkheim, with audaciously counterintuitive use of the terms "mechanical" and "organic solidarity," assigned the frank pejorative "mechanical" to the unquestioned and unchosen groupings of traditional society while appropriating for modern associations all the flourishing warmth of the corporal metaphor.[8] Marc Bloch also, writing almost a century after Michelet, cast his *Feudal Society* in implicit antithesis to the most valued aspects of modern life: Political sovereignty was fragmented and capricious, economic life incalculable, the cosmos unintelligible. Society and nature alike repelled human reason and evaded human control.[9]

Above all, radicals repudiated passive or involuntary subordination. They believed in the free individual and the democratic nation, and these two fidelities underlay their *civisme*. Concern for solidarity marked them no less than secularism. They were not individualists, nor indeed, liberals, in any simple sense. None imagined that society could be maintained by the transactions of self-regarding actors. Most assumed, with metaphors like Rousseau's general will or Durkheim's collective conscience, a common culture prerequisite to social life; and although both writers have been vilified for the supposedly totalitarian implications of this insight,[10] there is nothing of tyranny in it. Tocqueville, whose commitment to liberty cannot be questioned, took it for granted that "society can exist only when a great number of men consider a great number of things under the same aspect, when they hold the same opinions upon many subjects and when the same occurrences suggest the same thoughts and impressions to their minds."[11]

Radicals understood that a political community remained to be accomplished in France. They recognized that people differed, but their main concerns were profoundly egalitarian: At the same time that their

4

ethics attempted to distinguish the legitimate consequences of individuals' diversity from the illegitimate ones, their politics contrived situations in which men would encounter each other as fellows, as *semblables*. Thus, their preoccupation with schools and clubs, the radical effort to educate and uplift the nation (*instruire et moraliser*), that is much scorned today as an effort to discipline the vagabond poor for factory labor, might reasonably be seen as their determination to empower citizens. Their militant rationalism, too, is better understood if it is not regarded as insensitivity to metaphysical questions, but as an attempt to fashion a language of civility with no privileged speakers. Tireless *vulgarisateurs*, they believed that their truths were demonstrable; and in their lectures and popular libraries one sees, zealous and unabating, the philosophes' horror of the esoteric. Denis Brogan, who has great sympathy for the radicals, thoroughly understands this. His reservation is a sensible one: Radicals, like Catholics, "too often forget . . . that people do not always believe what they are taught."[12]

The radicals never expected schooling alone to produce civility: Continuous association for common causes, the enterprise of voluntary associations, must complete civic education. A positive flowering of such joint endeavors marked the 1860s and 1870s in France. Men in industry and commerce and in the learned professions, in concert with republican workers, assumed social responsibilities, creating for themselves public roles in countless associations, some of which were philanthropic and cultural, others avowedly political: industrial associations and chambers of commerce, free trade and protectionist lobbies, trade unions, cooperatives, mutual-aid societies, popular libraries, evening courses, lecture series, workers' choral societies, masonic lodges, circles for the *belles lettres*, animal husbandry and agronomy groups, and innumerable organizations for the protection of working women, nursing mothers, apprentices, and factory children.

Ample evidence exists to substantiate these activities. National, departmental, and municipal archives contain police dossiers on republican militants, and more decorous dissidents can be traced in the applications of numerous charitable and educational groups for the legal status of "public utility," a designation that conferred legal personality and the right to acquire property. Inquests pursuant to these demands required scrutiny of by-laws and membership lists including the names, addresses, and occupations of adherents and, sometimes, verbatim minutes of meetings. Although these data are formal and obviously could be falsified easily (one can imagine compelling reasons for inflating or minimizing membership) they give some sense of a group's tendencies. Furthermore, the liberalizing law of June 10, 1868, which permitted public meetings, made available more precise information; indeed, the hope of better gauging the opposition's strength may have been the law's primary intent. The prefect or his deputy might attend any authorized meeting to report on its size and temper or to adjourn a gathering judged to threaten public order. The new legislation further required that every meeting be underwritten by two or more sponsors, who would be legally liable for its consequences. Willingness to undertake this statutory responsibility attested stronger commitment than mere dues-paying membership, yet sponsors were never lacking for a wide range of political and cultural gatherings.

Evidence of sustained gregariousness is so overwhelming that "bourgeois sociability" has itself become an object of study. Maurice Agulhon, its most suggestive interpreter, contrasts the bourgeois *cercle*, a frankly political masculine society of equals meeting in a public place, with the aristocratic salon, where guests defer to a host and to the presence of ladies before whom certain topics would not be broached. Agulhon rightly supposes a link between the "structural democracy which constitutes the new sociability and the political democracy which constitutes the liberal, then the republican left which finally gains a majority for the middle classes." He maintains, with admirable clearheadedness, that this development was an improvement and frankly celebrates "those aspects of democratic progress which were not deplorable." He proposes also, and the research on which this book is based entirely concurs, that "mass politics" would consist in placing "an echelon of liaison" between preexisting groups: A party emerges not as a gathering of individuals but of circles.[13]

The Ligue de l'enseignement was just such a concatenation. Indeed, it was the most ambitious and influential one. Founded by Jean Macé in 1866 to "encourage education" and to "seek through legal means to change laws and practices incompatible with the freedom of conscience and the equality of citizens,"[14] its work is properly seen as the response of diverse progressives to the failures of 1848 and the subsequent inability of Left Bonapartists to hold the emperor to reformist policies.

The league acted as an umbrella for secular, popular, republican, radical, and simply charitable groups. It united, loosely, Protestant philanthropists, Saint-Simonian millionaires, members of the International, future communards, cooperative artisans, provincial teachers and professionals, entrepreneurs, and journalists. It drew upon existing, more conservative Parisian societies as well as upon provincial groups and, while professing to be a "school of decentralization," gave a unified thrust to activities that had previously been isolated, desultory, and apolitical. In defining free, compulsory education as the overriding national necessity, it set forth the social nostrum of the Third Republic. The organizers of the league deliberately set out to establish a secular voice and organization in French politics, a presence in every commune and department that would urge the existing government in a "modern" direction and provide an alternative to a society based on the Catholic Church. To ignore the Ligue de l'enseignement and its scores of affiliate and corresponding groups is to ignore the infrastructure of the Third Republic, the cadres patiently but actively preparing themselves to govern.

Certainly, much in the politics of any nation is contingent. If the emperor had not suffered military defeat, he would not have been deposed by freethinkers' circulating libraries in concert with the chambers of commerce. There was no historical necessity for the capitulation of Napoleon III or for his gratuitously stupid acceptance of the war that led to his downfall.[15] Nevertheless, I do believe that the character of French politics in the first decades of the Third Republic was determined, not uniquely but necessarily, by the ascendancy of men whose political positions had been strengthened and, sometimes, established in the secularist voluntary associations of the 1860s.

To be sure, there remain questions about these men and their radicalism. First, what connection should be supposed to exist between the opinions of any intellectuals and the notions, feelings, and conduct of other Frenchmen? Second, was radicalism, whatever its practical influences, itself coherent? Was it a set of miscellaneous prejudices or a body of thought able to sustain a tradition of moral reasoning? Finally, was radicalism perennially significant, or was it a disposition that was once liberating but had ceased to matter – or worse, had become positively obfuscatory? Was it an ideology in the vulgar sense that permitted bourgeois democrats to be, as Marx charged, "liberal with regard to the Middle Ages"?[16] In his weighty books, *Ambition, Love and Politics* and *Intellect, Taste and Anxiety*, Theodore Zeldin shows scant regard for the radicals. He does not conceal his distaste for them and puts forth for all three questions condemnatory answers, but his learned, puckish replies must not become canonical, because they are grievously inadequate.

Zeldin holds, first, that "intellectuals were essentially abnormal in their attitudes" and indeed, triply aberrant – "self-conscious, . . . unable to tolerate the contradictions of life," and disposed to seek "solutions of universal scope, and of an abstract nature."[17] Second, he dislikes radical intellectuals, in particular, on grounds of inconsistency: "They seemed to incarnate so many of the ambivalences in French society . . . They claimed to speak in the name of reason, logic, and principle, . . . but they were constantly allying with their supposed enemies, temporizing, compromising, and muddling through."[18] He also finds them hypocritical[19] and "much more elitist" than the Catholics,[20] and lastly, of course, he judges their politics, like all politics, largely nugatory after 1848. Nevertheless, another interpretation argues for a radicalism that was influential, coherent, and of continuing importance.

As to the first question, the suggestion that the zealotry of its intelligentsia imposed on France quarrels that the country might have been spared is an old one – some people thought Voltaire had caused the Revolution – and it is one that is often taken up by English critics of France. Zeldin's disdain does not compare to Burke's excoriations: "Happy if they had all continued to know their indissoluble union and their proper place! Happy if learning, not debauched by ambition, had been satisfied to continue the instructor and not aspired to be the master."[21] Zeldin's analysis, however, similarly misconstrues the relation between politics and belief, ideas and action. Unless it evokes more general experience, a writer's crotchet or the animus of a coterie will not resonate. Tocqueville, who attached considerable importance to the writings of the philosophes and physiocrats in his account of the Revolution, understood, nonetheless, that propaganda alone does not suffice. Thus, he explained, the ethical intuition of human equality, "the firebrand that set all Europe ablaze in the eighteenth century had been easily extinguished in the fifteenth."[22] People cannot act upon an idea unless the circumstances of their lives permit them to comprehend it.

Furthermore, radical ideas were not limited to a few rancorous pedants. Zeldin admits that the mischievous intellectuals were not all "highly educated; on the contrary, the autodidact, the bookloving artisan, the village pharmacist were much more typical of rank-and-file intellectuals."[23] Significantly, it was precisely such men who everywhere supported the Ligue de l'enseignement. Opinionated politics was peculiar to no occupation, class, or region. It was, on the contrary, ubiquitous and intrinsic to France.

Most important, one should not forget that ideas unite as well as divide. Sense cannot be made of French politics, or of any politics, if contemporary self-consciousness is not taken into account. To ignore the conceptions through which people defined themselves and identified friends and adversaries is not to be objective but to be, literally, impertinent. The Ligue de l'enseignement, like the revolutionary clubs of the 1790s whose aims it helped to realize, did not merely reflect social groupings, but hoped to establish "a new pattern of association."[24]

Eventually, the radicals' resolute sociability triumphed. For the social basis of republicanism became a reality, created over time by diverse men bound subjectively by memory and hope. As Zeldin himself recognizes, the republican clubs, circles, and electoral committees posed, finally, an alternative to the aristocratic clientele: Political affinities underlay the practices of doctors, lawyers, and notaries, the followings of printers, pharmacists, and veterinarians, the disbursement of charity, the weekly encounters of the market towns; and radical associations, in the second half of the nineteenth century, made possible the organization of French society on some basis other than the patronage of the chateaus and bishoprics.[25]

A radical point of view was, then, sufficiently apt and accessible to command broad popular assent. If it was not irrelevant, was it nonetheless shamefully flawed? Zeldin puts the radicals in difficult straits: if they refused to compromise he calls them doctrinaire and when they did strike bargains, opportunist. In fact, the radicals, who were neither rigid nor naive, were and remained meliorists convinced that concerted human action could make society more just and more free; and to that end they entered, characteristically, into two rapprochements (see Chapter 2). Procedural and substantive goals pressed radicals in two directions: With constitutional monarchists they shared a concern for civil liberty and parliamentary government; but it was the Left Bonapartists, those somewhat authoritarian modernizers, whose social programs they generally approved. In the 1860s this tension was evident as Thiers, speaking for the liberal opposition (who in the next decade would be "conservative republicans"), requested the "necessary liberties" of speech, press, and assembly while the young Jules Ferry demanded "necessary destructions" of those powers in society that thwarted democratization.[26]

The liberals, following the *thèse nobilaire*, tolerated privilege as an obstacle to tyranny and were disinclined to leveling. Their caution made many radicals, like some Jacobins before them, reluctant to separate themselves entirely from the emperor.[27] Many believed that his net effect, so to speak, might be or might be made to be progressive; and because the constitution made provision for amendment, the radicals could insist that their espousal of change not be interpreted as subversive. Many maintained a pragmatic fidelity to Napoleon III. A well-developed sense of the lesser evil prompted them to consolidate their gains or, at any rate, not jeopardize their *droits acquis*.[28]

The radicals' realism and flexibility have been often underestimated, often attacked. Some decry mindless tergiversations; others, like Peter Stearns, credit the bourgeoisie with a more instrumental confusion: "Suppleness, even polarity on leading issues, coexisted with common bonds – a clear formula for success and one that still dominates capitalist society."[29]

It is true that radicalism did encompass contradictions; but this testifies not only to the thoroughness with which it gauged its political chances, but also to a larger inclusiveness. Its richness seems the best refutation of Zeldin's other allegation that only rather odd people took its slogans seriously. Radicalism appealed broadly: Its coherence was not of a closed or syllogistic character. The power it continued to exercise over reason and imagination are better grasped if it is understood to be a persuasion, a sensibility, a tradition; and because it was a tradition, it could accommodate many dispositions and tendencies. It presented, as does any culture, antinomies, sets of poised opposites such as Lévi-Strauss finds basic to society and to thought. These are proof, not of duplicity or self-doubt, but of vitality, a power to appeal at many levels and to many people. No tradition is monolithic: Christianity, for example, can be fruitfully interpreted in terms of "the eternal combat between grace and law, . . . hierarchy and liberty, predestination and free will,"[30] as Michelet did in his *Jeanne D'Arc*.

So radicals were, at once or alternately, skeptical and enthusiastic, rational and mystic, libertarian and solidarist, nationalist and cosmopolitan, egalitarian and meritocratic, feminist and patriarchal, opportunistic and incorruptible. Each radical was, perhaps, unique and cleaved to an individual configuration of these elements; in various contexts, faced with new adversaries, individual radicals might arrange them in different hierarchies of importance: One might emphasize liberty or equality, peace or the civilizing mission, the greater absolute freedom of the modern individual or the different modes of his affiliation, but these disagreements were family quarrels (see Chapter 1). Radicals themselves explicitly defended the paradox of a "revolutionary tradition": "What is progress if not the intelligent furthering of an intelligent tradition."[31]

Zeldin would trivialize the radicals. Sanford J. Elwitt, though mightily suspicious, takes them more seriously, yet he, too, lacks an imaginative sympathy with them. One cannot fail to be amused that a professed Marxist deplores "comments on the morality of priests bordering on the salacious,"[32] when so many others have found the phrase "opiate of the people" itself lacking in respect.

Nevertheless, Elwitt, a good historian, understands that ideologies must be objectively plausible and, on many issues – railway expansion, education, and the rights to organize and to strike – he presents radical (or "petty bourgeois") solutions as, in their time, effectively progressive.[33] His chief failing is judging nineteenth-century bourgeois radicals by the proletarian standards of "advanced industrial society."[34] Were he to let socialist contemporaries speak for themselves, he would have to show them either in full accord with the radicals or similarly divided on major issues.

On the subject of the railroads, for example, Elwitt wishes to indicate that radicals were concerned with the creation of a national market – as, of course, many were. However, he shows them also to have been consistently opposed to monopoly, if uncertain (like socialists of the period) about specific remedies. Some favored increased competition;

some proposed regulation; some urged a form of nationalization, government repurchase of principal lines. They took, in fact, every conceivable leftist position except that of advocating accelerated capital concentration to hasten the system's decay, a formulation that also eluded French socialists.

On agricultural protection, interests diverged; and, with the Méline Tariff of 1892, the republic chose to exclude foreign foodstuffs, protecting peasant producers to the great disadvantage of the urban worker. Elwitt makes sense of the policy in this way: French industrialists chose to keep peasants on the land, preferring "to sacrifice the depressive effect on wages produced by a reserve army of labor in favor of conditions which appeared to sustain the social order."[35] The bourgeoisie is damned if it does enclose, damned if it doesn't.

Were the men who invoked the "principles of '89," then, poseurs, elitists, and hypocrites, or was there something authentic in the almost infinitely ramified web of sympathy and common judgment that kept like-minded men of the Center and Left in perennial alliance? I shall advance three arguments for the radicals.

First, the failure of republicans to transform France into a free and fraternal community does not prove they did not wish to do so. Those who fail to accomplish all they set out to achieve are not necessarily hypocrites: They may be thwarted by resistance stronger than any they could have imagined. Furthermore, if reformers identify wrongs that they are powerless to correct, they have still done something of importance, because an abuse cannot begin to be corrected until it is recognized as an abuse, not granted as a prerogative.

Second, the program of the Ligue de l'enseignement, the radical agenda – political democracy, secularization, education, and meritocracy – was, in the context of nineteenth-century France, plausible enough to be advanced in good faith by intelligent men. Moreover, it was a great deal more egalitarian than any proposals advanced by Catholics and was understood to be so by an overwhelming majority of French workers and by virtually all their political leaders. The radicals did not fabricate threats of reaction – monarchist and, later, fascist – to cow workers into moderating their economic demands: Rather, the logic of French politics forced the democratic Center and Left continuously to reach out to each other.

Last, even if radicals had deluded themselves or sought to delude others with revolutionary verbiage in which they had ceased to believe, one would still need to know what it was they said. Although their understanding of France and their proposals for its development need not be accepted as the only diagnosis or the only prescription, and although their generally flattering estimation of themselves and their achievements cannot be the last word, neither can they be disregarded: The subsequent history of France, which they greatly influenced, was, in large part, shaped according to their appreciation of their role and their task. Central to that self-understanding, and prerequisite to the considerable political success they eventually enjoyed, was an interpretation that was neither elitist nor self-congratulatory of their humiliating failures during the years from 1848 to 1851.

Unlike the Bourbons, republicans remembered their mistakes and learned from them. After the collapse of the Second Republic, French radicals developed – and many practiced – a secular ethic of participation and solidarity, *les moeurs républicaines*. Both their organization and their ethic were created in conscious response to the debacle of 1848 and enabled them to take and hold power, to shape the Third Republic in the face of repeated coups of the self-proclaimed Moral Order. Their earlier inadequacies, excessively familiar as the subject upon which Tocqueville, Marx, Michelet, and Flaubert agreed, were no less amply clear to the republicans themselves. It is ironic that they are defined for modern readers by those very failings they themselves acknowledged and struggled to correct.

The political interpretations of Tocqueville, Marx, and Michelet differed in important ways, but each expressed a longing shared by many Frenchmen for a public life, for a sphere in which citizens met one another in recognized fraternity. Their positions indicate the range of opposition to the Second Empire, and their writings anticipate its common themes. They expressed, in the most profound and self-conscious forms, the judgments of many active, practical men.

Tocqueville's constitutionalism influenced liberals like Edouard Laboulaye and Prévost-Paradol, and other, more jacobinical men, found his writings on civic culture suggestive. Tocqueville's witty and vituperative *Recollections* of 1848 was not printed until 1893, but its essence was available in his earlier writings and in speeches he had made in the Chamber of Deputies during the winter of 1847. He regretted an absence of genuine politics, of social intercourse, and of liberty: "What was most lacking, especially towards the end of the July Monarchy, was political life itself." He believed that by limiting participation, the exclusiveness of the *pays légal* impoverished even the notion of the public interest. The difficulty did not result from venality alone (although that certainly contributed to the "revolution of contempt"), but from a political solipsism. Limited to the experience of one social class, parliamentary debate lacked "passion and originality." Unfortunately, radicals knew the country no better. Reform proposals came, "nocturnal and precipitous," from febrile meetings in Parisian newspaper offices.[36] Politicians had no real links to the nation, and the Second Republic did nothing to establish these bonds. Ignorant of their fellows, the French had been unable to conduct a free government. Radicals felt the justice of Tocqueville's censure.

Similarly, it was not only French socialists like August Vermorel and Gustave Lefrançais who found Marx's *Eighteenth Brumaire* convincing. Jules Ferry, then a journalist and lawyer, prepared a voter's manual for the general election of 1863 that closely followed Marx's social analysis. "Persigny rests," he wrote, "upon the peasants and the functionaries," and he attacked the apolitical bourgeoisie, "that argumentative class which believes itself to be independent."[37] Prévost-Paradol, an Orleanist academician, echoed the regret that whereas in England the wealthy were public spirited and refractory, in France a man became timid as he grew rich.

Bourgeois liberals and radicals came to understand, with Marx, that the regime had acted to ensure that "every common interest was straightway severed from society . . . snatched from the activity of society's members." They saw perpetuated in the Second Empire the fatal asymmetry between the powers of the president and those of the National Assembly that Marx had seen in the constitution of the Second Republic: The executive retained the most crucial of royal prerogatives, for it alone disposed of a half-million offices. The center of an immense bureaucracy, it controlled patronage, administration, and thus, effectively, policy. Furthermore, the president, acting with the consent of his council of state and indifferent to the will of the legislature, might dissolve any elected municipal or general (departmental) council and replace it with a "commission" of his nominees. Republicans recognized that no parliamentary force could hope to exercise power in France until it "let civil society and public opinion create organs of their own, independent of government power,"[38] and in increasing numbers they came to consider a secular civic morality a prerequisite to republican government. Thus, the common critique of 1848 became the premise of republican self-criticism and revival.

Contemporary progressives drew several lessons from their acknowledged failure. First, they recognized that the victory of the united opposition in February 1848 had been deceptively easy. Louis Philippe had not contested the battle and had withdrawn before an uprising in Paris. Jubilant throngs had proclaimed the Second Republic and trusted in *la force des choses* to protect their victory, but this ready, nearly unanimous adherence obscured only briefly "the terrible originality of the facts"[39] – that workers and peasants understood their interests differently and would pursue them.

Second, the republicans learned that legal measures alone were insufficient to accomplish even their political goals. The new republic had decreed manhood suffrage and the right to work. Republicans had long argued that these two measures would assure a stable and popular government; differences remaining among citizens might be settled, without greed or violence, by the people's representatives. When the newly enfranchised electorate returned a markedly conservative constituent assembly, republicans were humiliated by the rooted strength of legitimist and Orleanist notables[40] in the country at large.

Worse shocks were to follow. The assembly took up the social question and entrusted to Louis Blanc the organization of national workshops. In the few months of its existence, the project became a dole rather than a source of employment: When it was eliminated workers faced with destitution or expulsion from Paris rose in revolt. There ensued the unanticipated horror of the June Days, a period marked by street fighting between the people and the republican National Guard.

In the face of popular violence, many republicans abandoned the cause. The revolutionary unity of the third estate had been, perhaps, a fiction from its beginnings, but it had once been morally compelling. Now, its chief beneficiaries disdained it and its victims scorned the petty bourgeois myth of the "people."[41] Bourgeois revolutionaries had learned that a republic of laws could not guarantee social peace.

It followed from this, as a third lesson, that a radical political organization was indispensable. Republicans understood that they lacked infrastructure: They could not reliably expect to win elections; they could not even maintain order. Many who had once assumed that a republican assembly could find peaceful solutions to the social question sought repressive means: In the absence of republican cadres, they turned to the army, the police, and a strong executive, the prince-president. In the aftermath of the June Days, the assembly divested itself of every shred of power and legitimacy that remained to it, including control over the military; enacted laws restricting the liberties of press, assembly, and association, and, in 1850, limited the right of suffrage itself.[42]

The same "party of order," legitimists, Orleanists, and frightened republicans, that took these extraordinary measures also strengthened the church, which was thought to be the most effective barrier to revolution. Ecclesiastics hastened to fortify this belief with statistics. Brother Philippe, Superior General of the Christian Brothers, rejoiced to find among the thousands arrested in June only seventeen past pupils of his order.[43] To strengthen this new holy alliance, French troops were sent to Italy to uphold the temporal claims of Pope Pius IX against the Garibaldini. This move was in violation both of the express will of the national assembly and of the French constitution, which forbade the use of French troops to oppose another people's fight for self-determination.

When, on June 13, 1849, the radical republican Alexandre-Auguste Ledru-Rollin led a public protest against the expedition, the demonstration was dispersed by armed troops. Ledru-Rollin escaped to England, and his supporters – the young Jean Macé among them – scattered. Macé learned from this misadventure the need to perfect what he later called the *métier d'organisateur*: Never again would he depend upon spontaneous support from the populace or from any arm of the state.

The flight of the red republicans led to shifts in domestic politics that underlined the fourth and, perhaps, the most fruitful lesson: the centrality of the schools issue. The Second Republic's first minister of public instruction, Hippolyte Carnot, son of the revolutionary general and regicide Lazare Carnot, had surrounded himself with men of conspicuous political color – among them, Edgar Quinet, Edouard Charton, Charles Renouvier, and Henri Martin. (Michelet had been invited to advise the ministry but declined, hoping to serve the Republic better by completing his *History of France*.)[44] They had prepared legislation requiring that primary education for children of both sexes be compulsory, free and independent, organizing republican popular education much as Condorcet had wished to do in 1792.[45] Carnot had abolished the requirement that applicant schoolmasters present a "certificate of morality" furnished by a clergyman and had done nothing to restore the teaching brothers chased from the schools of several municipalities. Furthermore, he encouraged teachers in their plans to hold evening courses for "citizen electors" and exhorted others to do the same.

His opponents attacked these instructions and seized upon a political indiscretion of Carnot to discredit his proposals. Carnot had correctly anticipated that monarchist notables would benefit from the electors' humility and enjoined schoolmasters in his famous circular of March 6, 1848, to remind voters that a representative of the people needed good judgment more than formal schooling.[46] He had sought to give voters an encouraging sense of broader eligibility, and his advice was unexceptionable (had not Descartes written that good sense was of all good things the most evenly distributed?), but monarchists gleefully derided the announcement, made by the republic's minister of education, that learning was irrelevant.

It was, of course, not Carnot's naivete they feared but his frank democracy, and the withdrawal of his project for free and compulsory schooling became a condition of conservative support for Louis Bonaparte in 1848.[47] This demand was met. Carnot's initiatives were abandoned, and he himself was eventually succeeded by Count Frédéric Falloux, the pious grandson of a legitimist cattle merchant ennobled in 1823. The loi Falloux, passed on March 15, 1850, and the administrative decrees that elaborated it, conceded to the church decisive control over

French education. The law reiterated the place of religion in the primary-school curriculum and permitted clergymen to inspect schools in order to satisfy themselves that the instruction there was orthodox. Towns might subsidize church schools rather than maintain secular public ones, and the state waived even those minimal certifying powers established by the loi Guizot in 1833 and permitted religious teachers to conduct classes without the "brevet of capacity" earned in examinations and required of all lay teachers. Girls, when schooled at all, were taught almost exclusively by nuns whose competence was guaranteed merely by a "letter of obedience" to their superior.[48] Philosophy and modern history were eliminated from the course of study in the *lycées*. Lastly, conservatives assailed the provincial normal schools from among whose graduates virtually all lay teachers were recruited. Their budget, their curriculum, and their prestige were substantially reduced; each of the 89 departments could choose to have them or not, and admission was no longer gained by competitive examinations but was dependent upon nomination by the mayor and the parish priest.

Thus, radicals inescapably judged the Second Republic a failure: It had given over its army and its schools to an extravagantly reactionary church. They had expected, nonetheless, that the people would defend any republican government, however imperfect; but when Louis Bonaparte, elected president overwhelmingly in December 1848, dissolved the National Assembly on the morning of December 2, 1851, there was no popular uprising in defense of the republic. Although many thousands were eventually convicted for protesting the coup, and although the infamous "mixed commissions" – so called because they included army officers as well as police and public prosecutors – scoured the departments for intransigents, there was no proof of widespread concern for republican government, and Louis Bonaparte was able to proclaim himself emperor the following year.

Estimates of the victims of the coup are difficult to evaluate. A roughly contemporary account listed some 8,000 killed, exiled, or imprisoned – among them some 89 members of the dissolved assembly. Some estimates go as high as 200,000, although this would have included many men who, like Georges Clemenceau's father, a republican doctor of Nantes, were pardoned before their sentences were carried out.[49] One must read these figures with some sense of self-correcting exaggeration. The government wished to be thought popular, and thus could not admit to having too many enemies, but it wished also to emphasize the necessity of strong measures and therefore required that the red menace be seen as a substantial one. Republican veracity, too, was subject to countervailing pressures. Primarily, of course, men who wished to carry on the fight would not court arrest, yet it was important to maintain that France had been taken forcibly and, later, candidates sought the unmistakable cachet that attached to having been a *proscrit du 2 décembre*. Lest republican opposition be minimized, it must be borne in mind that the Left had been scattered on at least two previous occasions – after the June Days and after the fiasco of June 13, 1849. Thus, many who might have protested were already *hors de combat*.

Nevertheless, the conclusion suggested by Louis Bonaparte's successes was drawn with striking unanimity: the bourgeoisie was unable and unfit to govern.[50] There were, to be sure, several bourgeoisies: a *grande bourgeoisie* of enormous wealth, the diverse *classes moyennes*, disposing of modest or meager resources, and a substantial class of peasant proprietors.[51] The nature of their work and the sources of their incomes varied greatly, and there were important differences of influence, opinion, and manner among these groups: What all bourgeois groupings incontestably shared was a common incapacity to deal with public issues. Bourgeois Frenchmen lacked organization and electoral and administrative cadres. They lacked the education such institutions would have provided, encounters with other classes, and an appreciation of the general needs of society. In consequence, they lacked the self-confidence and the moral authority to govern.

In the 1850s, radicals were chastened by the lessons of 1848; by the 1860s they were prepared to act upon them. Frenchmen had suffered in 1848 from the illusion that Michelet had described two years earlier as the "the false notion that we can with impunity isolate ourselves."[52] This error was seen to be at the root of the republican collapse and of the *sauve qui peut* reaction that followed the June Days.

When they reentered politics the republicans worked with a broader notion of civic life. In 1848 they had not been, in Michelet's sense, "sociable": They had conceived reform too narrowly and formally.[53] Now they understood the need to prepare the social basis for their revolution. Because conspicuous political action was forbidden until 1868, they began the task obliquely by organizing education societies. Article 291 of the penal code forbade the association of more than twenty people without the prior authorization of the departmental prefect, who had to consult with the police and, in practice, often also with his immediate superior, the minister of the interior. Association for charitable causes was more readily tolerated, and business ventures had the least difficulty. As a result, later radical groups sometimes incorporated themselves as profit-making enterprises.[54]

If the laws encouraged the use of educational and philanthropic societies as a cover for political meetings, the lessons of 1848 convinced republicans that these should not merely be front groups. For a republic to be legitimate, republican mores had to be created and upheld by a tissue of militantly secular (*laïc*) cells comparable to parish organiza-tion. A republic vulnerable to the impatience of workers or to the in-difference of peasants might equally be threatened by the religiosity of women, unwilling to support their husbands or to rear their sons in *civisme*.[55]

Republicans had come to recognize that relations within society, among classes, generations, and sexes, must be governed by a new dispensation. Bonds resting upon coercion and corrupted by dissimula-tion, servility, and cant were manifestly fragile. Republicans needed not only an organizational infrastructure, but also a new ethic capable of sustaining solidarity. Thus, republican mores, *les moeurs républicaines*, were revolutionary in their insistence upon civic participation and fraternal in their determination to embrace workers and peasants. Unabashedly bourgeois, their ethic proclaimed the greater utility and virtue of the productive classes. Self-righteously anticlerical, contemptuous of chiv-alric and monastic life, republicans also refused to give over women and children to the church.

The church, during this period, was unambiguously reactionary. Lib-eral Christians, Gallicans whose temperate optimism admitted, like Tocqueville's, of progressive revelation, were then to be found in the Catholic Church – where, indeed, one may find them still – but they were steadily losing. The pontificate of Pius IX is remembered for the doc-trine of the Immaculate Conception, the proclamation of papal infallibil-ity, and for the Syllabus of Errors best summarized in its last thesis: "The Roman Pontiff cannot, and ought not to, reconcile himself and come to terms with progress, liberalism, and modern civilization."[56]

Some have dismissed the radicals' anticlericalism as diversionary, but that is not the way that their proposals appeared to any contemporary French socialist. Their priorities made tactical sense even to those mil-itants who were neither moderate nor parliamentary. It was not, after all, simply a "bourgeois" army and national guard that could be relied upon to quell insurrection or break strikes. The symbolic Breton con-script, whose throat is cut in Emile Zola's *Germinal*, represented an al-most insuperable block to the leftward evolution of French society. French socialists, too, believed that conservatives manipulated a largely rural but essentially cross-class coalition by religious means.

In opposition to the power and privilege of the counterrevolutionary church – its exemption from laws restricting free association, its immu-nity from press censorship, its decisive control over education and pub-lic assistance[57] – republicans developed what would now be called a counterculture.

The need to institutionalize civic habits had been a Jacobin insight, the fostering of republican mores the expressed object of their republican catechisms. Carnot's notion of the schoolmaster's political role had been much the same as Condorcet's: both expected them to provide for adults the continuing education essential to active citizenship. But in 1848 the republic feared itself to be incapable of inspiring support or even obedience to its laws. The French expedition to Rome and the loi Falloux were the result of that feeling of inadequacy. Nothing, Quinet believed, could be salvaged after that "lack of faith," and he described the difference between 1789 and 1848 in religious terms: "The first believed itself able to save the world with its own spiritual energy . . . In France, any revolution that cannot find in itself a moral force great enough to sustain and save society is a revolution that will betray itself."[58]

For the radicals the principles of 1789 were an inexhaustible inspiration. Under the Second Empire, as during the July Monarchy, both government and opposition sought selectively to invoke the Revolution. Frenchmen continued to be preoccupied with its meaning: The antithesis Michelet described between social orders founded upon revelation or reason, hierarchy or equality, hereditary status or individual liberty served as an organizing antagonism. Politics is often a process of self-definition, and in France this struggle reached down to the deepest levels of personal identity. The man of the Revolution was a citizen, a worker, and the father of a family.[59]

In the nineteenth century, bourgeois radicals remained true to this vision of personal wholeness. They believed that only in a society governed by republican mores was such a personality possible. They believed, moreover, that until its citizens were educated in civic, not otherworldly, morals France could not sustain a democratic government. So they busied themselves with schools, lecture courses, and libraries and fought with their wives' confessors. These struggles were not trivial, either in conception or in achievement. Their effort to exercise and foster civic virtue underlay the first enduring national republican network achieved anywhere on the European continent. French radicals understood that a republic must rest upon shared assumptions of personal dignity, a dignity asserted first in the political sphere but unattainable if sought in that sphere only.

1 Defining the alternative society: *les moeurs républicaines*

> The quarrel about icons became so intense that it eventually became impossible for sensible men to propose a moderate solution, and this was because of its bearing on a very delicate issue – namely, power.
>
> Montesquieu, *Considerations on the Causes of the Greatness of the Romans and Their Decline*[1]

REPUBLICANS FELT THE NEED to create within existing society an alternative way of life, a counterculture affirming in all its relations the principles of 1789. In the decades following 1848, this concern, no less than the ban on direct political action, prompted their heightened emphasis on education as the most promising means of securing a republican moral order. Republican mores would accomplish three tasks that radicals held essential: first, the destruction of the moral, social, and political power of the Catholic Church, which they all believed to be counterrevolutionary; second, the self-affirmation of the new man, the assertion of his unique fitness to govern, the inevitability of his accession and his intrinsic solidarity with all productive workers; and third, the incorporation of women into republican society.

Their effort emerged from the failure of direct revolutionary action and in response to widely sensed practical imperatives, but it cannot be adequately understood as a wholly conscious political campaign. It drew upon deeper sources of energy and fulfilled profound psychological as well as strategic needs. French republicans wanted to reunite in one personality the masculine roles dispersed by the Old Regime among the three estates and to dignify the tasks degraded by it. They meant to govern as the king and nobility had done. They sought to become the spiritual fathers of their families, to invest physical paternity with the moral authority that the clergy had previously exercised. They saw themselves as materially productive and scientifically enlightened men and, as such, they laid claim to moral and civic autonomy.

These longings were intensified in the nineteenth century by a growing uneasiness with the division of labor. Men who were themselves engaged in specialized professions feared, with Rousseau, that the arm would be diminished by the tool. They sought in politics and in family life – and in the proper republican education that they expected to transform both those spheres – the full play of general faculties that might otherwise atrophy. They worried, too, about the brutalizing impact of mechanized work upon the laboring classes and the demoralizing effects of "melancholy leisure"[2] upon bourgeois women, because they believed that energy had to find expression. They believed that neither society nor the individual personality could be founded upon repression.

Bourgeois republicans were willing, like most who aspire to govern, to shoot those who challenged their supremacy, but they preferred not to rely on force. They were no less horrified than were conservatives by the prospect of civil war and were far less confident that popular protest could be disregarded or definitively subdued. It was this uneasiness with coercion – which was prudential as well as humanitarian – that characterized the radical position and underlay their concern for republican morals.

Men who, on these grounds, could not accept the coup of December 2[3] later insisted on looking beyond the suppression of the communes in 1871. Republicans such as Charles Floquet and Georges Clemenceau, the young mayor of the Eighteenth Arondissement of Paris, struggled throughout the spring of 1871 in the Union républicaine pour les droits de Paris to prevent armed confrontation. When they failed, they did not opt for the commune and die on its barricades; they did, however, amnesty the survivors and rehabilitate them as patriots. They raised money for the widows and children of those executed or deported, paid legal fees, and appropriated as martyrs the dead, who were, in any case, no longer able to argue against a policy of republican consolidation.

Early in the Third Republic, men like the social critic Charles Bigot warned the "ruling class," which he characterized as conservative republican, that it was both reckless and criminal to count upon "the police, the state of siege, and New Caledonia . . . After each bloody repression, one sees, from generation to generation, another and even bloodier revolt."[4] Radicals believed that their government would be stable only if it rested upon the comprehension and assent of the governed and then only if the spirit of its laws were internalized in personalities that found adequate expression in recognized social roles. The radicals understood, in sum, the crucial link between the socialization of the individual and the legitimation of the state. Their concern was manifest in the movement for free, compulsory, secular education described in Chapters 2 and 3; and the schools' agitation cannot be understood without an appreciation of its theoretical basis.

In the decades following 1848, many men, both eminent and obscure – Michelet, Quinet, Charles Renouvier ("the Republican Kant"), Prévost-Paradol, Anthime Corbon, Edouard Laboulaye, Etienne Vacherot, Alfred Naquet, Charles Sauvestre, and Jean Macé among them – contributed to a body of republican social thought. A generation later their doctrines were given systematic form in the social epistemology and ethics of Emile Durkheim, for whom the radical republicans created the first chair of sociology at the Sorbonne. In 1902, Durkheim reiterated Bigot's warning of 1876: "Truces, arrived at after violence, are never anything but provisional, and satisfy no one. Human passions stop only before a moral power they respect. If all authority of this kind is wanting, the law of the strongest prevails, and, latent or active, the state of war is necessarily chronic."[5]

CLERICALISM, THE ENEMY

The problem of order alone cannot explain the radicals' anticlericalism. Why, if they required a docile populace, conscientious workers, chaste and admiring wives, did they have to contrive new disciplines? Was it necessary to improve on the opiates at hand? Many bourgeois did see in religion, as traditionally understood and practiced, the best guarantee of the social order. Flaubert satirized their views in his *Dictionnaire des idées reçues*:

> *Religion*: Still one of the bases of society. Necessary for the people. A little goes a long way. "The religion of my fathers" must be uttered with unction.[6]

Other men, however, with no fewer interests to protect, affected no nostalgia for the old faith and did not find in the church the answers to their most troubling personal or political problems. Unlike Flaubert's bourgeois who defined themselves by their distance from the people,[7] radicals identified with popular struggles and found their moral identities in explicit opposition to the church; and although they differed among themselves on social, economic, and administrative issues, their commitment to a secular republic proved at critical moments to be their central allegiance.

These men did not dispute doctrine alone, but also questioned the social utility of traditional religion. In many quarters, the "dechristianization" of the people was assumed to have taken place already: Bigot, for example, warned *les classes dirigeantes* that their pretense of devotion was manifestly false: Their hypocrisy served only to complete the process of disenchantment that their earlier skepticism had begun. Freethinkers insisted that it was no longer prudent, if ever it had been, to ground morals on credulity: Revelation, they believed, had ceased to form the basis of cogent argument. The Reformation, Jansenism, and the Revolution itself had undermined the Catholic religion in France, and radicals believed that the brutal manner in which orthodoxy had triumphed over the Huguenots and destroyed Port Royal had irretriev-ably compromised its moral authority. As Léon Gambetta said, the church consisted of "the cadres of a discredited spiritual authority, too weak to secure order, [but] well-equipped to trouble it."[8]

Even writers who were disinclined to call this turn of events progress agreed with radicals that irreversible changes had taken place. Tocque-ville impressively accepted democracy as a "providential fact" that all historical forces, however disposed, promoted and that it was therefore impious to resist.

> It is not necessary that God himself should speak in order that we may discover the unquestionable signs of His will . . . If the men of our time should be convinced, by attentive observation and sincere reflection, that the gradual and progressive development of social equality is at once the past and the future of their history, this discovery alone would confer upon the change the sacred character of a divine decree.[9]

Cynics and puritans, legitimists and socialists agreed with radical re-publicans that there could be no return to the old habits of reverence. Pierre-Joseph Proudhon, like Michelet, assumed that there was a fun-damental conflict between the old religion, which was supernatural and based upon human subordination, and the unachieved ethic of the Revo-lution, which was immanent in man and the consequence of his dignity. He proclaimed, "La France a perdu ses moeurs," and cited in support of his distress the words of Pierre-Paul Royer-Collard, a constitutional monarchist of moderate disposition who lamented during the Restora-tion, "Society is crumbling. There is nothing left but memories, regrets, utopias, lunacies, and despair."[10] Honoré de Balzac, although he wrote about two imaginary Christian utopias in *Le Médecin de campagne* and *Le Curé de village*, more often portrayed churchmen as being consumed like other men by vanity and greed, and similarly, he emphasized the inabili-ty of aristocrats, genuine or *arrivistes*, to govern – indeed, even to with-stand – their villainous tenantry.[11] Restoration of the old order he reluctantly judged not to be a practical proposition.

Attempts to invoke old principles appeared to be either travesty or delusion. One thinks of the consecration of Charles X or, more gro-tesque still, the Sacrilege Law of 1826, which proposed to make certain forms of public discourtesy to religion punishable by death – although not, as one pious deputy urged, by drawing and quartering.

After *faits accomplis*, other modifications were required to make men and institutions consistent. Prévost-Paradol, an Orleanist member of the French Academy, cautioned that once the "sentiment of birth" is lost, no force on earth can reawaken it. Whatever one's personal preferences, he believed (and like many writers, he preferred to regard monarchist or republican sentiments as matters of taste), democracy had been the work of history: civilization attenuates natural inequalities and equality emerges, as Tocqueville believed it did, inevitably. Prévost-Paradol assumed that every society experiences conflict among rival classes and warned that although the form and the duration of the conflict may vary, the issue is certain: The result must be a democratic society that may temporarily sustain an undemocratic government but that tends naturally to develop its "appropriate" political institutions.

Among the innovations that Prévost-Paradol recommended was full disestablishment of the church. No French government since 1789, he wrote, had been able to escape the choice between the church and revolution; yet he admitted no irreconcilable antagonism and promised an end to the *Kulturkampf* on the day that the church became a "free association." Clerics required only the right to meet, organize, and teach – three freedoms that anyone might exercise in the new France. A church, dependent like other organizations upon these liberties, would thus become a bulwark of freedom. He did not say that this would be the reverse of its present position but he hinted at what others made explicit – an avowed complicity of the church with the counterrevolution: "We are proceeding towards the complete separation of church and state and *no significant change can take place in the government of France without separation.*"[12]

For this reason, radicals found religious toleration an insufficient policy and, with Jules Ferry, called for "necessary destructions" as well as for the "necessary liberties" envisioned by liberal Orleanists and others of the "Thiers Party." (The constitutionalist *tiers parti*, neither Bonapartist nor republican, neither clerical nor *laïc*, a third force and self-acclaimed *juste milieu* in parliament, was punningly called after its ablest leader.) The church retained significant, probably decisive, control over important aspects of national life: Although generous by nineteenth-century standards to dissenting Christians and to Jews,[13] the various French constitutions had granted special status to the Catholic Church as the religion of the "majority of Frenchmen": The Revolution, in attempting to nationalize, to supersede, and, finally, to regulate the Church, left little, in institutional terms, save impieties for future regimes to expiate.[14]

The Concordat of 1801 between Napoleon and Pope Pius VII guaranteed a publicly subsidized clerical establishment, partly self-administering and in close relation with Rome; ministers of all "recognized cults" were salaried. *Laïcs* delighted in the theological implications of this open-handedness:

Q. Was Calvin a heretic?
A. Are preachers paid? Yes? Well, then, no.

Q. Is the *Koran* a true book? (This, after the annexation of Morocco.)
A. Is the *khadi* on the payroll? Then, it must be.

Nevertheless, the *budget des cultes* was paid chiefly to Catholics.[15] This subsidy was accepted by the church as perpetual reimbursement for incomes from lands that had been sold by the Revolutionary government, the ownership of which the Pope agreed in 1801 not to contest. Ecclesiastics naturally viewed these payments as unconditional reparations, whereas Erastians within several administrations, as well as in the opposition, saw them as salaries paid to a species of functionary in the expectation of loyal service.

Despite acrimonious dispute about the nature of these payments, they were duly made, and church programs of every kind benefited from direct and indirect subsidy. The church was also closely associated with the state power in the administration of public education and assistance: Clergymen were involved, *ex officio*, in academic administration at every level and served on the *bureaux de bienfaisance* of the Second Empire, just as they had during the Restoration and the July Monarchy. The parish priest was legally entitled to "inspect" schools and had a hand also in choosing those deserving poor who were entitled to the limited number of free places in communal schools.[16]

At issue, then, were not things indifferent but important social powers and a principle: Popular sovereignty or tested expertise must direct public institutions and disburse public funds.[17] The radicals' solicitude for civil marriage and their passion for civil funerals, seemingly trivial preoccupations, constituted a refusal to accept church monopoly of the essential rites of life. Beneath the symbolic conflict they were fighting for control of the rudimentary but basic apparatus of social services, schools, hospitals, and the dole: control of communication and patronage. Republicans were convinced that the church systematically thwarted their individual and joint success. They charged that Catholic groups published lists of pious artisans and shopkeepers whom the *bien-pensant* might patronize to the detriment of their freethinking competitors. Balzac had written during the Restoration that "provincial men of business were bound to profess political opinions of some sort if they meant to secure custom; they were forced to choose for themselves between the patronage of the Liberals on the one hand or the Royalists on the other."[18] Republican prefects complained of the practice well into the 1880s, and even later schoolmasters deplored "ferocious reprisals" for political or religious dissent.[19]

In an epoch when party was little more than a network of patron-client relations, in an economy of small-scale enterprises dependent upon local markets, religious divisions corresponded to patterns of solidarity, personal exchanges of goods and services in which political commitment and moral authority were daily manifest in the most inescapable ways.

Clerics were, moreover, incontestably free to speak, publish, and organize as laymen were not; and although the church was by no means monolithic – liberal Catholics may even have exaggerated their disagreements with secular reformers in order to forestall ultramontane criticism – after 1848 French Catholics resumed open hostility to republican government, and Catholic writers from the rabid Louis Veuillot to the politic Charles de Montalembert rallied to Louis Napoleon's coup in terms that expressly equated republicanism with the most lurid depravity.

Three days after December 2, Veuillot called upon the readers of *l'Univers* to support the government. "Its cause is that of social order." The prince-president had preempted a civil war in which decent people would fight, not merely for "their political opinions, nor even to preserve their goods, but to save the lives of their wives and children."[20] Montalembert's endorsement, withheld just a fortnight, was no less unstinting. He urged an affirmative vote in the next week's plebiscite:

> To vote against Louis Napoleon is to vindicate the socialist revolution . . . To call upon a dictatorship of reds to replace the dictatorship of a prince who has, for three years, rendered incomparable services to the cause of order and of Catholicism . . . to vote for Louis Napoleon is not to approve all that he has done; it is to choose between him and the total ruin of France . . . It is to arm the temporal power, the only power possible today, with the force necessary to subdue the army of crime . . . to defend our churches, our homes, our wives against those whose covetous lusts respect nothing . . . In the great struggle of the two forces that between them contest the world, I believe, in acting thus, to be once again as always of the party of Catholicism against the revolution.[21]

Republicans, anathematized and constrained to refute association of their cause with anarchy and license, charged that it was Roman Catholicism, not secular rationalism, that was deracinating, amoral, and perverse. It was not they who were antinomian: Republican mores were a sterner discipline, a life at once more exigent and more free. A lay intelligentsia, many of whom were victims of the coup or voluntary exiles, began earnestly to preach a secular morality.[22]

Of course, this was not the first time that dissidents had expressed themselves in the popular idiom of anticlericalism. Rabelais and the philosophes had been vigorous practitioners; and immediately before the revolution of 1848, Michelet and Quinet had jointly explored its political and psychological ramifications in *The Jesuits* (1843) and *Ultramontanism* (1844), in Michelet's *The Priest, Woman, and the Family* (1845) and *The*

People (1846), and Quinet's *The Education of the People.*[23] After 1848, republican secularists increasingly sought a functional equivalent for France of the Protestant Reformation, a moral basis with which to secure modern society against political reaction.

> Where religious revolution has preceded political revolution, there are certain moral advances that no one dreams of undoing. Wherever, on the contrary, a political revolution is made without modifications in national religion, you see, in the same moment, incredible progress and lapses more unbelievable still . . . We pass the day [the revolutionary *journée*] asking whether we shall be governed in the evening by Babeuf, or by Gregory VII, or by both men jointly.[24]

A nation's religion is its "law of laws," Quinet wrote, and underlies all others: he considered Britain to be episcopal and aristocratic, the United States, congregational and democratic, and both constitutions to depend upon a national religious consensus. "All that you say of liberty in a republic presupposes that you have had a religious revolution."[25]

Eighty years of dishearteningly incomplete success made French republicans impatient with the indecent longevity of institutions that, they insisted, rational men had abandoned generations before. "Indecent," it must be emphasized, was precisely the term with which Catholic doctrine and devotion were attacked. The word most frequently used to describe them was *malsain;* and militant secularists undertook the crudest and most banal priest baiting. Charles Sauvestre, an early enthusiast of the Ligue de l'enseignement and a contributor to the Left Bonapartist *Opinion nationale,* which published Macé's initial appeals to organize, enjoyed great success with a book that he called *Monita secreta,* which purported to be a manual prepared for Jesuits by the last librarian of the order in France before 1789.

Sauvestre made much of "mental reservations" and casuistry, of the unwholesome moral effects of absolution and indulgences, of dispensations for the rich and misery for the poor. Priests were portrayed as do-nothings and poseurs and clerical and chivalric ideals confounded in a self-righteously bourgeois attack: For example, he characterized Ignatius Loyola as a "soldier of fortune" prone to "romanesque ambitions." Religious devotions were dismissed as "sick fantasies . . . that distract from work."[26]

Further, Sauvestre shared with virtually all freethinkers the conviction that celibate life must produce fantasies, and perhaps deeds, of a prurient nature – the worry that moved the pharmacist Homais in Flaubert's *Madame Bovary* to urge regular phlebotomies for priests.[27] Sauvestre deplored the examinations of conscience for which, he alleged, schoolchildren were taught ritual self-accusations of the most unsuitable sort and cautioned against eroticism in religious metaphor: "There is a good deal too much flesh about it . . . ," he suspected, of a young communicant's meditations on the Heavenly Bridegroom. Sauvestre saw therein intimations of an unwholesome ecstasy, a sensual religiosity like that of the Ursuline boarding school in which Emma Bovary's destruction commenced.

Flaubert himself, although he mocked the vulgar anticlericalism of Homais, dwelled upon the identification of the erotic and the mystical in Emma's mind: "The comparisons of fiancé, husband, celestial lover and of eternal marriage that recurred in the sermons aroused unexpected pleasures in the depths of her soul." Indeed, it was the sensuality and luxury of her devotions that made the book so offensive to those who prosecuted Flaubert. Adultery was nothing new in French fiction; but Emma alternated between sexual and religious diversions and signaled each new consolation with purchases – a riding habit, a whip, a reliquary. Dying, she pressed upon a crucifix "a kiss more passionate than [any] she had ever given a lover."[28] It was for this that Flaubert was charged with *outrage à la morale publique et religieuse et aux bonnes moeurs* in 1857 and on those grounds that Marie-Antoine-Jules Sénard, who had been president of the National Assembly and minister of the interior during the Second Republic, successfully defended him against the imperial prosecutor: "The author poses the question, 'Have you done what you should for the education of your daughters? The religion you have given them, is it one that will sustain them through the storms of life, or is it nothing but a mass of carnal superstitions?'"[29]

Anticlerical writers were not, then, simply political pornographers, although scandal had ever done invaluable service to the republican cause. (As Richard Cobb has observed, *Les Liaisons dangereuses* damaged the old regime far more than Rousseau's *Contrat social* ever could.) Implicit in their attack – and bound up inextricably with sexual innuendo – were two crucial assertions: First, they maintained that traditional religion did not assure good conduct: Either its miraculous beliefs promoted skepticism and cynicism, or its "magical" sacraments destroyed character. Second, they expressly attacked Roman Catholicism as a socially isolating, rather than a unifying force. Republicans, concerned with *l'enracinement* no less than with liberty, attacked clerics as men *ni de leur temps ni de leur pays*, estranged both from their compatriots and from history.

Liberal Catholics concurred to some extent in both criticisms. Tocqueville, recalling an earlier period when "homage due to saints and angels became an almost idolatrous worship for most Christians," counseled the church to attend more to the substance of religion, lest it become a "band of fanatic zealots in the midst of a skeptical multitude." Along with other Gallicans he regretted the growing ultramontanism of the clergy, which he believed to be the saddest consequence of the sale of

church properties. Men without families, he thought, could attach themselves to their country only through the land. If they must be property-
less as well as childless, what stake could they have in France? They
would be driven, in spite of themselves, to identify with Rome.[30] Radicals, unsurprisingly, dwelt even longer on this presumed allegiance to a
foreign despot.

The radical ethic was an ethic of engagement. Secularists found the
notion of cloistered virtue altogether abhorrent and, furthermore, implausible. Radicals were, accordingly, harsher with monks than with
parish priests – *guerre au moine, paix au curé*,[31] Paul Bert said in 1883 – but
their general indictment of the Catholic clergy emphasized obligations
not undertaken. With Rabelais, they preferred riches, marriage, and
disciplined liberty to poverty, chastity, and obedience.[32] No Christian
teaching was attacked more furiously than Saint Paul's grudging advice
to marry, if one must, rather than burn. Edouard Lockroy summed up
their indignant critique in the Chamber of Deputies in 1880:

> Those men who have voluntarily separated themselves from the
> world . . . who consider the state of marriage an inferior state, for
> whom paternity is a dishonor and almost a crime, who have a celes-
> tial [home] that they prefer to their earthly one . . . consider work a
> punishment, a chastisement . . . "Because you have sinned . . . you
> shall earn your bread by the sweat of your brow."[33]

Dissatisfaction with the quietistic aspects of Christianity and an interest in the figure of the patriarch led many radicals to a distinct philo-
semitism. Maria Deraismes, a founder of the League for the Rights of
Women, reproached the French clergy in 1879: "Christianity is in this
respect much beneath mosaicism [Desraismes's agnosticism drove her
to curious terminological lengths], which infinitely better accords with
nature." In popular fiction, Erckmann-Chatrian's genial rabbi David
Sichel diligently promotes a marriage between the confirmed bachelor,
L'Ami Fritz, and a blooming young Anabaptist.[34]

Balzac's parish priest in *Le médecin de campagne* had insisted that patriotism could promote only occasional and momentary forgetfulness of self,
whereas Christianity presented "systematic opposition to the depraved
tendencies of man."[35] Radicals disputed this. They believed that precisely those commitments that distinguished them from priests – work, fa-
therhood, and citizenship – formed the basis of a more methodical morality.

Michelet, the most suggestive of the radical polemicists, argued that
Catholic devotion brought about the "annihilation of personality." His
notions of morality rested explicitly upon a preference for ethical over
sacramental approaches to salvation: He caricatured the believer as su-
perstitious, lax, and dependent and his – or more generally her – rela-

tion with a confessor as precluding at once autonomy and human loyalty. The practice of confession received his especial disapproval. He assumed, as did many *laïcs*, that it must produce cycles of sin and repentance, self-abandon and self-abasement: It discouraged the development of a continuously ethical personality. On similar grounds the ferociously chaste Proudhon had opposed the cult of Mary Magdalen, and Quinet advanced a curiously puritanical argument in favor of divorce. The Bourbon Restoration, Quinet wrote, in refusing to admit adultery as grounds for dissolution of marriage, had implicitly condoned the offense.[36]

Michelet's emphasis on psychological, rather than logical necessity enabled him to ignore, for example, the orthodox requirement that a resolve to sin no more be part of contrition and thus requisite to absolution. In developing his attack on the church, he anticipated the distinction that Max Weber would later make between a religious *doctrine* and "the practical impulses to action which are founded in the psychological and practical contexts of religion," its "economic ethic."[37] In response to a hypothetical objection that he was attacking a seventeenth-century quietism that was no longer canonical, Michelet declared himself justified in separating the spirit of a doctrine and the methods associated with its practice from the *letter* of the doctrine, which, he emphasized, the first two frequently survive.[38]

Michelet's style and his argument – which was sometimes tendentious but more often charged with sibylline acumen – were inseparable, and fellow academics mistrusted both. Undeterred, Michelet persisted in attacking simultaneously habits of mind, modes of expression, and social practices. He assumed in the ranks of his adversaries a like union of moral and aesthetic preferences. His revulsion against the baroque, the art of the Counter-Reformation, strengthened his conviction that the aim of clerical education was ornamental, that taste, no less than character, was corrupted by it: "A taste for littleness and humility . . . for the least of creation, little children, little birds, little lambs, little bees, authorizes with the Jesuits minuteness, baseness of style, narrowness, pettiness of heart . . . The essential [aim is] to make souls feeble and false, to make the small very small and the simple [into] idiots."[39]

The same obsession with humility, an insistence upon the sinfulness of pride, Michelet further argued, led "evil sophists" to countenance, and possibly to encourage, sins of the flesh. According to him, the *directeur de l'âme* feared that if the flesh held itself aloof from sin, the spirit would grow proud. Therefore, the body had to falter in order to humble the mind. It was an outrageous canard, and yet the accusation resonated and found real assent. Michelet had caught the emotional core of the grievances of well-conducted lapsed Catholics – that the church, although brutal with principled heretics, showed itself to be indulgent with feckless sinners. The moralists whom this policy so enraged concluded that the church was more concerned with exacting submission than with promoting virtue.

Radical anticlericalism cannot be explained as some Marxist and Catholic historians would suggest, as a diversionary maneuver merely, but the more astute radicals did see in anticlericalism an inspiring alternative to class conflict. Quinet candidly described its advantages: "Social wars disorganize a nation; religious wars do nothing comparable. In religious struggles, each party contains all elements of society, great and small, rich and poor, the nation in its entirety is represented in each religious faction."[40] To my knowledge, Quinet never considered the possibility that class and religious affiliations might correspond. The clash of material interests plainly dismayed him: Such struggles were not edifying ones, and in them "all moral superiority vanished." He asserted that conservatives were left with no instinct except that of preserving their advantages, and those willing to support the weak had to expect ruin and oblivion, because "the poor have nothing to give, even that vapor called glory." However, Quinet presented a more serious objection to class war: it admitted of no solution. No group actually involved in production (clerics presumably were either expendable or capable of reeducation) could be permanently excluded from national life. Class war could end only in bloody impasse, whereas a religious struggle would permit reconciliation of the bourgeoisie and the people, and of men and women, on a new plane of reason and fellowship.

THE NEW MAN, *PUR ET DUR*

The radical anticleric, like all scrupulous dissenters, demanded that others see his protest as he himself saw it, not as a shirking of duty but as a quest for a more adequate ethic. The *laïcs* prided themselves upon the tradition of republicans who were *purs et durs*, and the imperial police were occasionally forced to pay rueful tribute to this characterization. They noted, for example, of one Lyonnais militant his "irreproachable conduct, regular habits, advanced opinions."[41] Renan recalled, with as much indignation as his tranquil soul could muster, that many accused him of leaving the seminary so that he might more conveniently misbehave. Nothing, he protested, could be more false. On leaving Saint-Sulpice he adopted by preference "the manners of a Protestant pastor." A freethinker, he wrote, had to have perfect decorum in his personal life, because a man could not permit himself two rebellions at one time.[42]

Although their ideal man was self-controlled, the radicals did not deny passion: On the contrary, they demanded its rehabilitation as a human capacity that was no less honorable than reason. Anticlerics believed sustained repression to be impossible for a personality or for a society, and they concluded from this that priests were hypocrites and reactionaries, fools. Republican mores depended upon an acceptance of instinctual energy and upon its legitimation: Social unrest and personal demoralization resulted from attempts to suppress what could not be denied. Corbon put the axiom in its most purely Baconian form, maintaining that human energies, like every other natural force, injured man only until he was able "to understand and use them."[43] Michelet, too, pleaded for the legitimate grievances of the instincts. A remarkable catalogue of the chagrins, anxieties, and humiliations incident to each occupation, in the section "Servitudes and Hatreds" of *The People*, presented a sense of impotence as the chief misery of the factory worker. When a worker's body was subjected to a mechanical process that he could neither control nor understand, Michelet wrote, "he feels himself to be so little a man" that in leaving the factory he urgently seeks the "liveliest exaltation of human faculties . . . a sense of immense liberty, that exaltation may be drunkenness, most often, love."[44] Radicals believed that education in science and political economy would make industry's hitherto incomprehensible ways intelligible and that men who grasped the process as a whole would enter into it with self-respect, and perhaps could even improve it.

Above all, it was in politics that radicals expected to provide a sphere for the "exercise of faculties that work neither engages nor develops . . . It preserves many energetic natures from demoralization." Thus, Corbon fought the stereotype of the socialist ne'er-do-well: "He passes in a cabaret all his time not better spent beating his wife,"[45] as Tocqueville described one militant with whom he was acquainted. Corbon defended the people's "great and legitimate need for a public life." If it should be denied "a broad intellectual participation in the general movement of things, . . . it will squander its generous sap."[46] Corbon wrote "sap," not "blood" – he understood that threats of bloodshed were ill-suited to the early years of the Liberal Empire – but he substituted a more audacious thought: the onanistic futility of victories *sans lendemain*, of political action without issue.

Radicals believed that if every man could become, like the *sans-culotte*, a citizen, worker, and *père de famille*, the duties thus necessarily undertaken would develop both reason and sympathy. The ghastly irony that this ideal – *travail, famille, patrie* – was expressed many decades later on the coins of the Vichy government proves only that any ideal is susceptible to corruption. The radicals were not protofascists because they believed work honorable, political engagement essential, and sexual love and parenthood worthier commitments than celibacy, nor did their con-

cern for these virtues make them "fundamentally" or "merely conservative."[47] They themselves would have denied that conservatives supported labor and monogamy; their adversaries, the radicals would have
said, lived by unearned increment and the double standard. The principles of 1789, radical republicans asserted, held the necessary wisdom:
"The unhappiness of the times and the frailty of our spirits have re-
tarded their glorious and definitive manifestation . . . and it is this infidelity to ourselves that accounts for our moral misery and our servitude."[48]

The central thought is "this infidelity to ourselves." With Proudhon,
republicans regarded the problem as one of political identity: Their critical achievement – of moral imagination and of social invention – would
be a modern masculinity. They contrasted this manhood, "powerful in
acts, fruitful in works,"[49] with the clerical life, which they considered to
be irrational, unnatural, and above all, unproductive. The language of
potency and fertility was reiterated ceaselessly and in a variety of contexts: Scientific truth, political agitation, capital investment, light itself
were all described as *fécond*. The celebration of productivity was linked,
certainly, to the boast of the bourgeois republican that he too was a
worker and shared the common heritage of the laboring third estate, a
basis on which the solidarity of the bourgeoisie and the workers might
possibly be prolonged.

A work ethic was incontestably part of the republican myth. The
young Clemenceau is purported to have asked his father, a provincial
republican doctor facing deportation to North Africa after *le 2 décembre*,
how he might avenge him. Clemenceau *père* replied, "Work!" The republicans were busy men. ("Aide-toi, le ciel t'aidera"[50] was a secularist
maxim as well as the name of a republican secret society.) They emphat-
ically denied *dérogeance*: Trade did not unfit a man for nobler pursuits.
Men of the *nouvelles couches* – commercial and industrial notables and poor
professionals – confident that they understood political economy, the
management of men, and the march of history, were ready to apply
their talents to the direction of the state.

Increasingly, capitalist standards of conduct became familiar in political argument. The "imperative mandate," an extreme form of direct
representation in which a legislator agreed to follow the wishes of his
constituents on issues specified during the campaign, was spoken of as
a "contract." Clients, who were presumed to know their own interests,
instructed their "agents." Gambetta, who popularized the term "nouvelles couches," was himself contemptuously described by opponents as
the "travelling salesman of the republic." His "profession of faith" before the electors of Belleville accepted an engagement to carry out the
wishes of his constituents: "Thus, we shall contract publicly. . . ."[51]

Jean Macé suggested a different type of imperative mandate: The candidate would set forth what he intended to do and sign his "billet"; and the carrying out of his pledges became, then, a matter of common honesty.[52] Macé's baldest statement of this position appeared in *Jacques Bonhomme à ses députés*: "Businessman or deputy, can an honest man be anything other than a machine for keeping promises?"[53]

Ultimately, radicals trusted in reason, nature, and history. In their more confident moments, they considered themselves part of a universal brotherhood. They watched with visceral concern the struggles of foreign progressives[54] and saw in every victory over vestiges of feudalism the promise of their own eventual ascendance. The triumph of the North in the American Civil War was cause for jubilation. William Seward had early prophesied war on the basis of comparative history: "Did any property [sic] class ever reform itself? Did the patricians of old Rome, the *noblesse* and clergy in France, the landholders in Ireland, the landed aristocracy in England?"[55] Clemenceau, reporting on the Reconstruction period in America for *Le Temps* (a Parisian daily) recognized in men like Thaddeus Stevens and Charles Sumner fighters whose fundamentally democratic cause was akin to his own. Clemenceau characterized Southern society as one that was systematically perverted by slavery: "Private as well as public manners, deeply affected by such a 'peculiar institution,' have evolved certain customs, a whole complex of ideas and sentiments . . . a nondescript of delicate refinement and all villainy."[56]

Like the abolitionists in America, French radicals engaged in elaborate and self-congratulatory statistical comparisons correlating schools, libraries, hospitals, inventions, and industrial productivity, per capita with the degree of human emancipation.[57] During the 1860s the Ligue de l'enseignement would distribute Manier's *cartes d'ignorance*, maps that suggested a link between ignorance and misery as well as the intimate connection between high literacy rates and every other conceivable good.

The radical republicans, rationalist and egalitarian by conviction, expected all fair-minded people to share their confidence in human progress. Etienne Vacherot, for example, willingly disclaimed originality in his discussion of democracy, maintaining that political ideas lack authority without a degree of generality and cannot be realized until they become obvious to all. Visionary politics, he wrote in 1860, are the politics of irrelevance or despair: Platitudinous complacency bodes better. Vacherot's affectation of banality did not reassure the authorities, who found his *La Démocratie* sufficiently provoking to warrant putting its author in jail. But many agreed. Dr. Guépin, the cheerful freemason, wrote that the great industrialists and savants who proclaimed that "everything is socializing itself" were no longer isolated dreamers, but "the most elevated representatives of the vigorous groups of men who surround and support them."[58] Despite their profound individuality, these men expressed commonly held beliefs that had been established in their shared experience of science and industry. They knew that events are related by sequences of cause and effect: They saw, in history, law, necessity, and progress.

Alas, Guépin continued, this knowledge was not immediately accessible to all. Elegant idlers, of course, comprehended only "intrigues, gestures, accident, caprice, and whim"; but more tragically, a rational view of life was also denied to many men and to all women. Poor men and most women were excluded from the crucial experiences of the century – education, politics, and work – in which reason can be exercised. They did not find in their lives verification of the truths that were axiomatic to the enlightened; and the same economic forces that made men accessories to machines also trivialized women. Both working men and economically redundant ladies suffered "the greatest deprivation . . . to pass through life without understanding it."[59]

The bourgeois was himself diminished by these developments, because they made it difficult for him to sympathize with, or even to comprehend, the plight of the others. Michelet's *Le Peuple*, written in 1846, was only one of the early efforts at reconciliation. Republican artists, for their part, published collections of engravings depicting popular occupations. Courbet illustrated one, *Les Métiers*, which announced its purposes thus: "The work has for its object to paint popular manners, to put the leisure class in rapport with the people, to initiate the public into the existence of artisans, [which is] too much disdained, too little known."[60]

Radicals were dismayed to find Frenchmen mutually unintelligible. An illiterate man could not belong to his country or his times: Like the cleric he lived apart – *ni de son temps, ni de son pays* – and he could not be reasoned with. It was just this – the ability of the church to communicate with those in society still inaccessible to rational argument – that frustrated anticlerics: "The priests have been permitted to undertake among the poorer classes the most dangerous initiatives: meetings of workers, homes for apprentices, associations of domestics who report to the priests . . . The unity of action and the monopoly of association, surely these are two great forces."[61]

Remembering the White Terror, bourgeois republicans feared a reactionary rabble. The "Church and King mob," like the *lumpenproletariat* it so markedly resembled, had been an all-too-familiar phenomenon. Corbon had insisted upon the thoroughly conservative character of the desperate and semi-criminal poor.[62] Republicans were convinced after the June Days, if they had not been before, that to ignore these "irrational" beings was as rash as it was irresponsible. It remained for bourgeois men to share their beliefs with the dispossessed, to establish "a certain community of ideas and sentiments that permits the members of a society to draw closer to one another, to understand and respect each other in the most unequal circumstances." Radicals described themselves as men who refused to accept "the desolating thesis . . . [that] the brutalization of part of the human race is inevitable."[63] The magnanimous saw their fellows wronged and diminished; the prudent understood that unrelieved wretchedness threatened the social order.

It is true that in their hopes for better relations with workers, the radicals' egalitarianism was fraught with real conflict: They certainly wished for the voluntary union of equals, but they wanted hegemony, too. The resolution of these tensions depended upon a peculiar conception of the division of labor: They imagined a modern economy of specialists united by common purpose and by a large, indeed, empathetic understanding among fellow workers. Both Charles Renouvier and the chemist Alfred Naquet (better known for his sponsorship of the divorce bill in the Third Republic) anticipated Durkheim's account of organic solidarity.[64] Increasing division of labor, they held, heightened both individuality and interdependence. Specialization developed and differentiated modern individuals, who thus needed one another more than omnicompetent primitives were supposed to do; moreover, advanced individuals were judged able to acknowledge and will their intensified solidarity.

Radicals insisted, too, that functional differentiation did not have to imply political inequality. Indeed, in the twentieth century, Alain would find hierarchy acceptable *only* as a means to equality. "Inequality among agents, equality among citizens": Thus, a judge was superior to the judged so that he might judge all fairly.[65] "Rights," Naquet insisted, "are not proportional to capacities." In 1870 Jules Ferry similarly rejoiced that employer and employee were no longer master and servant, but parties to a contract, each with specified rights and responsibilities.[66] Elwitt asserts that Ferry "welcomed the growing separation of labor and capital,"[67] but obviously, it is independence, not division, that Ferry celebrated. One would not for a moment contest that Ferry presented an imperfect account of industrial relations, but the moral is properly radical. Consent replaces deference; subordination is limited to that which is essential for tasks jointly agreed upon – and the radicals were determined that the essentials be agreed upon.

Education would make the potentially threatening oppressed both autonomous and tractable. The radicals hoped that schooling would make workers as reasonable and self-satisfied as it was credited with making the bourgeoisie. It would teach them to reject utopias, which were in the nature of things demonstrably unattainable, and would instruct them in the theodicy of supply and demand that accounted so well for their condition. Charles Robert, an early champion of the Ligue de l'enseignement, attributed the docility of Lancashire workers during the cotton famine of the 1860s to the "happy discussion of the truths of political economy."[68]

Similar arguments were made by a school inspector, Cèlestin Hippeau, in a report on public education in America prepared for Victor Duruy and relied upon also by Ferry. In America, Hippeau found,

> no pretended defender of religious faith has ever seriously questioned whether or not to educate all citizens, rich and poor, men and women, rural and urban . . . ; nor is it deemed cruel to open vistas of culture to those doomed later to abandon these pursuits for more mundane occupations, because nothing is taught that does not elevate, refine, and uplift.[69]

Americans expect only benign consequences from education, Hippeau argued, because Americans genuinely believe that social status must be earned, and not result from an "accident of birth." As Ferry, too, was to stress, inequality of education worked in France to perpetuate that "regime of caste" that all other social forces were struggling to overcome. Liquidity was a more evident truth than concentration of capital; and Guépin, for example, recalled, with full assent, Condorcet's belief that fortunes tend naturally to equality, save when disparities are perpetuated by "aritficial means." Significantly, it was the church that defended primogeniture.[70]

Although radicals expected France to develop in this agreeable, egalitarian, and just direction they were plagued with fears that it might not. Failures, remembered and anticipated, tormented French progressives. Repeated experience with *revolutions manquées* no doubt taught them a prescient shrewdness that happier lands might occasionally have done well to heed. (Georges Clemenceau, with a *vendéen's* grasp of the essentials, predicted that Reconstruction would fail in the American South, because "every inch of land has been left in the hands of the former rebels," and he noted that among the Union commanders only the German "forty-eighter" Carl Schurz shared his worry.)[71] The past's dead hand had throttled them before. Rage, terror, and loathing underlay the radicals' brilliant optimism, and the emotional coherence of the rationalist ethic – all that made it so broadly and immensely appealing – depended upon the interrelatedness of their hopes and fears. Manichaean antitheses patterned their writings: struggles between light and shadow, fertility and barrenness, life and death.

Peter Gay, writing with great wisdom about the Enlightenment, understood that the philosophes themselves had not been optimists but dualists who saw "two irreconcilable patterns of life, thought, and feeling." They believed that Reason and Superstition struggled for mastery within every epoch and neither ever reigned unchallenged. Their hopes for progress rested upon the possibility that history might not prove irredeemably cyclical, that the Gothic night that had fallen upon the Stoics and Epicureans would not redescend upon them. Light imagery came as naturally to them as it did to the Albigensians and as it would do to their heirs, nineteenth century radicals. Alain expressed the same apprehension in a 1911 essay on "Progress." "Barbarism," he wrote, "follows us like our shadow . . . The spring has always the same winter to vanquish."[72]

It was the church that represented the dark power – decadent and discredited but powerfully, meretriciously attractive and emasculating. Quinet described France as Laocoön and his children crushed by the black snakes of clericalism. His symbolism was apt. Laocoön was, of course, the only Trojan man who was not deceived about the military peril inherent in a seemingly pious offering.) Vacherot, too, used a drastic image to express his country's plight: Samson and Delilah.[73] However strong a man, however unshakeable his convictions, his work could be undone and his posterity corrupted by a lesser creature.

WOMEN: "HE WHO HOLDS THE WOMAN HOLDS ALL"

The virility that republicans wanted to affirm in work and in politics required another crucial ratification, the reassurance of conjugal love. It was not patriotism or industrial productivity alone, but also ties between husband and wife, father and child that the church was alleged to subvert.[74] Radicals argued that the church, while professing to strengthen the family, had little use for those "rights of the *père de famille*" that it never failed to invoke in opposition to compulsory schooling. "The priest seeks to substitute his authority for the natural authority, . . . the husband's."[75]

In 1858, the Mortara scandal underscored radical allegations that priests viewed earthly attachments as "something stolen from God."[76] The small son of a Bolognese Jewish family, baptized during a serious illness by his Christian nurse, was kidnapped by the woman after his unexpected recovery. She escaped with the boy to the papal territories, where Pius IX upheld her refusal to relinquish him to "apostasy." Napoleon III, whose troops still protected the Pope's temporal sovereignty, was under intense domestic pressure to demand the child's release, but he was unable to move the Pope.

The Mortara case, however exceptional, was taken to epitomize the struggle between paternal and priestly authority. It is impossible to imagine a more conventional French quarrel than that fought, generation after generation, between freethinking husbands and pious wives.[77] Indeed, women's presumed clerical bias deprived them of the vote until the establishment of the Fourth Republic – when their supposed conservatism probably militated for franchise – and denied them a legal voice in their children's education until 1971. The lack of harmony between men's and women's religious beliefs presented problems at many levels: It denied romantic love complete *épanchement*,[78] piqued the husband's *amour-propre* and troubled his wife's confidence in him, and laid bare to children the moral and metaphysical confusion of their elders. It was, in short, unfailingly productive of chagrin and grief.

Significantly, in the revival of secularist energy immediately before and during the early years of the Third Republic, these private troubles were acknowledged, politicized, and held to be amenable to collective action. Moreover, radicals believed that their resolution was inextricably joined to the solution of other problems. The support of women became in the minds of many progressives the sine qua non of free government. "How can they be indifferent?" Jules Simon asked in *L'Ecole*. "Men make laws," Quinet wrote, "Women shall make the mores."[79] The Republic, Michelet had warned in 1845, would never be secure so long as "our wives and our daughters are brought up *by our enemies*, enemies of the modern spirit, of liberty, and of the family." Perhaps no words of his were more quoted in the sixties than these: "There is a grave *dissentiment* in the family, and the gravest of all [sic]. We can speak to our mothers, our wives, and our daughters about subjects we discuss with those who mean nothing to us . . . never of things that touch the heart or the moral life."[80]

Michelet himself had suffered and lost one of those "unequal combats of human affection and mystical prestige."[81] Shortly before he wrote *Du Prêtre, de la Femme, et de la Famille*, Michelet's mistress, the mother of his student (and later son-in-law) Alfred Dumesnil, died of cancer. Mme Dumesnil had fallen ill soon after consenting to live openly with him. When medical treatment failed to cure her, she sought relief in mesmerism, appealed to several charlatans, and turned finally to a priest, Abbé Coeur, an urbane churchman whose influence over her quickly surpassed that of her notorious friend.

Du Prêtre was all too obviously the infuriated response of a man spurned. Michelet, characteristically, spoke openly of adultery, impotence, and frigidity. Both he and Quinet attributed to the medieval church the idea that love was impossible in marriage: The woman's heart belonged to a troubador or cleric; only her body remained to her husband. "He to whom the mind belongs, holds the whole person"; so the confessor leaves the husband, "the soul's widower," only a "dead, inert, lifeless possession."[82] Michelet feared that the priest would excel the husband – not in virility but in complaisance. The bourgeois laudably immersed in work ignores his family, so the cleric wins the soul of the woman and the mind of the child by default, by sharing their most trivial concerns (as the husband and father cannot) and indulging their weakness. He dwelt, too, upon the humiliation of obtaining "that which belongs to you" only through the authorization and indulgence of another – a plaint echoed by Jean Barois, who dismisses his wife's fondness for him as a "little licit flame" sanctioned by her mother and her confessor.[83]

In his revulsion against religious sentimentality, Michelet compared Guido's *Annunciation* to a "seraphic seduction," but his most astonishing critique was reserved for the cult of the Sacred Heart. He attacked this enthusiasm – which was to assume political significance in the 1870s, when some Catholics urged the National Assembly to atone for the "sins" of the Paris Commune by dedicating the nation to the Sacré Coeur,[84] – as decadent sadoeroticism. "When a faith degenerates," he wrote, it "hates all ideas and wants nothing that cannot be touched." For systematic argument, for the chaste clarity of exposition, it substitutes a "mute sign"; and the heart itself, "that organ, powerfully influenced by the revolutions of the blood, is not less powerful than sex itself . . . in it all loves are mingled indiscriminately . . . it lends itself marvelously well to the language of double-entendre."[85] Finally, he dismissed the devotion as a concession to modern delicacy, a surrogate for an older, even more objectionable preoccupation with the mystery of the Virgin Birth.[86]

Above all, Michelet lamented the moral divorce in marriage, which posed in microcosm the dissensions in society – the displacement of affection and loyalty, the dissociation of personality (because it was nothing less) that inhibited wholehearted and effective action. The pervasiveness of this theme in novels, in the correspondence of bureaucrats and the diatribes of the opposition, and in the projected statutes for libraries and coeducational schools makes clear that Michelet's private anguish was an archetypical one.

Moderate men expressed their unabashed longing to reign supreme at home. Hippolyte Taine, for instance, described an English family – wife, children, and servants – gathered to hear their master read a sermon and prayers: "By this community and this direction of moral sentiment, the master succeeds in holding before his household and even before his children his true, legitimate and complete role."[87] Taine's wish for an ampler patriarchal dignity was expressed in many forms. Men asked for comprehension as well as for authority, for sympathetic support in their professional and political actions. Vacherot complained that women were unable to comprehend their husbands' aspirations because they had been educated exclusively to answer the commands of the church or fashionable society: "With the first she calls all striving after truth, pride, and with the second she calls a devotion to justice, folly."[88]

This problem, and the related one of being undermined in one's *métier* because women were ignorant or suspicious of science, rankled.[89] Louis Legrand, a deputy from the department of the Nord, was honored by the Academy of Moral and Political Sciences in 1870 for a work, *Le Mariage et les moeurs en France*, that, though far from egalitarian (spouses were to be joined in the "hierarchical relation of love"), nevertheless asked for informed submission: Current female education, Legrand echoed Vacherot, could produce only a housekeeper or a fashionable woman. Neither course seriously educated a girl. Although an entirely domestic curriculum might preserve her virtue, "chastity, however respectable, has neither great charm nor great ascendancy when it is accompanied by silliness (*sottise*). Man thirsts for sympathy, consolation, feelings, hopes."[90]

This estrangement, distressing in bourgeois households, proved ruinous for the poor. Jules Simon's *L'Ouvrière*, a report on working-class family life, accounted for the existence of much popular misery by citing the decline of domesticity among the poor. Among those who were moved by this picture was Jules Ferry. Writing in 1870, he promised that female education would substitute for the cabaret the "enlightened hearthside, animated by conversation, embellished with reading."[91]

Quinet, too, saw eugenic peril in the undereducation of women. Natural selection depended upon the ability of women to recognize increasingly advanced men: "The male wants to please the female; it is one of the organic causes of progress in nature." Naquet agreed with him that indiscriminate mating would not improve the race. "To couple without love is an anti-social act," he said. When women are adequately educated, they will reason better, men will love them better, and all will benefit, for it is love that discerns worth and makes an instinctual act redound to the common good.[92]

Radicals believed that the secular education of women was politically and socially imperative; and if the response of the clergy to their overtures was any index of the importance that ecclesiastics attached to the continuing orthodoxy of women, *laïcs* chose their target well. Victor

Duruy, the combative secularist whom Napoleon III designated as his minister of public instruction in 1863, asked after government losses in the general elections of that year, "How much of our current difficulty results from the education of our girls by those who are neither of their time nor of their country?"[93] Subsequently, Duruy's plan to provide secular secondary education for girls would provoke a violent political storm. In 1867 Duruy authorized nationally a series of courses, usually taught by *lycée* faculty in town halls, that young ladies, accompanied by their mothers or maids, might attend. The project was denounced by Félix Dupanloup, the not illiberal bishop of Orléans, as part of a conspiracy of freethinkers to corrupt Christian Frenchwomen.[94] His pamphlet, *Woman, Christian and French* (1868) followed close upon *Atheism and the Social Peril* (1866).

Dupanloup's extreme agitation might be explained by some statistics from a survey that he initiated shortly after his elevation to the see of Orléans in 1850. At that time only 11 percent of the general population of the diocese, but 67 percent of women aged thirteen to twenty, received communion at Easter. Paschal communion was perhaps not the best sign of devotion – because some of the faithful probably felt that pilgrimages were more inspiriting – but it was the conventional indicator of regular practice. Communicants had been accordingly analyzed by age and sex, and it had emerged that young women, precisely that group whose faith secular education was expected to undermine, were the most (indeed the only) reliably orthodox group.[95]

The entire French church opposed Duruy's project: ultramontanes and liberals alike. Auguste Cochin, who had long argued for political moderation and religious tolerance, rejoiced to see the church intervene in politics in its "rightful sphere."[96]

Duruy fought back and appealed to Empress Eugénie, who was known to be devout, in terms that she found irresistible. Those who argue, he pleaded, that a French girl cannot be in the presence of a man without danger (although, of course, he had recommended that the girls be chaperoned) were those who advocate a return to the seclusion of the harem. He knew – as she did – that Frenchwomen were "more valiant and more pure," that they wished not only a community of sentiment with their husbands, but also "a community of ideas, so that their souls can better be but one." The empress had no daughter, but her two nieces were sent to the Paris classes.[97]

In a confidential circular to the rectors of the several provincial academies, Duruy emphasized that the secular education of girls would greatly augment the "moral influence" of the University and continued: "We shall have contributed to the disappearance of the intellectual divorce that too often exists between husband and wife. How many times harmony in a marriage is troubled by difference in education, sentiment, and ideas that prevent the two spouses from understanding one another and that force them to live in two separate and contrary worlds."[98]

Secularists in the opposition welcomed Duruy's initiatives, and his ouster from the cabinet in 1869 was taken as proof that only a republic might accomplish reforms of such magnitude. Jules Ferry, in his celebrated lecture on equality read to the Society for Elementary Education, paid tribute to Duruy and recalled to his anti-Bonapartist audience the clerical opposition to Duruy's proposals: "You remember that clamor of bishops . . . The bishops knew it well, [that] he who holds the woman, holds all, at first, because she holds the child, later, because she holds the husband, not perhaps, the young husband . . . but the husband exhausted and disillusioned with life."[99]

Ferry, the republican *éminence jeune*, no less than the minister who would be reckoned his illustrious predecessor, reiterated Michelet's description of marriage in France: "Equality of education, unity reestablished in the family! There is today a barrier between men and women, between husband and wife . . . Most apparently harmonious marriages [are] in truth divided by the most profound differences of opinion, taste, and sentiment . . ."[100]

From women, no less than from workers, bourgeois republicans wanted something more than acquiescence. Indeed, in the 1860s and 1870s, relations between the sexes became paradigmatic of other encounters between social superiors and their subordinates. Macé, for example, recalled the fatal insouciance of 1848: "Certainly, it was agreeable to believe one held the people like a bride, who would follow one anywhere." Marx had written even more harshly of the same events that "a nation and a woman are not forgiven the unguarded hour when the first adventurer that came along could violate them."[101] Radicals believed that relations hitherto characterized by force and fraud – and thus weakened by hypocrisy, deceit, and evasion – must be made frank, consensual, and freely chosen. Honest men sensed the parallel deficiencies of the marital and social bond. Was it liberty they wished for others or merely the absence of opposition? Jules Ferry faced the issue candidly. Equality, he cautioned, is resisted by two sorts of vanity: "pride of class and pride of sex, this latter is worse, more persistent, more ferocious . . . In the heart of the best of us, there is a sultan."[102]

Indeed, the radicals' solicitude for the education of women has not received unmixed approbation. Even John Stuart Mill, no friend of revealed religion, cast doubt upon the designs of "certain liberal and progressive French writers" on their wives' liberty of conscience.[103] More recently, Theodore Zeldin has gone so far as to suggest that the church might "be appreciated positively as one of the most important ways by which women began to liberate themselves from the domination of men." He offers no evidence for this, and he does acknowledge that "the Church never thought of itself as doing any such thing."[104] Furthermore, his extraordinary revision neglects entirely a central difficulty, the fact – which no radical ever lost sight of – that priests were also men. More important, however asymmetrical the relations between husband and wife in the nineteenth century, their inequality did not begin to approach that which obtained between clergy and laity. The church, becoming increasingly hierarchical, was on the point of declaring itself infallible. No autocrat who knew himself to be human was putting forth claims remotely like that.

In their relations with women, as with workers, radicals relied upon a certain idea of the division of labor. They saw perfection achieved through complementarity of roles. Michelet, who often argued in this vein, believed that France must be guided by the "instinct of the simple," as well as by the reason of the learned. Naquet insisted upon the "absolute equality of the reasoning and affective faculties."[105] It was, after all, a generation enthralled by the androgyny of genius, with a Fourierist confidence in the free play of multifarious faculties. Radicals advocated that women be more thoroughly educated because they accepted a sexual division of labor as something natural, akin to the "hierarchy of talent" that they expected education to establish in the economy. Republican women were as welcome as republican workers and as essential. Hippeau argued that education was like nourishment: Observing the coeducational refectory at Oberlin College, admirable for its decorum and fellowship, he had been struck by an awareness that reading the same books cannot change women into men any more than does their sharing the same food. Each person assimilates knowledge according to the laws of his or her organism: There are good and bad diets, weak or vigorous spirits, but there can be no confusion of gender.[106] Education does not unsex; nor does it unfit anyone for any useful task.

Laïc arguments in favor of coeducation provided an extremely characteristic example of secularist reasoning. Republican mores depended upon internalization, not upon surveillance: (As expressed by Elisa Lemonnier, a collaborator of Mme Charles Sauvestre in the early vocational education of women, "No girl is adequately chaperoned unless she chaperons herself."[107] It was the hope of its supporters that secular education would develop faculties that enabled both men and women to withstand temptation. It was insufficient ethically – and perhaps also not feasible – merely to avoid occasions of sin. Reason and judgment must be disciplined by experience. *Laïcs* inveighed against memorization, against catechisms, and designed *leçons des choses*, which they hoped would better approximate real choices. Reality incontestably required the society of the other sex: Men and women did best to learn early in life that work and duty are the essential context for love.

Nevertheless, sex segregation obtained almost absolutely in French schools, and Catholics opposed mixed schools in principle, if not always in practice – with dire results for the education of girls. Jules Simon reported in 1865 that 19,312 communes made no provision whatsoever for the education of girls.[108] Hippeau cited the perfect order in American schools as proof that coeducation was not itself evil. Far from promoting promiscuity, the presence of young women had made college men courteous: Boys at Oberlin refrained not only from "vicious practices," but even from smoking. Monsignor Dupanloup, attacking Duruy, Hippeau's esteemed chief, had feared that "more than one marriage might result" between professors and students. Was marriage, then, such a bad thing? Did the church not intend women to marry? Was a convent the proper place to prepare for marriage? Far too often girls entered into "duties for which they were extremely ill-prepared."[109]

Hippeau contrasted convent schooling with higher education of girls in America: There they had before them the truths of real life. A report in favor of coeducation prepared for the departmental council of the Yonne, based on observations of Swiss schools, pressed the same argument: Mixed schools enabled both boys and girls to distinguish appearance from reality early in the life, to judge character wisely; and they provided experiences that some families did not furnish: "Who has not observed that boys without sisters are turbulent, that girls without brothers are sentimental?" The report noted, too, with satisfaction, that there were fewer illegitimate births in cantons with coeducation.[110]

Coeducation, then, produced not mannish women but better women. Hippeau recalled with evident rapture a defense of regicide offered by a seventeen-year-old American girl at the Packer Collegiate Institute in Brooklyn Heights, New York. Another student opposed capital punishment altogether, but she believed that the execution of Charles I was justified because he had "violated the laws of his country."[111] What Hippeau applauded was not, indeed, her conclusions, but the habituation to reasoning and self-expression and to mutually tolerant debate. Dupanloup's writings had celebrated womanhood, sublime in Mary as virgin and widow;[112] republicans wanted mothers of the Gracchi.

Republicans sought to educate women because when they were unschooled they threatened disruption: No domestic or political settlement was proof against their restless and unenlightened passions. Emma Bovary's transgressions were those expected of the *femme désoeuvrée*.[113] Even nondomestic employment was sometimes recommended, precisely in order to make women better wives and mothers. Michelet congratulated the commercial classes for involving women in business: Shared responsibilities enabled women to appreciate their husbands' cares and taught them a sympathy and prudence unattainable for more sheltered ladies, who were not likely (short of bankruptcy) even to hear about their husbands' business. Guépin saw moral value in the "religion of labor for both sexes,"[114] and so he incorporated it in a revised initiation rite that he prepared for the freemasons.[115] Work alone, unenlightened by proper schooling, was insufficient. Only when each person understood his own duties, when he justly valued the labor of others, could cooperation be satisfying and fruitful.

SCHOOL, THE NEW CHURCH

Secular democrats saw the school as the new church. Citizens might sit side by side on its benches and receive that intuition of equality, that "confraternity of ideas," that religion had ceased to assure.

Ferry foresaw "an egalitarian nation, one nation animated by that spirit of the whole and that confraternity of ideas that is the strength of all true democracies . . . [can be achieved] if, among the two classes [there is] that first rapprochement that results from the commingling of rich and poor on the benches of a school."[116] This vision derived from an almost identical passage in *Le Peuple*. Michelet had hoped, twenty years earlier, that "if only both children, rich and poor, have sat altogether on the benches of the same school, if joined in friendship though divided in career . . . they will preserve in their disinterested, innocent friendship, the sacred knot of the City."[117] Ferry did not acknowledge Michelet in his talk but alluded to Hippeau's report, which endorsed not only free, compulsory primary education but also the American comprehensive high school: "To unite in the same schools, to seat on the same benches, and to provide a common education for the children of all strata, is the most certain method of preserving that spirit of equality that is the supreme law of all truly democratic institutions."[118]

Constructive anticlericals labored to recreate moral community: The "idea of mutual dignity"[119] that Proudhon saw as essential to every social institution, nation, commune, or family, they all held to be incompatible with stratified morality, with skepticism for the few and mystification for the many. Taine described with evident wonder and relief the Anglican Book of Common Prayer. There was nothing in it, he wrote, that an educated man could not accept, "at least symbolically." He took a historian's pleasure in its frankly eclectic nature: The prayers were dated, their historical origins acknowledged – "the faithful are informed on history and criticism" – there was no reason that later editions might not even include *éclaircissements* furnished by modern biblical criticism. Above all, he welcomed a religious atmosphere in which a "cultivated man" might, without intellectual sacrifice, remain in communication with simple people: "On the fundamental point, which is the moral emotion, everyone is in accord. . . ." Some French liberals hoped that Protestantism might furnish an inclusive faith; and, to that end, Edouard Laboulaye translated the works of the Boston Unitarian William Ellery Channing.[120] Others felt that authentic reunion must be founded in French historic experience, in the Revolution.

Anticlericalism was historically a republican enthusiasm, although its political nuances ranged vastly, from Taine's anglophile longing for an unembarrassing creed preached by a gentlemanly clergy in underdecorated churches to the cerebral iconoclasm of Auguste Blanqui, for whom unbelief heralded social revolution. Blanqui wrote in December of 1864: "Indifference to philosophical questions indicates a lack of maturity and decision in political ideas. One cannot seriously change a society in its political and social order without destroying the philosophical idea that is its foundation."[121] Its ethical tone varied, too, from the prudery associated with British and American puritanism to the Brechtian rebellion of the *communard* Jules Vallès – who rejected his family's *bien-pensant* meanness for the more feeling world of labor, "where fathers cried and mothers laughed."[122] The anticlerical faith, like any vigorous tradition, was riddled with family quarrels, cherished antagonisms, mutually contradictory wishes. These did not prevent the tradition from exercising an inescapable hold over its adherents.

It has become conventional to speak slightingly of the religious aspects of republicanism, as though the "mere substitution" of one set of beliefs for another was somehow dishonest or historically negligible. The proselytizing *laïcs* saw, on the contrary, that an essential sphere of life had eluded democratization. Quinet, in 1843, struck a note that all republicans would echo in the 1860s. In a valedictory lecture, he exhorted the privileged youth of the Collège de France to share a distinctly eucharistic "bread of science" with their unknown brothers. "You have contracted here an obligation to them . . . to defend their rights, their moral existence . . . Share then and multiply the bread of the spirit."[123] Other, more prosaic writers spoke of education as wholesome and essential nourishment, stressing that it was not a dangerous stimulant, but Quinet evoked loaves and fishes, a miracle of generosity, and enjoined fraternity.

Radicals did not hold, as is sometimes alleged, an idealistic theory of social change. They did believe, however – as they had every reason to believe – that political and social institutions develop unevenly and that some institutions mightily resist and retard the concurrent development of others. Vacherot expressed their nonmechanistic optimism: "The force of events provokes revolutions. By his moral improvement and his personal action, man alone creates, establishes, and organizes the societies which emerge from them."[124] In response to repeated political failures, radicals set about the task they felt incumbent upon them, the organization of republican society. Unsurprisingly, the issue around which they organized was education.

2   Organizing the
alternative society

The middle classes are about to resume their fractious ways.
                    Subprefect's reports, Sens (Yonne),
                                        January 1862

The democratic party holds itself in readiness,
prepared to profit from eventualities that it believes will
come about sooner or later.
                    Police report, Lyon (Rhône), October 1863[1]

IN 1885, when one-third of the Chamber of Deputies were members of the *Ligue de l'enseignement* and Jean Macé himself was a senator, the Burgundian freethinker Paul Bert asked him if he had known all along what he was doing. Wherever, Bert said, there was a *société d'instruction*, "the republican party found itself already organized." Macé assured Bert (or so he told the general assembly of the league gathered at Lille) that, of course, he had.[2] Certainly, Macé had never undertaken to overthrow the Second Empire; but he had intended to establish in France a secular presence, civic activities, and, above all, a means of influence that was everywhere commensurate with Catholic influence. He was able to accomplish this for a variety of reasons, not the least of which was his own enviable moral composure; he united a serene commitment to enlightenment and democracy with an opportunism no less imperturbable. Jean Macé, an archetypical, rather than original propagandist for republican mores, seems largely responsible for the league's success. Accordingly, Macé the man must be considered first.

JEAN MACÉ, ORGANISATEUR, VULGARISATEUR

Macé must be seen as a perfect, quixotic *quarante-huitard*, and he did not discourage a picaresque image. "I am the son of a drayman; I am a drayman for ideas."[3] Born in 1815, the son of a Parisian working man and a Norman peasant woman, Macé's precocity and his mother's piety attracted the attention of the vicar of Saint-Eustache, who made him a choirboy and obtained for him a scholarship at the collège Stanislas.[4]

Whatever the priest and the boy's mother may have hoped that classical learning to prompt, Macé's recollections of the college center upon the introduction of natural science into the curriculum after 1830, something he saw as a welcome but inadequate consequence of limited political progress. ("Imagine, my dears, just one hour each week to apprehend the wonders of Creation.")[5] He won a prize, and Geoffroy Saint-Hilaire predicted for him a career as a naturalist.[6] There is no record, however, of his having had further education in science.

Macé served briefly in the army and, at some point, married. Very little is known about either engagement, and he was unapologetic about his lack of achievement during the missing decade. "I never thought a stone's purpose should be to gather moss."[7]

In 1848, at thirty-three, Macé began his apprenticeship in the *métier d'organisateur* on a propaganda bureau, La Solidarité républicaine, which distributed republican and socialist writings (some of them his own) in the provinces. He opposed Louis Bonaparte in the presidential elections of 1848, suggesting that the chief argument for Bonaparte's presidency – the need for a permanent, solid symbol of national unity – supported more compellingly the candidacy of the Arch of Triumph.[8]

During the Second Republic (as he continued to do for the rest of his life) Macé urged the dignity of civic engagement. He saw political self-assertion as a manifestation of self-respect and posited "the duty of every man to esteem himself the equal of another and the duty, in consequence, to consider that man his equal."[9] Thus, humility was no virtue, but an insult to fellow citizens: "He who fears me offends me; he who dares not speak before me thinks me intolerant. He who suffers for me and dares not tell, thinks me unjust . . . Such a one must despise me."[10]

His courtesy book for the new man, *Les Vertus d'un républicain*,[11] rested upon a premise from Montesquieu: Constitutions rely on custom; positive law is never exhaustive and *politesse* must make up for the gaps in the Code. Macé was convinced that a republic required a special *savoir vivre*: Fraternal love, he said, was the first imperative, reciprocal egalitarianism the next, and universal suffrage was the crucial legal expression of those duties.

In two *Lettres d'un garde national à son voisin*, published under the pseudonym Jean Moreau, he specifically rejected the "addition of capacities," which widened the test of eligibility for the vote from an exclusively material one – the payment of two hundred francs in direct taxes – to include holders of certain degrees and members of licensed professions. The soldier reminded his propertied neighbor that their fathers had fought together to destroy privilege in 1789, and so they must object to the reconstitution of privilege in the form of an electoral caste. Even if the law purported to reward "intelligence" or "usefulness," this was simply to "transfer the absurdity." Macé's guardsman objected to this –

although he was puzzled that others did, because it might add a measure of moral force to the cruder standard of wealth. Besides, as a practical matter the addition of capacities would not much alter the electorate, because opportunities for education were so deplorably limited. However, good sense was not restricted to members of the upper middle class: He raised a strong artisanal voice, "there are a thousand capacities."[12] In *Le Petit catéchisme républicain*, Macé reiterated that "no one is ignorant of his own needs or of the needs of others whose lot is similar to his own."[13]

In 1848, at his most "revolutionary," Macé spoke of himself as bourgeois in language, dress, and habits. Nevertheless, he said, he felt his "conscience in revolt"[14] and dedicated his *Profession de foi d'un communiste*, written in the early spring of 1848, to his friends and initiators in socialism. Their intellectual fellowship, he hoped, presaged a union of material interests: "This communion of intelligences by which humanity progresses, is it not a fine example to give to those who have such difficulty imagining the communion of interests?"[15] Macé was, irresistably, conciliatory and plausible.

Thus, for Macé socialism arose as a cooperation in accordance with laws that, once well-established, would impose themselves on all intelligences. Later, as a Radical senator, he deplored "that ferocious socialism of the state," still preferring a Fourierist free association of free persons that would replace the anarchy of competition by "prudent and benevolent" communal action.[16] His notion that society might be saved by foresight revealed how akin to bourgeois thought socialism might be. Each expected activity to be serious and fruitful: Opponents were do-nothings and poseurs, and the socialist horror of "waste," vainglorious military or religious display, was not unlike middle-class notions of thrift. There was no antagonism of mood or style between Macé's libertarian socialism and the perceived self-interest or moral sentiments of bourgeois and artisanal Frenchmen. In 1848 Macé acknowledged in Saint-Simonian fashion the existence of two classes, those who work and those who make others work, but he believed consideration of the "social question" should be deferred until republican institutions were securely established. A democratic government, he expected, would necessarily concern itself with economic justice. "Soyez républicain d'abord."[17]

After the events of June 13, 1849, Macé fled Paris and lived for four or five months under an assumed name in Normandy. He traveled through France as a correspondent of *La République* and became thoroughly convinced that Louis Bonaparte had been elected president in 1848 because he incarnated, however illegitimately, the Revolution. Macé never ceased to believe that France could be united only in an acceptance of the principles of 1789. He later described himself as having belonged, during that unhappy time, "body and soul to the political fever."[18] Actually, Macé turned, more promptly than many of his contemporaries, to education – specifically, the education of young ladies – directly after the coup of 2 *décembre* and in consequence of it.

In his republican travels Macé had once stopped at Beblenheim in Alsace with a message for a friend's daughter who was at boarding school there. The headmistress, a Mlle Verenet, was a woman with an impeccably progressive genealogy: Her grandfather had been one of the last bailiffs of Riquewhir, an apanage of the Protestant princes of Montbéliard, and her father had been a chemist of "advanced views."[19] As Macé told it, and there was always an ingratiatingly accidental air to his accomplishments, he dropped in, found the science mistress having difficulty in explaining a problem in physics, offered a few clarifying suggestions, and was begged to stay on. The situation appealed to him, and he took refuge there in December 1851. (It is not clear that he was in immediate danger, but prudence may well have suggested lying low.)

Teaching suited him, he found, and convinced him that he should seek ". . . in the happiness of intellectual and moral paternity, the first of the social functions."[20] He and his "dear wife" were childless, and Macé seems to have been tenderly attached to his pupils. He began also to write for children: stories, plays, a fanciful arithmetic primer, and a remarkable introduction to human physiology as well as to the political and scientific quarrels of the nineteenth century, *L'Histoire d'une bouchée de pain.*

True to the gracious androgyny of his age, he saw the teacher as both father and mother and likened his little books to mother's milk: "There is something, too, of the nurse . . . in those who take the purest part of their intelligence and heart and transform it, so to speak, into milk, so that they can give your awakening soul [*votre âme naissante*] nourishment it can digest without too much effort."[21]

Had Macé's papers not been destroyed, one might read his children's books less closely; but there could not exist a more charged polemic, a more complete artifact of *mentalité* than his *Mouthful of Bread.* He addressed the book to a little girl[22] and, through it, introduced her to all the points of view with which she should sympathize intelligently. The conceit, simply, was to follow a morsel through the body, explaining digestion, circulation, respiration, and in passing, the dignity of labor, the interdependence of classes, the inevitability of progress, the unity of creation, and the advantages of republican government. Macé even managed an attack, delicately phrased but unmistakable, upon celibacy.

He asked the child why she eats and anticipated her answer, "Because it tastes so good." Of course it tastes good, but it is also essential that you nourish yourself.

> To each duty God has imposed, he has joined a pleasure to reward you for fulfilling that duty . . . You will understand this better when you are older . . . You will scarcely now be able to believe that what I am telling you has been the subject of the most terrible arguments among big people, and I regret to say, that it still is . . . Suppose a loving mother gave her child a toy; will she imagine her child taking great pleasure in it or destroying it and tossing it away? A child should enjoy parents' gifts in perfect good conscience, remembering from whom they have come, and giving thanks from the bottom of her heart. Thus should men do with these other pleasures of which we have spoken.[23]

God, who has made nothing without a purpose, is the author of all delight.

A serene deism, argued from Design, suffuses the entire book. *Le bon Dieu*, sublime *Bricoleur*, destroys in order to create, "constructs that which shall be out of the debris of that which has been."[24] Thus, a mouse becomes a cat; grass, a cow; and the swallowed bread, flesh and blood. Macé hinted that transubstantiation is accomplished daily by every living thing.

History works similar changes: The thousand small societies of which France was composed in the Middle Ages have consented, "with good grace" (Macé preferred consensual change), to dissolve themselves in order to live again on a higher plane.[25] This rebirth created a more complex order: Like so many republican thinkers, Macé understood progress as increasing differentiation and heightened interdependence. He restated the point in a discussion of invertebrates: Savages, like segments of an earthworm, can break off from the whole and go their way alone, but the organs of advanced forms, whether mammals or republics, survive only in reciprocity.[26]

A frugal Providence, governing nature and society, thus makes a rough sketch, which He refines and elaborates through endless variations. Macé wholeheartedly embraced the "transformist" evolution of Etienne Geoffroy Saint-Hilaire, which denied separate creation. Macé mocked academicians who refused to recognize their likeness to worms and oysters: No one is demeaned by similitude with any of God's creatures. Invoking Pascal,[27] he said, "If God can embrace the whole universe with his love, we can, at least, accord it our respect."[28]

Macé was evidently fascinated by this mystical fellowship of great and small, simple and *évolué*: His most arresting images, perhaps suggested by Michelet's natural histories, *L'Oiseau, La Montagne*, and, especially, *La Mer*, evoke freedom, love, and the miraculous richness of blood, milk, sap, sea water, all fluids charged with the germs of life.[29] In nineteenth-century French science, "germ" had a meaning closer to a modern notion of a gene than to that of a bacterium. He did, indeed, recommend that his little reader ask Papa to lend her M. Michelet's beautiful new book on the sea.[30] Macé suggested many consultations with Papa, perhaps deliberately strengthening the girl's reliance upon her father's counsel.

It is not surprising that Macé's pedagogy showed a Froebelian acceptance of the energy and activity of the child ("It is one of the laws of [God] that little children . . . cannot stay too long in the same place")[31] and great concern for observation and experiment. He made resourceful use of the kitchen and the sewing basket, instructing his young reader: Next time you have rabbit, note its teeth; when Cook cleans a chicken, ask her to show you the little green gland attached to the liver; make a tube with a scrap of linen, fill it with water and stich up both ends, the water will ooze through the cloth, as it does through what we call bodily "tissue." There was, too, an unflagging eagerness to broach all those scholarly quarrels that Macé infused with moral significance and, withal, a gentle, self-deprecating tone: "Forgive me for dwelling too much on things that I find interesting without perhaps considering enough whether you would find them interesting, too."[32]

The things that Macé found most interesting invariably suggested political lessons – above all, equality: "The king's truffled capon and the peasant's black bread are all one to the small intestine."[33] Before one can eat, the food must be grown and prepared; therefore, a chapter on the hand preceded one on the mouth. Opposable thumbs received due attention, but Macé subordinated them, too, to a moral point. Deeds not words; the mouth says "I love you," the hand proves it. Above all, never fear to clasp the hand, hard and dirty, of one who labors. It is in your service that those hands were soiled and calloused. Many people will deny this fraternity, as they try to ignore evolution, and decry leveling. ("You will hear, dear child, people who owe everything to our great Revolution pretend to despise it.") It was not nobility that was suppressed in 1789, but ignobility. Now everyone was free to develop his highest faculties.[34]

Macé's natural history throbs with controversy; so, too, his *Théâtre*. He recommended the study of dramatics for girls because it made them self-possessed and taught them otherwise tedious facts effortlessly, by appealing to their love of costume. His history and geography tableaus, as well as an anti-Linnaean *Revolt of the Flowers* (Macé favored Cuvier's "natural" classifications), were little more than occasions for dressing up, but most of his plays had messages. The duties that he emphasized were appropriate to well-to-do married women: consideration toward servants; attention to children's lessons and husbands' laundry; prompt payment of bills, especially those rendered by the genteel poor like seamstresses, who, he made plain, might need the money for that night's dinner.[35]

Macé's longest play, *Les Ricochets*, set in a stuffy German principality with subversive "French ideas" as something of a running gag, must have been received well in Alsace. A mistaken-identity farce, it has predictable but genuinely comic moments. A princess, returning home on her majority, seeks a companion. Three families, the noble Hohenkopfs, the banker Geldhaus, and Petermann, drapers, present their daughters, each giving compelling reasons that the offspring of their immediate inferior is quite impossible. "What a pity," the princess remarks, "there isn't a fourth letter. I'd be fascinated to learn what shoemakers think of washerwomen." Each family has been told to wait for her at a particular bench in the garden. She arrives, dressed like a peasant girl, and encounters snubs from all and the barest suggestion of an undue familiarity – nothing like full-blown *droit de seigneur* – from Hohenkopf. Finally, an authentic peasant, Gretchen, the godchild of her old nurse, appears. The disguise is now suspected, and all fawn upon the simple girl – to the great amusement of the princess, who, of course, chooses Gretchen as her particular friend.[36]

The play that Macé regarded as his most ambitious, perhaps "too ambitious," *The Anniversary of Waterloo*, shows Peace and War disputing over four fallen soldiers: French, German, British, and Russian. Peace resurrects them so that they may speak for themselves about their sacrifice. They find they have no quarrel with one another, and each has left a grieving woman. Hearing a veiled daughter, sister, wife, or mother mourn, each believes she weeps for him. There are unveilings and stupefaction: "Unknown to me! An Englishwoman!" Yes, Peace concludes, "Nature everywhere speaks the same language."[37]

Although antimilitarist, Macé was not a pacifist ("While the wolves remain, we must keep the sheepdogs"),[38] but he took every occasion to praise other forms of courage. Apropos, for example, of rattlesnakes:

> Their poison works through the blood. Were you to swallow it, my dear, and of course you must not, it could not hurt you. How do I know that? Dear child, you would not believe what scientists are capable of doing in the service of truth. You must not be persuaded that all heroism takes place on the battlefield.[39]

Macé's several books were sold as part of the Hetzel *Bibliothèque d'éducation et de récréation*, which published many other popular writers of a decorously advanced cast.[40] Thus, Macé found himself in the 1860s a happy man, a wary optimist, rested from the fevers of the Second Empire, disabused but not despairing, an educational writer of growing reputation, established congenially in an eastern Protestant enclave – *pour mieux sauter*.

Hence the legend that Macé, a provincial professor, launched on November 15, 1866, a nationwide movement with a simple appeal to his fellow citizens in a Paris newspaper; but this folktale greatly underestimates both Macé's realism and the ripeness of local, national, and associational *milieux*. The Ligue de l'enseignement benefited greatly from three kinds of opportunities: first, the increasing sophistication of the democratic opposition in exploiting disunity within the Liberal Empire and the University; second, the ongoing efforts of established educational societies of various political tendencies; and third, the special attention given popular education in Alsace by the great paternalists of Mulhouse. Macé's activities both presupposed and advanced the centrality of the schools issue: He knew that the moment was auspicious and he seized it. What, then, of the France into which he sprang?

THE THREE OPPORTUNITIES

The Liberal Empire and the two rapprochements. Political alignments began to shift in the years between the general elections of 1857 and 1863. The Cobden-Chevalier Treaty of 1860 established a significant measure of free trade between France and England. The emperor undertook also to champion Italian unification. At home he conceded broader powers, chiefly the rights of interpellation and item scrutiny of the budget, to the Chamber of Deputies. When, in 1864, French troops were withdrawn from Rome, Pius IX responded with the *Syllabus of Errors*, which was promptly banned in France. The imbroglio with the pope, like the commercial treaty with Britain, cut deeply and in two directions. Clericals and protectionists who had for a decade relied on Louis Napoleon to save the social order began to reconsider the uses of liberty. They found themselves in procedural agreement with liberal parliamentarians, many of whom were secularists. Anticlericals, on the other hand, along with some confident and competitive industrialists, gained a new appreciation of Bonapartism.

Selective collaboration with the empire became thinkable for many who had long abstained from politics. An adventurist foreign policy in support of "oppressed nationalities" like the Italians had ever been the most reliably appealing feature of both Napoleons. Moreover, worsening relations with the Vatican were welcomed as a gauge of more general domestic intentions by many previously irreconcilable to the regime.

The change was already in evidence by the parliamentary elections of

1863. When, in 1857 and the by-elections of 1858, five acknowledged opponents of the regime, "the Cinq," were elected to parliament, other successful candidates – like Cavaignac, Lamartine, and Jules Simon – could not be seated because they refused the oath of allegiance to the emperor. There was a generational split – an immensely painful one and one not measured in age alone – between the *sermentistes* and the *non-sermentistes*, as the Alsatian editor Nefftzer of *Le Temps* described those willing and unwilling to take the oath.[41] The difference should not be confounded with degrees of substantive radicalism, although it does indicate that complicity with the "crime of 2 December" remained an issue.

In 1863 former republicans sensed an opportunity to reenter public life. Attracted programmatically by the administration, they began to accept the requisite oath of allegiance as a pledge to support, not the person of the emperor, but the constitution itself. At the same time the growing parliamentarianism of the regime's conservative opponents tempted them to join a "loyal opposition." Radicals were thus drawn into two contradictory but useful rapprochements, into sympathy with the government's policies and into procedural agreement and tactical alliance with constitutional monarchists.

In the general elections of 1863, legitimist, Orleanist, and republican candidates undertook to support any other opponent of the regime in the second round of voting. The "Liberal Union" failed even as an electoral strategy: Its members were profoundly divided and their party discipline ill developed. Radicals, especially, complained that royalists would not vote for them under any circumstances; furthermore, as Theodore Zeldin has shown, official candidates were so shrewdly chosen that they were, in general, more acceptable to the majority in any constituency than any single independent candidate.[42]

Nevertheless, in 1865 an attempt was made to prolong and enlarge that coalition, such as it had been, and to give the opposition some shared substance. A group in Lorraine solicited the views of prominent men and published their replies as the Nancy Program (*le projet de Nancy*). A nineteenth-century variant of the *thèse nobilaire* emerged from a broad spectrum of thought: Encourage *civisme* and sociability; restore municipal and parliamentary liberties to restrain and direct the central administration; permit the Chamber of Deputies to control expenditure and initiate legislation; abolish Article 291 of the penal code, which forbade unauthorized association; make functionaries, immune from prosecution under Article 75 of the Constitution of the Year VIII, responsible like other citizens for their actions and transfer their powers increasingly into the sphere of voluntary and "natural" associations. Replies in this vein came from republicans such as Carnot, Simon, Vacherot, Clamageran, Morin, and Jules Ferry, and from Montalembert, Cochin, Falloux, and Berryer among the Catholics. All sought, as Macé would, to reanimate old groupings or to establish new ones.[43]

The Nancy Program is recalled chiefly as another testament to decentralization as a theme of the opposition, abandoned without shame or regret once the apparatus of the state became available. In fact, it was marred less by disingenuousness than by serious ongoing arguments at cross purposes. Nothing better illustrates this than the two complementary but irreconcilable slogans of the opposition: Thiers's "necessary liberties" of speech, press, and assembly and Ferry's surprisingly incendiary "necessary destruction."[44] Secularists believed that Napoleon III might be trusted to accomplish the most essential razing, the disestablishment of Catholic power.

Although men like Ferry expected that education would gradually free French minds from *les ténèbres*, there remained for them the problem of cadres. However "dechristianized" France had become, no one questioned that the church was organized in France as no other group could yet hope to be. The Catholic Church was the only organization in France comparable to the government in the extent of its administrative competence and the generality of its expressed purpose. This unargued fact posed problems – particularly, if the emperor made good his promises of "sincere elections," an end to the system of official candidates supported by official favors and harassment. Something, democrats assumed, would have to be done to counteract clerical influence and the political consequences of the church's near-monopoly of education and philanthropy.

Here the dissolution in 1861 of the Société-Saint-Vincent-de-Paul by Minister of the Interior Victor Fialin, duc de Persigny, had been seen by many as decidedly encouraging. This was the first action taken under the empire against a Catholic organization. The group's purpose was ostensibly pastoral: It sought to succor the poor and to overcome religious indifference among workers. Persigny was dubious: "Must Christian charity organize itself in the form of a secret society?"[45] An anticleric of sorts, Persigny acted, it seems – with little malice or relish – as a policeman and an Erastian. He permitted local activities but forbade central or provincial associations; an institutional nexus was unacceptable.

In the varying responses to Persigny's action, early in the decade, it is easy to foresee the subsequent lack of success of the Nancy Program. Liberals were distressed to see the strictures routinely applied to republican and workingmen's groups extended to Catholic organizations. Edouard Laboulaye – like Tocqueville, much influenced by travels in America – protested that no one laboring in a good cause should be harassed: "Whether charity be dispensed by the Saint-Vincent-de-Paul society or by the freemasons, there can be no harm."[46] Self governing voluntary association he judged the proper mode for those many beneficent activities that fell between public and private spheres of competence. Concentrations of power were better curbed by countervailing ones than by forcible dissolution. Should association lead to disorder – and Laboulaye believed that it would have the opposite effect and expressly recommended workers' coalitions as vehicles for the peaceful resolution of industrial disputes – the law could deal with violence. The right to organize was precarious in France and it was central to liberals' notions of men acting freely. Men like Laboulaye saw the worrying of the Catholics as another arbitrary attack on those social forces they relied upon to resist the peremptory state.

Radicals were less concerned: They knew that the administration had no need of precedents to do away with them. Furthermore, the radical secularists had a finer sense of competing elites. Liberal constitutionalists could more plausibly attempt alliance with Catholic parliamentarians; and, more important, unlike the radicals the moderates prided themselves on a certain lack of programmatic imagination. "Youth," Laboulaye regretted, was all too easily seduced by the "symmetry and unity of social transformations accomplished by fiat. Age alone understands the impotence of all administrative mechanisms and that liberty alone can supply the infinite variety of social needs."[47]

Indeed, the government was beginning to concern itself with "an infinite variety of social needs," showing itself to be conspicuously (some felt excessively) progressive. There were many intimations of this, although some of the more telling ones were hidden in administrative directives rather than promulgated as laws.[48] Publicly, the entry into the cabinet in 1863 of Victor Duruy, a popular historian and publicist whose first service to his sovereign had been the preparation of *Les papes, princes d'Italie* in support of the new foreign policy, presaged – or so many hoped – important domestic consequences of the emperor's rift with Rome.

Duruy's appointment was welcomed by many republicans, who were eager to help him enact their common *desideratum*, secular public education. The new minister of public instruction did not, at first, disappoint them. He quickly affirmed the combative character of his office, reasserting the University's right to inspect those religious schools that were, as permitted by the loi Falloux, "serving the function of public schools." That law, he reminded Louis Napoleon, allowed civil authorities to "verify that it [instruction] was not contrary to morality, the constitution, and the laws." He underscored the propriety, the urgency of this surveillance: "Sire, they are conspiring against you and against our society. These are the most dangerous enemies of your son . . ."[49]

Next, Duruy introduced the legislation that radicals awaited: compulsory, free primary education. He proposed, too, a longer, broader secondary curriculum for the commercial classes, workers, and women. He plainly believed that universal schooling was a historical imperative and seemed to have had the impression that this opinion was widely held. It had become a commonplace, he later wrote, that compulsory primary education was the "indispensable corollary" of universal suffrage. This was, perhaps, not a flattering approach to take with a ruler who had fared so well with an ill-educated electorate, but Duruy insisted upon the political wisdom of his plans. He wrote to the emperor on February 6, 1865, urging him to preempt the social issue with sweeping and magnanimous action on education. He quoted the son of the well-known republican François Arago as rejoicing in the misapprehension that Napoleon III was not, in truth, liberal enough to create free, obligatory primary schools. Were he to propose it, this republican personage was supposed to have said, he would deal the party a blow from which it would be very difficult to recover.[50]

An important piece of legislation would be triply useful, Duruy continued. It would steal the republicans' thunder; it would dish the Orleanists, who had never ceased to take credit for Guizot's law of 1833; lastly, as to the clericals, whom he cast as the emperor's most intractable adversaries, they could be fought only with light.[51] Duruy did not invent prudential arguments for policies to which he was already committed: The school issue had arisen frequently in elections contested by republicans in 1863. In the department of Yonne, for example, the opposition candidate in Auxerre, M. Rampont-Lechin, whose election posters minutely informed voters of their rights under the law,[52] called strenuously, if vaguely, for a "serious education for all." Edouard Charton, publisher of the *Magasin pittoresque* and an aide to Hippolyte Carnot in 1848, while campaigning at Sens, demanded a "free extension of education, which alone can make citizens equal."[53]

Popular concern for education persisted, as was duly noted in monthly police reports on *l'esprit public*. A Lyonnais police commissioner wrote in March of 1867 that the workers were indifferent to the posturings of the parliamentary opposition. Bruited then was a threatened discontinuation of the emperor's yearly Address to the Chamber, an occasion cherished by orators because the replies they were entitled to make afforded their only opportunity for general invective against the government. The commissioner reported that the populace cared little for speeches but concerned itself earnestly about educational matters. Nothing, he said, excited such interest among the laboring masses as discussions of primary instruction.[54]

Under the Liberal Empire the balance of forces within official circles and in the nation at large for a consistently reformist domestic program was subject to continual reinterpretation by myriad policemen and functionaries: Some loyally served the regime by relaying any shred of information that might help to win an election; some attempted to serve the regime more ambitiously by counseling the better course, adding that this was also the popular will; a small number evidently saw the empire as secondary and instrumental to prior programmatic ends.

Indeed, more essential to the effectiveness of the Ligue de l'enseignement than the sum of policy pressures at any particular moment was this very divergence in official positions; for within the government, as within the opposition, systematic and contradictory positions were emerging. As the opposition was divided between programmatic reformers willing to support the government and conservatives whose deepening hostility led them to emphasize the right to dissent, so there were corresponding developments within officialdom. Some, especially within the University, welcomed popular support and urged the mobilization of public pressure in support of administrative initiatives; others, fearful that the democratic genie, once freed, would never be gotten back into the bottle of correct procedure, sought to exclude "political" considerations of all sorts from their work and, like the parliamentarians, emphasized procedural values. Ironically, in their aspirations to disinterested professionalism, they confirmed the opposition's bitterest accusations of bureaucratic arrogance and insensitivity.

The league would thrive in an ambiance of collaboration, protest, cooptation, endorsement, and occasional persecution. The schools movement depended upon conventional and irregular relations among private citizens, local elected officials, educational bureaucrats, and national political figures and appeared to an extent a continuation of efforts that had never been wholly abandoned to circumvent or repeal the loi Falloux. It is important to remember that even in the early 1850s when the supposed political consequences of irreligion are said to have been so widely feared, measures were taken in many quarters to protect secular education and to preserve lay institutions. In Mulhouse, the municipal council, dominated by the families who would be Macé's early supporters, struggled to preserve the city's religiously mixed common schools. The general council of the Yonne exercised its options to retain a normal school and formally protested the decree of March 24, 1851, that eliminated natural science from its curriculum and abolished competitive entrance exams. In Bourg-en-Bresse freemasons championed and subsidized secular private schools.[55]

In Lyon, the *inspecteur primaire* praised the exemplary work of the Society for the Promotion of Primary Instruction in the Rhône, which was supported by the vigorous Saint-Simonian Arlès-Dufour and many other wealthy *laïcs*. The inspector assured the prefect that its nineteen secular schools – ten for boys, nine for girls – were conducted by teachers "already distinguished in the normal schools from which they have come." He recommended that its patronage be extended to suburban secular schools where the teachers were not the best and were moreover deprived of "counsel and encouragement." For, he warned, ". . . the law of 1850, in destroying the local committees, has left the lay teacher no defense against the *curé* who gives vehement preference to religious teachers." The secular schoolmaster was particularly vulnerable now, because the new law provided that he might be dismissed without a hearing.

Significantly, the inspector foresaw a need for centralized lay organization. Of course, he recognized that there might be self-constituted local groups, but they could not compare in strength or prestige with the departmental society. "Should there arise a storm of reaction against lay education, the Lyonnais teacher will know he has nothing to fear. The Society is there, strong in its unity, confident of the moral value of the great majority of its members and of the social position of practically all."[56] Complicity was thus long established among supporters of lay schools, in the University and in politics as well as in citizens' groups, precursors of the Ligue de l'enseignement. Duruy's appointment had promised authoritative patronage for these arrangements, and many of his ablest subordinates urged him to enlist the support of the secularist groups. He could not bring himself to do this, and his reluctance will be discussed in the next section.

Unfortunately for Duruy, the emperor to whom he was martially loyal never adequately supported him.[57] Isolated within the cabinet, save for the sympathetic friendship of Michel Chevalier, and always mistrusted by his colleagues in the Ministry of the Interior, Duruy could not secure a commitment to free, compulsory primary schooling. The school law of April 10, 1867 (curiously and sadly not called the loi Duruy), permitted municipalities to tax themselves to establish *gratuité* and provided for departmental and national subsidies when local maximums had been voted. It was an important measure, but it fell far short of what he had wished to accomplish and short, too, of what the opposition was demanding. Appropriations were never adequate, and Duruy was left with hopes that Jules Simon derided as "the incredible pretension of creating schools without money."[58]

Lastly, Duruy's initiatives in feminine education had brought him into bitter combat with the French church. His humiliating dismissal in 1869 served to clarify the uses of Left Bonapartism.[59] A sacrifice to the clericals, Duruy's career made manifest the limits of reform under the empire. Serving the emperor so faithfully, Duruy served the republic better by forcing radicals once more into frank opposition.

Louis Napoleon spoke often of liberty as the "crown of his edifice." He did not, as many readily grasped, imagine liberty to be his government's foundation; but he occasionally made inspiriting pronouncements about "individual initiative." The most-often quoted of these – "Individual initiative, exercising itself with an indefatigable ardor, relieves the government from being the sole promoter of the vital forces of a nation" – came more and more to be invoked by groups whose aims the administration had thwarted, the local circle of the Ligue de l'enseignement at Rheims, for example.[60]

Radical secularists, who had lost their man in the cabinet, were thrown back on their own resources. Acquaintaince with liberals inspired by Tocqueville had reminded them of the uses of voluntary associations. Increasingly, they created for themselves opportunities for constructive public action. They seized upon old antistatist arguments – because it was clear that nothing remained to be gotten by being *bons sujets* – and turned the *thèse nobilaire* in new insurgent directions. As local control might be used to preserve established power, so, too, it could be used to create new centers of power. The Ligue de l'enseignement would develop in voluntary organizations the modernist cadres hitherto lacking in France.

The educational societies, politics and philanthropy. These cadres were already incipient; popular education had been the object of genteel charity since the Restoration. Macé would draw upon many established national and provincial groups: the Société d'instruction élémentaire, the Association polytechnique and the Association philotechnique, the Société pour la promotion de l'instruction élémentaire du Rhône, the Philomathique at Bordeaux, numerous local sociétés des connaissances utiles, and the burgeoning popular library movement of which the Franklin Society was a notable example. Some of these groups cherished touching and extravagant hopes; others inclined to Samuel Johnson's sober conclusion that ignorance had been tried but had failed to produce the wished-for results. There were differences of political nuance among them as well.

The two most important groups, the Société d'instruction élémentaire (henceforth, SIE) and the polytechnicians – those from which the league drew its most eminent supporters – attracted members of many political tendencies, although the SIE tended to voice the sentiments of the liberal opposition and the Association polytechnique (AP) inclined to Left Bonapartism. That a new, more popular organization could draw upon both preexisting groups corroborates the rapprochement of radical secularists with progressives inside and liberals outside the government.

Education provided a common ground, although by no means a neutral one; and, although the government held schooling to be an unimpeachable good, the societies' activities were always somewhat suspect. There was general hostility toward any activity outside those regular channels through which all legitimate wishes might be expressed and, if worthy, granted. There were fears that the academic hierarchy might be subverted by outside patronage of teachers. Attempts to organize and reward schoolmasters – above all, the political possibility that teachers might mediate relations between the people and the professionals – worried the imperial administration and every subsequent minister of education (including Jules Simon and Jules Ferry).[61] Special watchfulness surrounded any group capable of maintaining regular communication with workers: Indeed, many adherents felt an almost irresistible temptation to turn their philanthropic reputation to political advantage. Nevertheless, members disagreed (often bitterly) about the place of politics in the curriculum itself. In all these ways, the earlier groups' experiences prefigured the league's.

A vignette from the archives captures much about these skirmishes. The SIE, organized during the Restoration by men like Benjamin Constant and Alphonse de Lamartine and rewarded with the status of "public utility" in 1831, had ever been an irreproachably respectable group concerned with adult literacy and teacher training. Nevertheless, it did not escape suspicion. In 1850, the prefect of the Pas-de-Calais warned the minister of public instruction that SIE had chosen as its correspondent in the district one "M. de la Rozière, who vaunts himself on being a socialist." Delarosière (the name is spelled both ways) had recruited a following "among men notoriously hostile to the government, who award medals to teachers we are obliged to dismiss on account of the exaltation of their political opinions and who seem to present themselves as the protectors of those who make a virtue of their insubordination."[62]

Delarosière himself, casting about for something to do, typified well the restless malaise that followed Louis Bonaparte's election. A member of the local school board, he "corresponded" with the SIE in Paris, and one can imagine the status that this conferred or was expected to confer. The Archives of the Ministry of Public Instruction preserve three "faire part" letters that Delarosière wrote upon assuming these responsibilities (and perhaps simultaneously on resuming the practice of law in the Pas-de-Calais). The first, to the parish priest, suggested that first communion be withheld from children who could not read. (This attempt to relate literacy to preparedness for communion was of great importance, because for many rural children first communion meant the end of schooling.) The second letter, to the mayor, urged that the welfare bureau deny support to families who were not sending their children to school. This suggestion was accompanied by an offer of his professional services. The third was a circular to teachers, whom he urged to present themselves for the society's prizes. These were awarded on the basis of "new methods, the number and assiduity of their students, special projects they have undertaken." He also recommended – and the prefect was quick to sense a political danger – that teachers inform him of *tracasseries* they suffered on the part of "enemies of *laïc* instruction." Delarosière recalled to schoolmasters the "numerous means" offered to members of their profession for proving their zeal. "Lastly, to cooperate, to contribute in augmenting as much as possible the legitimate influence I should like to see attached to your modest functions," Delarosière offered his service as a lawyer to all needy persons. He did omit in his letter to schoolmasters the mention of past royal patronage that he included in the letters to the *curé* and the mayor.[63]

Like many provincial professionals, Delarosière identified himself with Parisian movements and personages in order to build a clientele, to create a political base for himself, and, perhaps, merely to relieve the tedium and bitterly felt irrelevance of provincial life. The SIE was quick to dissociate itself from struggling provincials of dubious political hue. Macé would be less intolerant of ambition.

The Second Empire attempted to withdraw educational matters from local politics. Administrative correspondence of the period suggests that this was done expressly to diminish republican and Orleanist influence in the countryside. The subprefect at Aire (Pas-de-Calais) who so feared the baneful effects of Delarosière was advised by his superiors to take no action that might call attention to the man and to await a new law that would "disencumber us of him."[64] Article 17 of the loi Guizot, which established local school committees, did provide for their dissolution and replacement by a special commission on which no one sat by right (that is, refractory mayors and notables might be excluded), but the imposition of direct control was understood in 1833 to be an exceptional measure. In 1854 powers of appointment, supervision, and discipline were concentrated within the administrative hierarchy: Henceforth, the prefect would hire teachers. Denied regular political means, men of substance and insurgents alike would work obliquely, through philanthropic associations.

Nevertheless, under the Liberal Empire the SIE seemed to be a safe expression of "salon opposition": reasonable men who were content to pursue their goals within the empire. Contributors in 1866,[65] besides the minister Victor Duruy, included the comte Boulay de la Meurthe, a senator and member of the Conseil général d'instruction public; Ferdinand Buisson, later the author of *La Foi laïque* and director of primary education during the period of Radical ascendancy in the Third Republic; Adolphe Crémieux, Léon Gambetta's patron; the deputies Jules Simon, (author of *L'Ecole* and the opposition spokesman on educational matters), Jules Favre, Alexandre-Thomas Marie, Pierre-Clément-Eugène Pelletan (or perhaps it is his nephew Charles-Camille Pelletan), Picard. Others were young lawyers and journalists who became members of the Ligue de l'enseignement and would come to power with the republic: Jules Ferry and Charles Defodon, who was later the editor of *Manual général de l'instruction*; Frédéric Morin, André Rouselle, Charles Sauvestre, and Benjamin-Joseph-Agénor Bardoux at Clermond. Among corresponding societies in the provinces was listed Arlès-Dufour's Société d'instruction primaire du Rhône at Lyon.[66]

The society was quick to welcome Duruy's initiative in popular education. Its acting president, M. Malapert, welcomed rumors that the new minister would revise the basic law governing primary education. "We have never considered the law of 1850 a definitive work," he wrote, and he mentioned five reforms that the society would propose in a study it expected to complete in December of 1863. The first imperative was obligatory primary education. Second, the French language had to be part of this obligatory education, in order to preserve and complete national unity. Third, *brevets*, certificates of competence, would be required of all teachers. "Letters of obedience" from ecclesiastical superiors could no longer substitute for tested academic qualifications. Fourth, all schools had to submit to evaluation of their pedagogy. Lastly, the society hoped to restore a local voice in the administration and character of education: "We should view with pleasure the [re]establishment of local committees." The letter concluded with the warmest expressions of confidence in Duruy: "Enough said of these reforms, it is not to you that their urgency must be proved."[67] Malapert promised the society's ardent cooperation. Duruy's reply was a guarded one, modestly reminding Malapart of his very brief incumbency. He urged the society to complete its study and assured Malapert that he would appreciate further communication.

The SIE, Duruy observed in 1868, had been created in the spirit of perfect accord with the government. Nevertheless, it could not be trusted to act freely. Its recent past presidents, among them M. Marie (who was conspicuous in the parliamentary opposition) and the incumbent Jules Simon, did not inspire him with confidence.[68] The society already enjoyed the status of "public utility," the right to collect and dispense funds and to open independent schools, and the "tendencies" displayed by its members necessitated vigilant surveillance. In fact, the SIE was scarcely able to do more than discuss classical books, present medals, and hear an annual oration, "but it would like to expand, to send out on every side travelling orators[69] charged with speaking and teaching in its name." Duruy felt obliged to discourage these plans. The group was not out of control, but Duruy considered that its progress – from the presidency of Boulay de la Meurthe, a moderate Orleanist, to that of Jules Simon – suggested the many dangers that one courted in granting any association "extended powers and a general character."[70]

The society was certainly not revolutionary. Its monthly bulletin, the *Journal d'éducation populaire*, prescribed workers' education as the guarantee of social peace and women's as the promise of moral elevation. It was, however, despite professions of tolerance, openly secularist. "The future belongs to men who know how to reconcile human and social necessities." Teachers must be laymen, for if a man is a citizen and the head of a family, a proper sense of his rights and duties "arises for him out of the milieu in which he is necessarily engaged."[71] Liberal notables believed that those responsibilities were essential to the formation of character. To this end, the society asked that schoolmasters receive decent pay and enjoy working conditions consonant with their status as society's most respectable functionary. Thus, before there was a republican schoolmaster, or a Ligue de l'enseignement to extol him, his essential characteristics had been sketched by the SIE.

The league's other major precursor, the Association polytechnique, dated from 1830. Students of the Ecole Polytechnique, elated by the Trois Glorieuses, went to share their learning with the heroes of the uprising, who were recovering from their wounds at Saint-Cloud. Subsequently, the polytechnicians stressed scientific and technical education: They offered vocational courses at the Hôtel de Ville, and, almost immediately, two professors suspected of introducing political topics into their lectures were dropped after a "serious investigation" of the charges.[72]

Political schisms periodically split the group. In 1848 another period of "deplorable dissension" would arise as members debated their relation to the new republic. The polytechnicians differed, as would the members of the Ligue de l'enseignement at Marseille, on curricular issues, too. Complaints persisted that the group had become an organization for foremen, that it had neglected general éducation to advance the careers of substantial artisans and mechanics.

Men opposed to a narrowly vocational program dissociated themselves from the Association polytechnique[73] and established the Association philotechnique. Several attempts at reconciliation failed, and official preference was given the *polytechniciens*, but the Philotechnique persevered. In 1863–64, its *conseil de patronage* resembled that of the SIE and included most of the wealthier Parisians who would rally to the Ligue de l'enseignement.[74] In the early years of the Third Republic, officers of the Philotechnique congratulated themselves that they had remained devoted to the fundamental problem of mass literacy, whereas the *polytechniciens* taught applied science to workers already adept and *rangé*.

To some extent, the Association polytechnique probably did serve as a source of trained and steady manpower. Its officers did not pretend otherwise. As early as 1835, Auguste Perdonnet, whose ideas were to dominate the group, defended his refusal to give courses in reading and writing, taught adequately, he said, by others, and explicitly disavowed "moral" education: "We are in the mainstream of progress; we shall be able to maintain ourselves there and to advance. Some say . . . instruction is incomplete . . . dangerous, rather than useful to workers who, proud of their 'demiscience,' puff themselves up with vanity and end up lazy and disputatious."[75] Instead, Perdonnet countered, his group restricted itself to subjects that were morally neutral and of immediate practical value. His members agreed on scientific truth and on nothing else. At attempt to proselytize on other grounds would destroy the group.[76]

The disinclination for politics, the preference for *connaissances utiles* suggest an easy accommodation with Bonapartism. The AP flourished under the Second Empire. By 1860, scientific and technical courses similar to those taught by the polytechnicians in Paris were organized in Bordeaux, Rouen, Lille, Lyon, Mulhouse, and le Creusot, and there was talk of establishing popular libraries.[77] The library of the Third Arrondissement of Paris, often credited with being the first popular library in France, was formed partly by worker-members and partly by "subscribers" to the AP. Perdonnet cleverly described it as a "mutual-aid society" for the "needs of the intelligence." This was a happy choice of words, because these organizations were in particular favor with the emperor, who encouraged them and watched over them closely, usually naming their presidents,[78] hoping that they might provide an alternative to trade unions. Victor Duruy might have found in these groups allies in his struggle for "professional" or vocational education, but he was reluctant to permit any significant degree of extragovernmental organization and consistently refused to allow extended "federal" association.[79]

By 1867, there were no less than sixteen provincial societies under the patronage of the AP, and at Lyon Perdonnet spoke of education as "wholly a work of conciliation; to us belongs not the light that burns but the light that illuminates."[80] This light, of so specific and benign a character, was widely diffused. Ties existed between the polytechnicians in Paris and the Saint-Simonians in the Chamber of Commerce at Lyon. Arlès-Dufour, the Lyonnais philanthropist, sponsored the Société d'enseignement professionnel du Rhône, as well as the Société d'instruction primaire du Rhône: He was among the first adherents of the Ligue de l'enseignement and summoned to Lyon, on Jean Macé's recommendation, Charles Gaumont to teach vocational courses and political economy of the most orthodox sort.[81]

Some Republicans (like Ferrouillat) were hostile, insisting that *l'enseignement professionel* meant complicity with the empire. Curiously, the procurer-general at Lyon was dubious, too. He did not share Duruy's or the Chamber of Commerce's confidence in the appeasing virtues of education:

> Dangers and infractions originate in the passions. Instruction does not always help in correcting them[;] it may happen, to the contrary, that they grow with an expanded horizon, with more elevated thoughts.
> Instruction does not accomplish its miracles unless it is closely joined with religious and moral education. The town laborer is more intelligent than the countryman; nevertheless, the former does not offer to society the same guarantees of morality and steadiness.[82]

The thriving of provincial affiliates naturally suggested a reorganization of the AP. Duruy, although he utterly disdained most of the prosecutor's views, shared his apprehensions about the polytechnicians' projects:

> I foresee the gravest difficulties in giving to the chief of such a society, whoever he may be, effective powers, a right to direct the actions and the finances of thousands of workers that the society unites in many departments. . . . One could animate them all with the same spirit and move them all in the same direction.[83]

Before he grudgingly approved their revised statutes, he made certain that the Paris sections exercised no authority over local groups. He required, furthermore, that the program of instruction be yearly submitted to the ministry and that the government concur in the choice of the group's president. It would be imprudent, he reiterated, to permit too much independence to an organization that "united such a large number of workers and that can exercise the greatest influence over them."[84]

Why was Duruy so reluctant to unleash these groups? He was involved in bitter struggles with the Chamber of Deputies, pilloried by conservatives, forced always to settle for less. Why were the alumni of the Ecole polytechnique – with its cult of science and its historic associations with the Napoleonic armies – not welcomed as allies? They all but embodied his strongest argument for popular education, vital national interests. British industry and the Prussian army dominated most Frenchmen's estimate of their international position; they were troubled by the supposedly superior attainments of the two Protestant countries.

Military defeat had not yet capped the argument, but the commercial treaty with England negotiated by Michel Chevalier, one of Duruy's few influential supporters, made the skill and discipline of English workers a pressing problem. Education could be presented explicitly as an alternative to commercial protection; and although conservatives argued that schooling made people *raisonneurs* – lazy, dissatisfied, and deracinated – advocates of useful knowlege promised that just as classical education fitted men to govern, technical training prepared them to work.

Victory Duruy, who feared that the emperor's enemies would exploit popular education for their own political ends, had always urged that these efforts be preempted. To that end, he frequently protected the established educational societies, as he would the young league, from the disapproval of the minister of the interior. His own powers of authorization were limited, however,[85] and he himself did not trust all those who shared his concern for schooling to share also his fealty to Napoleon III. In this, he was quite right.

Duruy's antagonist, Dupanloup, bishop of Orleans, had declaimed against the multiplication of libraries, "this horrifying diffusion of skepticism . . . popular libraries, school libraries, communal libraries."[86] Libraries occasioned much anxiety, too, for the minister of the interior. Sanford Elwitt has argued that in response to this orgy of self-improvement, the Liberal Empire, in 1864, patronized, or perhaps actually instigated, the organization of the Franklin Society – a circumstance that, in his judgment, casts suspicion on those subsequently associated with the group.[87] There is evidence that the imperial administration had high hopes for the Franklin Society. Certainly, Jean Macé, in organizing the Communal Library Society of the Haut-Rhin, insisted on maintaining his group's independence of it, making slighting references to previous attempts to foist books on communities "from above."[88]

More important, however, than the administration's plans for the Franklin Society were the group's plans for itself. Elwitt consistently underestimates the rapidity with which increasingly militant secular democrats moved into organizations that had been the preserve of the more tractable salon opposition. In April of 1864, just two years after the creation of the Franklin Society, the minister of the interior, in a confidential circular, directed the special attention of his prefects to popular libraries sponsored by voluntary associations, including the Franklin Society, "authorized by one of my predecessors." (Such indiscretions are never committed by incumbents.)

> I cannot urge you to too great a solicitude on this important point. As much as it may be appropriate to support and facilitate efforts to moralize and instruct the people, so much is it indispensable to

preserve them from the disastrous effects that antisocial doctrines and troublesome books will produce upon them.[89]

To that end, the minister reiterated that libraries must everywhere submit to certain formalities. Although he left the details to the discretion of local officials (he imagined that they might mitigate rules designed for the more troublesome *grandes villes*), he emphasized that libraries were to be considered "circles." The analogy, he believed, was incontestable. Therefore, a library's president, and its administrative council if it had one, must be chosen or agreed to by the prefect and its catalogue examined by him *yearly* to insure that it contained

> only useful, professional books, belonging to that body of wholesome literature proper to elevate and educate. One must eliminate with a just severity novels whose reading can leave a regrettable impression; equal care must be taken to eliminate books of social or religious polemic, and those that, under the pretext of political economy, serve only to propagate dangerous and subversive theories.[90]

The minister felt it almost unnecessary to remind his subordinates (as indeed it must have been) that these distressing bands must never be convoked in general assembly without prior authorization, and he concluded with an insistence upon absolute confidentiality for the circular's contents. He may have required secrecy so urgently because he suspected his colleague in the Ministry of Public Instruction was himself circumspectly fostering the creation of libraries.

Another circular, two years later, alerted prefects to the possibility that "certain notabilities of the opposition, and particularly certain deputies of Paris," might attempt to pervert the many "scientific, literary, agricultural, or philanthropic solemnities" over which they were invited to preside in the departments, seizing the occasion to make speeches that would serve their own personal interests or those of their party. The government refused to furnish its adversaries with such opportunities, and the prefects were asked to arrange that speakers not be brought from afar to do mischief. These observations applied with particular force to educational overtures to workers. The minister protested, "the government, which has always shown such active solicitude for everything that concerns the instruction of the laboring classes, cannot allow hostile parties to come and reap the benefits of its efforts, nor permit them to forge from the government's own triumphs a weapon with which to combat it."[91]

The Ligue de l'enseignement would incorporate the issues, and gradually the membership, of its predecessors. Like them, it would be encouraged by Duruy so long as it seconded imperial policy, rebuffed by him when its purposes and the empire's diverged. Nevertheless, the league, in the very definition of its purposes, would transcend its predecessors. It would take education out of the realm of enlightened charity and into the sphere of *civisme*. Education would be made the central political issue, and the campaign for schooling itself used to educate citizens, to train a class that was eager for political roles to take political initiatives.

Alsace, Macé, and the mulhousiens. The immediate context for Macé's venture was Alsace, especially the textile center of Mulhouse, and France could not have offered him a more suitable one. In a collection of essays, *La Morale en action, le mouvement de la propagande intellectuelle en Alsace*, Macé described his early collaboration with Paul Odent, the prefect of the Haut-Rhin, and, more significantly, with the great paternalists, the Dollfus and Engel-Dollfus, Thierry-Mieg, Koechlin, and Kestner families. By the time he undertook to organize the league, he was their established familiar: He contributed to their newspaper, *L'Industriel alsacien*; he had been initiated into their masonic lodge, the *Parfaite Harmonie*, at Mulhouse.[92]

The men who first patronized Macé were descendants of the Protestant oligarchy of Strasbourg and Mulhouse, Calvinist burghers and magistrates transformed, as they could so predictably be, into paternalistic entrepreneurs. Their prosperity rested upon a potentially explosive coincidence of religious, linguistic, and social divisions: a Protestant and Jewish French-speaking *patronat* and a Catholic German-speaking "floating population" of South German and Swiss migrant laborers. The Société industrielle of Mulhouse, attempting to create a disciplined and bilingual work force,[93] and profoundly suspicious of the Catholic clergy, perennially demanded compulsory primary education.

In this period Alsatian scholars, too, paid careful attention to the religious aspects of citizenship. The Protestant faculty of theology at Strasbourg, a chief vehicle for the introduction of German new criticism into France, helped in developing what it held to be more acceptable versions of the New Testament, and Neffzter of *Le Temps* popularized them with his *Revue Germanique*.[94] Denis Fustel de Coulanges, perhaps the finest mind at work in the province then, argued in *La Cité Antique* (1864) that the *polis* had been united, as any human community must be, by belief, "something necessary, something stronger than material force, more respectable than interest, surer than a philosophical theory, more unchangeable than a convention, something that should dwell equally in all hearts and should be all powerful there."[95]

The mulhousiens had long hoped that common schooling might somewhat attenuate religious and social division. In 1831, the mayor, André Koechlin, whose brother was a Protestant pastor, established an interdenominational school explicitly intended to inspire more fellow feeling. As a school inspector explained a few years later, "They had felt it appropriate to offer the same education to all to prepare the children for a social fusion, if not a religious one." Social experimentation was accompanied here, as it would be forty years later in the municipal schools of Paris, Lyon, and Bordeaux, with innovations in pedagogy. The inspector noted approvingly, "The child never gives an answer that he cannot explain rationally."[96]

The Société industrielle and the city council did not, of course, foresee a classless society. The scale of fees at the communal elementary schools gives some sense of the city's educational priorities. A minimal schooling was underwritten by the city for all; during the first three years, trifling fees were required for both boys and girls. After the third grade the fees rose sharply with each grade level, and more precipitously for girls than for boys.[97] It is easy to see at what point capital investment became luxury consumption.

A report prepared for the city council in 1846 described even more explicitly four classes of children within the city. The poorest children were to be schooled for three years, and they were expected at the end of that time to speak, read, and write both French and German. Children of a slightly better class were educated for five years. The sons of skilled artisans and foremen might aspire to "superior primary instruction," which would include mechanical and commercial training, modern history, and foreign language – not classical language, but "langues vivantes." Lastly, there were those boys whose parents would send them to college. It was not a utopian program, but Mulhouse was making *some* provision for the education of children of both sexes when Guizot himself remained committed to the absolute right of the *père de famille* to educate his children or not, as he chose. In February of 1831 the bulletin of the Société industrielle disagreed with Guizot: "Neither individual liberty nor the authority of parents can be invoked as valid objections to a measure that can prevent the frightening debasement of the working classes.[98]

The society repeatedly petitioned for schools legislation. Under the pseudonym Daniel Ortleib, Jean Macé himself published two "Letters from an Alsatian peasant" in the *Industriel Alsacien* in December of 1861 and January of 1862, in support of the formal *voeux* of the Société industrielle de Mulhouse for compulsory schooling.[99] The letters convey a subdued but unmistakable impression that only the electorate's ignorance permitted the current regime to function. The peasants were discomfited by their unsolicited franchise, and "feeling ourselves incapable of it [self-government], we all went in one great movement, looking for someone who could govern in our place . . . What exists today is there because we have willed it."[100] Universal education, however, would inaugurate a freer collaboration. Macé anticipated Duruy's arguments about the political consequences of such a measure: "At this signal many will respond, even among those you might consider ill-disposed towards you. Here they all have a great interest . . . Here is the true reconciliation between the small and the great."[101]

Nevertheless, Macé's letters, however agnostic as to political forms, contained two allusions that were profoundly offensive to Catholics: one was a characterization of the loi Falloux as a law made for the "greater glory of ignorance,"[102] the other a pointed reference to the Mortara affair. Arguing that obligatory instruction did not require the indoctrination of a child with ideas offensive to his father, but merely that he be educated in some manner, Macé wrote, "We are not asking that children be kidnapped."[103]

Macé was next associated with the Mulhousiens in the organization of the Communal Library Society of the Haut-Rhin. Jean Dollfus and Charles Thierry-Mieg served with him on its administrative council. In July 1863 Macé called for an *agitation à l'anglaise* that would enlist social energies of every sort.[104] He had, he claimed, for years urged Frenchmen not to delay civic action until the day came "when a decree comes to proclaim absolute intellectual freedom. Before emancipation by decree . . . there is another of which you alone can be the artisans."[105]

The Communal Library Society was designed to foster local initiatives. Unlike the Franklin Society, it did not itself undertake to create libraries but subsidized them where funds were needed. Furthermore, it declined absolutely to furnish books or to dictate their choice, something that Macé characterized as "an act of presumption." In August 1863, Macé wrote again in the *Industriel alsacien*, confident of enlisting the support of the "intellectual elite" of each commune. He reiterated that the choice of books would be entrusted to local committees: The new enterprise required a sentiment of personal responsibility. "Direction from on high is not what is lacking in our communes."[106]

Macé hoped, too, that citizens would find themselves able to set aside their differences for the common good. He enjoined the "mutual sacrifice of our personal inclinations" and noted that at Ribeauville the masters of the three denominational schools had established a mixed committee. The grand rabbi of the central consistory had written to the rabbis of the Haut-Rhin, urging cooperation with the "liberal tendencies" of the group: "We Israelites especially have everything to gain from the progress of civilization[,] which removes barriers between citizens." Macé added that libraries that owed their foundation to the "enlightened zeal" of a "large number of pastors and priests" were not necessarily of an exclusively confessional character. Macé always took care, as he would in the leadership of the league, to present a concrete task, some manifestly useful project. He encouraged common action "devoted exclusively to the questions that unite us and ignoring those which divide. In this way alone can the war on ignorance take on a truly national character."[107]

Unlike the secret societies that republicans organized during the Restoration and the July Monarchy – conspiratorial in their means and all-encompassing in their aims – the organizations of the sixties suited the increasing realism and respectability of bourgeois republicans. They ceased to be plotters and undertook unexceptionable public services. Charles Sauvestre would say in 1874 that the new men of the republic were men of deeds, not words, who had prepared for politics by "real services" to the nation.[108] With a mixture of flattery and exhortation, Macé aroused the *civisme* of local notables. In the absence of meaningful political activity, and with the blessings of the prefect, he sought to establish spheres of competence, a sense of social priorities that only the assumption of civic responsibility could teach.

As decentralization would create public roles for the "intellectual elite" of each Alsatian commune, so Macé thought association would strengthen the civic sense of the poor. Organization, he felt, had different but equally necessary lessons for peasants and for workers. As both joined with the bourgeoisie in public-spirited action, workers were made aware of individual rights and peasants taught to appreciate the common good. For urban workers Macé approved the formula adopted by the library of the Amis de l'instruction of the Third Arrondissement of Paris: "A man is strengthened by association and dignified by dues paying . . . His reading becomes a right"; but this sense of private property, so essential for a man "in the heart of working-class agglomerations," was overdeveloped and injurious in the peasant. Accordingly, Macé recommended that no dues be collected from library members in the countryside.[109] In rural areas, the only libraries known to people were private ones, and these ran directly counter to the ends he hoped to achieve. "It is a question of establishing in the commune a literary and scientific patrimony . . . that it has hitherto been without. Dues paying creates a private property limited to members of the association." Furthermore, libraries need not be expensive: Books would probably be donated. The only expenditure that Macé anticipated was for bookplates, a *cachet* to set public volumes apart from all others.[110]

The theme of "two patrimonies" – one material, divisible, and intrinsically private, and the other an inexhaustible common heritage – was one to which Macé returned.

> The ceaseless labor of past generations has produced two patrimonies, one material, one intellectual, subject to two different laws of transmission. The first, divisible and destructable by consumption, inherited by families; this is the cause of social inequality and antagonism. The normal function of the second serves to reestablish the harmony destroyed by the other.[111]

Macé's concern for this new public good, no less than for the autonomy of each library, led him to decline fusion with the Franklin Society.[112] He suggested that instead of circulating libraries emanating from Paris, the Franklin Society foster permanent departmental associations, to create "communal property of a new nature, an instrument of intellectual culture . . . placed in the public domain in the countryside."[113] He preferred independence of action at all levels. "Unity of aspiration" he believed to be the only legitimate and profitable centralization in intellectual matters. Prudence may have dictated his refusal, because the government consistently opposed federated voluntary associations, but Macé also believed in local initiatives. Participants got a clear sense of local needs and priorities, and, of course, a decentralized movement could not be destroyed with one administrative blow.

Macé liked to emphasize tasks that could be done *at the moment.*This tendency was evident in his characterization, in that early period, of German achievements in the absence of political liberty: "The lower ranks of the [German] people were flooded with ideas. *When the day comes*, there will be a people that finds itself ready, with life everywhere, that lacks nothing today but centralization."[114] Might not "the day" be for France "le jour de gloire" about which the *Marseillaise* sang? This thought, later more pithily expressed ("The snake does not shed its skin until the new is formed beneath"),[115] was never absent from Macé's writings. The Ligue de l'enseignement was its practical expression.

THE LIGUE DE L'ENSEIGNEMENT, "SCHOOL OF DECENTRALIZATION"

In the fall of 1866, Jean Macé described the activities of a Belgian Ligue de l'enseignement working through legal means to change laws incompatible with the liberty of conscience and equality of citizens or not conducive to the progress of education. He commended its efforts to offer young women a more serious curriculum, improve the social position of teachers, and encourage adult education. He emphasized, perhaps exaggerated, the popular character of the group, then two years old: "The people themselves prepare their entry into political life, by organizing societies of instruction, as in England and America, where the bourgeoisie figure only as supporters of the popular effort."

Macé's article appeared in *L'Opinion nationale*, a paper directed by the Saint-Simonian Adolphe Guéroult and patronized by a "red" Bonapartist coterie surrounding the emperor's cousin Prince Napoleon.[116] On November 15, the same paper carried Macé's *Premier Appel* for a French counterpart to the laudable Belgian enterprise. He called for the "cooperation of all good citizens" and hoped that their Ligue de l'enseignement would always enjoy the "consent of authority." "One takes one's country as it is when one wants to work for it," he said.[117]

In the following month he received sixty-eight expressions of support. The first three, commemorated today by a plaque in the league's Paris headquarters, came from one Mamy, a conductor on the Paris–Lyon railroad, Jean Petit, a stonecutter, and a policeman named Larmier. Others were less obscure. Guéroult joined, promising the support of his paper. Arlès-Dufour and four younger members of his family, all describing themselves as "manufacturers," and Flotard, a notable republican, responded from Lyon. There were many Bordelais also: Gounouilhou, the publisher, and several Lavertujons, including André, Gambetta's friend and editor of the *Gironde*, who told Macé that success was assured because his supporters were humble people like those who first rallied to history's other great movements. The economist Léon Walras, whose own social program relied upon primary and technical education, cooperatives, and credit unions, and who had attempted the previous year to unite all Parisian cooperatives,[118] was another early adherent. Another was Doctor Guépin of Nantes – one of the most venerable provincial republicans. Guépin had campaigned in 1849 for an alliance of workers and bourgeois to confound "the adversaries of our fathers," men who ruined the schools and free institutions of France, because their reign of "moral terror" depended upon the brutalization of the masses. He welcomed the league as an appropriate vehicle for the energies of the "practical and thinking part of the nation."[119]

Macé intended to keep from prominence in his movement men of "too determined a political color." He wished to minimize, too, the role of official personages, unless their patronage became essential to the group's survival. Nevertheless, many of his earliest supporters were already influential; others were intent on becoming so. Indeed, it was not oblivion that Macé offered them, for he had long insisted that local activity should multiply, not disrupt, ties between Paris and the provinces.[120] Nevertheless, he remained acutely conscious of the political constraints under which he worked, writing to Charles Buls, secretary of the Belgian Ligue de l'enseignement, that he believed himself to be working "among a people who have abdicated and who must be put back in possession of themselves without destroying anything."[121]

From the beginning Macé disavowed direction of the league, protesting that he hoped only to establish communication among "all those decent and committed energies that believe themselves powerless because they feel themselves isolated."[122] He knew that an immense variety of sympathetic groups existed already "under a thousand different names." Several of his earliest adherents were directors of established educational societies: Gérard, the general agent of the Société Philotechnique; Schrader, the director of adult education for the Société Philomatique at Bordeaux; and the president of the Cercle des Travailleurs du Quartier des Brotteaux at Lyon. The "societies for useful knowledge" at Moulin, Rheims, Bordeaux, Nîmes, Cognac, Toulon, Périgeux, Montbéliard, Strasbourg, and Mulhouse affiliated with the league, as did many cooperatives and, curiously, nine spiritualist groups.[123]

What is more important, freemasons rallied to the league, both individually and in support of the "collective adherences" of their lodges. French freemasonry was traditionally universalistic and progressive.[124] Many lodges had been suppressed in the attempt to destroy republican organization that followed the coup, and figuring notably among the "venerables" purged by Prince Marat, whom Napoleon III had made grand master for France, were the Saint-Simonian Viénot at Rouen and the feminist Léon Richer, editor of *Les Droits des femmes* – both league activists.[125] Masons had probably been consistently more anticlerical than anti-Bonapartist, and their numbers greatly increased under the Liberal Empire. There were 244 "ateliers" in 1858 and 392 in 1870, many of them already committed to educational projects.[126]

Disputes over atheism and hierarchy divided French masonry during the 1860s, but both the official *Monde maçonnique* and the more aggressively radical *L'Action maçonnique* reported the league's waxing fortunes with evident pleasure. The *Monde maçonnique* reprinted Macé's projected statutes in February of 1867, noting with approval his insistence upon the local circle "administering itself and determining on the spot the best use for its resources." In May it again called attention to Macé's "welcome, bold, and timely" enterprise, claiming for it already 2,109 adherents and applauding once more its openness and flexibility: "No direction, no program, no preconceived or imposed ideas, only one enemy, ignorance . . . an organization contrary to all precedents . . ."[127]

No less vigorous support came from *L'Action maçonnique*, a paper that shared many of Macé's preoccupations: "Every idea must enter into common practice before it establishes itself in institutions." ("Toute idée doit passer dans les moeurs avant de s'affermer dans les institutions.") With these words from Comte, its editors had announced their intention to accomplish through freemasonry the incorporation of righteous ideas into French life. *L'Action maçonnique* followed educational activities closely. It reported that in Marseille elementary notions indispensable to the worthy exercise of citizenship had been taught by freemasons in free evening courses for the past eighteen months, and in Bordeaux lodges supported a "collective work of public popular education" – principally, lectures for workers on political economy. The freemason Vacca had become president of the local league circle in Metz and hoped to make it a source of cooperative as well as educational initiatives. In February 1868 the paper reported that Brother Macé's movement had attracted some five thousand members.[128]

In October 1868 a Société coopérative d'enseignement libre was formed by freemasons, with their expressed aim the moral and intellectual autonomy of each member as well as the provision of serious technical training. The membership of this new group, like the staff of *L'Action maçonnique*, made plain the breadth of support for secular schooling. Bourgeois democrats like Léon Richer and the young Ernest Hendlé, a conspicuously effective prefect under the Third Republic, cooperated with socialists and future *communards* like Paule Minck and Gustave Lefrançais. Lefrançais, who later recalled freemasonry with contempt as "the most insipid and religious of charitable societies," in this period contributed regular articles on such perennial *laïc* enthusiasms as divorce, civil marriage, and masonic baptism.[129] The collaboration of republicans and socialists, grounded in common commitment to *la morale indépendante*, contributed greatly to official uneasiness about the league.

Victor Duruy felt for this fraternity his predictable misgivings. As early as December 1866, he had written unfavorably about the league to the rector of the Academy of Strasbourg. In the same month he acknowledged to the minister of the interior that it might become an "occasion for political maneuvers" and discouraged support for it among members of the *corps enseignant*, though he did not positively forbid their membership.[130]

Duruy explained at length his feelings about citizen involvement in education:

> Far from having the pretension to realize all desirable progress in matters of public instruction by the sole hand of the state alone, I am persuaded that individual action is the indispensable auxiliary of government action . . . But . . . if the action that one seeks to exercise over public or private education is confounded with political scheming or if it pretends to manifest itself by the creation of an institution *formed in imitation of the Government itself*, with a chief, a central council, a budget, and agents obeying orders from on high . . . [then] despite my preference for individual action . . . there will be an emphatic veto.[131]

Thus, Duruy could not approve the league's statutes as they appeared in the magazine *L'Ecole* on December 15, 1867. Articles 4 and 5 provided for considerable local autonomy but foresaw also a central agency nominated and paid by members, disposing of a budget and publishing a bulletin. Duruy could accept local groups like Vacca's in Metz, which had been warmly endorsed by the prefect of the Moselle. He agreed, too, to the circulation of a bulletin, but a federal bond he found simply unacceptable.

Faced with these objections and acting at least partly from genuine conviction about the uses of decentralization, Macé recast his plans to emphasize local circles, each entirely free to act as it wished, to collect and dispense its own funds. With this constitution Macé was able to preside over a striking breadth of endeavor. He sought, however, to keep his adherents cognizant of each other's schemes and hoped for a general congress in Paris during the Universal Èxposition of 1867. That wish was denied.

The regime was by no means unanimously unsympathetic, however. A few prefects and several academic officials welcomed creation of league circles to countervail clerical pressures against Duruy's innovations. They urged their chief to foster secularist groups and benefit from them. Paul Odent, prefect of the Haut-Rhin and Macé's associate in the departmental library society, remained his ardent backer, as was the prefect of the neighboring Moselle. M. Leroy de Boiseaumarie, confident of his ability to direct the intellectual currents of his department, early authorized league circles in the Seine-Inférieure. M. de Saint-Pulgent, the knowledgeable prefect of the Dordogne who held intelligence to be a "productive force," approved the work also.[132]

Duruy did consent to meet with Macé in 1868 and seemed to be contemplating a public endorsement. This was not to be accomplished under the empire.[133] Insofar as Duruy did protect the league, he acted in consequence of invidious comparisons with Catholic groups. He upheld the inoffensive characterization of the league as religiously "neutral" – that is, preferring to entrust doctrinal instruction to family and church – and thus repudiated the position taken by the minister of the interior, who construed its purpose to be irreligious and therefore illegal.

Duruy also disagreed with the Ministry of the Interior, over the latitude that Catholic groups should be permitted. Confronted with Duruy's initiatives, particularly the *caisses d'école* – voluntary associations permitted by the law of April 10, 1867, to encourage school attendance and endowed, toward that end, with the right to receive donations and bequests and, of course, to assemble legally – those intent on preserving Catholic influence redoubled their efforts. The vicomte de Melun and Charles de Montalembert, among others, petitioned to establish a Société générale d'éducation et d'enseignement. The minister of the interior, who in these matters was required to consult with his colleague in the Ministry of Public Instruction, implicitly rebuked Duruy for favoring secularist groups while withholding approval from persons seeking to "propagate and perfect education supported by the principles of the Catholic religion."[134]

Duruy was frankly hostile to Melun and Montalembert: "I would fear to see the projected society meddle in the direction of public education . . . You have asked me to note . . . that this society has no other purpose but to act upon 'private' educational establishments that it shall create . . . private establishments whose number will never be considerable."[135] He doubted that their purpose was so modest and insisted that he, not the minister of the interior, had to decide what might or might not be prejudicial to the "political and scholastic interests" of public education. The minister of the interior, he acknowledged, exercised final authority over associations, but he recalled that his colleague's predecessor, Persigny, had recently felt obliged to dissolve the Société Saint-Vincent-de-Paul, which had created 813 circles in nine years (1852–61), "a vast body obeying a single direction." Surely, it was folly to permit reconstitution of clerical power. One should not confer legal standing and civil personality when one will have eventually to rescind the authorization "with *éclat,* at the cost of irritating debate."[136] He did not question Melun's moderation or good faith but dismissed as imaginary the vicomte's fears that atheism would penetrate the schools. Clergymen, aided by teachers, gave religious instruction in accordance with the loi Falloux. Local clergy, as Duruy had every reason to know, were zealous in the enforcement of this law, and he could not see their need for additional support.

The project, Duruy feared, was nothing but an organization of war against the public schools, to "gather together *en un faisceau* all the influences which might be grouped around that idea."[137] Not content with liberty and subsidy, they sought the destruction of the state system of education. Duruy reiterated his rectors' assurances of the perfect political orthodoxy of lay schoolmasters, and communicated too their uneasiness concerning religious teachers.

And in truth, Duruy received reports continually of clerical harassment of lay instructors. At Rennes in the Ille-et-Vilaine where Kerdrel, a legitimist deputy, had proposed a *société de l'enseignement libre,* "a Christian endeavor to raise the moral and intellectual level of humanity," A. de Chateauneuf, the inspector of the Academy of Rennes cautioned, in December of 1868, that it was nothing but the revival of the dissolved Société-Saint-Vincent-de-Paul. He claimed that new membership lists had been printed separately to disguise the fact that it was a "resurrection effected *en bloc"* and deplored the occasional complicity of elected officials in the "druidism" of the people. "I have never encountered so little probity, loyalty or morality, for it is all one, nor so much ignorance, nor so much religion." The rector at Rennes thought that he exaggerated but agreed that the society posed a real political threat and that the invectives of the clergy against public schools had done education irreparable harm in the West.[138]

The bureaucratic response to lay and Catholic organization revealed French officialdom itself to be as divided as the nation, lacking, perhaps, the extreme positions but composed of some men urging reconciliation with the church, and others convinced that the Second Empire must build a modern society based on the Declaration of the Rights of Man and the Citizen and the Napoleonic Code and persisting in seeing those documents as complementary. Louis Maggiolo, an inspector attached to the Academy of Nancy and an energetic provincial supporter of Duruy, found strong sympathy for the University among men of the opposition. In a confidential appraisal of cooperation to be expected in the elections of 1869, Maggiolo reported that Duruy had, if anything, *more* partisans in the opposition. *L'Impartial de la Meurthe et des Vosges* had "rendered signal services" in the controversial organization of secondary courses for girls. He acknowledged, too, the aid of *L'Indépendant de la Moselle*, which he described as the *moniteur* of the Ligue de l'enseignement, and of the invaluable *Courrier de la Moselle*, which sought out and broadcasted ecclesiastical scandals. The vehemence of the clerical press, he thought, had rallied moderate men to the government and to the minister's views on education. "Clerical hyperbole . . . has helped me establish, without engaging myself personally, the Ligue de l'enseignement[,] which shall be a counterweight to the congregation." Maggiolo wrote again to assure Duruy that although the honorable M. Macé had been urged to become a candidate himself in the next elections, he had formally declined to do so on August 29, 1868.[139] He thus anticipated and tried to allay Duruy's fears that Macé would politicize his struggle. Maggiolo's career prospered in the Third Republic and he became rector at Nancy, where his exertions in documenting illiteracy[140] and resettling (perhaps in regions where republicanism might waver) the eighteen hundred Alsatian teachers who had taught their *dernière classe* revealed him to be an ardent and enterprising administrator.[141]

There were, no doubt, other Maggiolos (and it would be interesting to see how they fared under the republic), but many imperial functionaries discerned dangerous tendencies in the league and did not believe that it could be made to serve the interests of the government.

Sanford Elwitt is mistaken in the assertion that "none of the early foundations (of the league) ran afoul of the law."[142] At Rheims authorization was three times denied to men "linked by a community of principles and ideas" to newspapers that were violently hostile to the dynasty.[143] The president of the proposed "circle" of the league was Félix Cadet, professor of philosophy at the local *lycée* and of political economy at the classes of the Société industrielle. (Later, he became *inspecteur primaire* of the Seine.) Other officers, A. Thomas, professor at the Ecole de Médecine, and J. Warnier, judge of the Tribunal de Commerce, member of the Chamber of Commerce and president of the Société industrielle, were both elected deputies in 1871. The group enjoyed the support of two municipal councillors, and all but three petitioners were also members of the Société industrielle of Rheims. The prefect found nothing objectionable in the work itself but regretted that it had not been undertaken by sounder men.[144]

In November of 1868 a letter with 124 signatures petitioned Victor Duruy to conduct an investigation to determine whether the group was worthy of legal authorization. Adherents argued that many such authorizations had already been granted (circles of the league were legally established at Metz, Dieppe, Rouen, LeHavre, Colmar, and Nancy, as cited in the petition of November 1868) and that the minister, whose sympathy for workers was so manifest, could not disapprove of their enterprise. Rheims, they reminded him, was a city with twenty-five thousand workers. Their supporters would invoke, ominously, the thought imputed by Condorcet to the uneducated poor: "In my ignorance I know nothing of society but its injustice."[145]

If the project itself was praiseworthy, their persons must be the obstacle. They protested their respectability: "Professors at the *lycée*, at the school of medicine, businessmen many of whom represent their fellow citizens on the Commercial Tribunal, the Chamber of Commerce, and the Municipal Council."[146] One must admit that such men were not "in certain spheres . . . free from philosophic, economic, or political engagements . . . They have erred, if it is an error, in reflecting on the events, the needs, and the ideas present around them and each had arrived at opinions on these matters that he believes confirm truth and progress."[147]

Nevertheless, because they all recognized that education required for its development "a serene atmosphere," they had undertaken to abstain from religious and political arguments "with a will and a certainty of remaining faithful to their commitment."[148]

The Radical press championed the league members. At the height of the controversy *L'Indépendant rémois* reprinted from the *Gironde* a letter from Jules Simon questioning the emperor's concern for education and criticizing Duruy's effectiveness, if not his sincerity; and in October 1868 Gustave Isambert had written for *Le Temps* a provocative account of the first refusal. The administration had neglected even to give a pretext, the semblance of a justification for its refusal. Isambert there-fore proposed that the newspapers supported by the prefecture might as well be shut down: "The policy of silence" had no need for such organs. As Macé had done elsewhere, Isambert argued against the ab-surdity of prior authorization: The group had to be organized in order to solicit permission to organize, but it could take no other action. Judg-ments therefore had to be made on persons, and, Isambert protested, these petitioners presented "toute surface désirable." The state was powerless to act without popular assent in most matters, Isambert as-serted. To assume it could act without citizen participation in education was merely ridiculous: "This great initiator of liberty [Napoleon III] who pretends to make of us a free people begins with fear of you, of me, of talent, of independence, of the clergy, of politics . . . Indeed I can think of nothing of which he is not afraid."[149]

Werle, the mayor of Rheims, suggested a compromise. Authorization for a circle of the Ligue would not be granted, but the Société indus-trielle, which already sponsored popular and technical courses and whose membership corresponded almost exactly to that of the proposed organization, would extend its patronage to any educational projects that its members wished to undertake. The mayor's compromise was rejected. Members judged it contrary to their aims: "To provoke and sustain, whenever it can, private initiative; far from wishing to absorb the manifestations of this initiative, so rare among us, it seeks to respect them."[150]

The league's provisional committee decided that firmness was re-quired for the "education of the public intelligence." This undertaking, they stressed, was not the work of a coterie but of that "notable and honorable portion" of the city that had placed in letters of gold in its meeting room the emperor's call for individual initiative. The prefect persisted in his advice that in view of the coming elections, the group was too dangerous to countenance. Consequently, the circle at Rheims remained outside the law until February 1872, when its petition was successfully resubmitted by its president, the deputy, Thomas. In 1877 the group was again under surveillance. The prefect of the Moral Order was incensed by its resilience. When the educational societies were dis-solved, gymnastic societies arose: "When one studies these diverse so-cieties, what is most striking is their persistence [in acting] under one name or under another."[151]

Some imperial functionaries, like the vigilant prefect of the Marne, felt certain that the league constituted a political threat. Was it, in fact, covertly republican? The question cannot be answered in precisely these terms, because an adequate response requires consideration of those refined and enlarged notions of republicanism that the failures of the

Second Republic suggested to thoughtful men. Certainly, Macé himself was not conspiratorial, and even circles like the Association phocéenne – which included Blanquist members – devoted themselves predominantly to lawful activities. On the other hand, the group was never merely a charity that emphasized education. Its philanthropic projects were undertaken to create the preconditions for a democratic, if not a formally republican government. The group's tone was therefore meliorist and, although critical, exaggeratedly judicious. It was given to pronouncements exemplified by the words of an unsuccessful candidate for the Chamber of Deputies in 1863 who declared himself "like the government dedicated to the principles of 1789 but fearful that our forefathers would have difficulty recognizing their handiwork [in our laws]."[152]

The decentralized form that Macé favored enabled the league to embrace a wide range of activities and – perhaps more essential to its success – precluded divisive and definitive national positions on social, economic, and political questions. Macé encouraged his adherents to cultivate their own gardens; and until the fruit was ripe, few would see the orchard for the trees.

Often, groups organized *caisses d'école*, giving whatever aid was necessary to enable needy children to take advantage of the free education voted by their towns. Clothing, books, and school supplies were provided and, in some cases, there were nurseries for younger siblings whom school-aged children would otherwise be required to look after.

Some circles concerned with pedagogy supported *salles d'asiles* modelled on Froebelian kindergartens. At Moulin, members of the league sponsored a vocational school offering agricultural and industrial courses and maintained an experimental kindergarten. They had plans for a popular library and expressed their frequently mentioned hope of evolving into a cooperative society.[153] At Epinal and Algiers members decided that the most pressing local need was secular education for girls and so created schools for them, giving preference for admission to members' daughters. In general, however, circles did not establish private secular schools; and Macé stressed that the most important aspect of the school at Epinal was the pressure that it implicitly exerted upon the municipal council.[154] The league did not intend to supplant the state system but rather to infuse public schools with a character it could approve.

Most league circles tried fervently to increase and regularize school attendance, which in this period was scant and fitful. *Fréquentation*, the French term, was in fact a most inapposite one.[155] The demands of agriculture – an occupation in which even the very young and unskilled might be employed tending animals, weeding, or, like Hardy's Jude, as living scarecrows – took peasant children from the classroom continually. City children had, apart from the hope of earning enough to feed themselves, responsibilities for infant siblings as well as the attractions of the street to keep them from school. League members hoped to entice children and their parents – sometimes with prizes for perseverance, sometimes with winter clothing and shoes – to come to school and to attend consistently. A group at Bauge (Maine-et-Loire) of "workers, merchants, and farmers" – of whom five admitted to being themselves illiterate – offered a cash prize to the teacher who enrolled the largest number of unschooled adults in proportion to the population of his commune and another prize to the schoolmaster who received the largest number of nonpaying students above the number that the municipal council required him at accept. The "prize" was really compensation to the schoolmaster, whose salary was made up in part by his students' fees, an attempt to ensure that teachers did not pay in unremunerated labor the costs of expanded schooling.[156]

The league circle at LeHavre sought to reopen the issue of compulsory attendance abandoned by Duruy in 1867. Jules Siegfried, its founder and president, argued that although private efforts were certainly praiseworthy – he himself had long been associated with them – legislation was required. He recalled the frequent petitions of other groups – like the Industrial Society of Mulhouse, of which he was also a member – for legal obligation. Various forms of direct and indirect compulsion, some said to exist abroad, ought to be considered: fines, imprisonments, or literacy tests for suffrage after some date. Perhaps negligent parents should be deprived of *their* civil rights. Ingenious arguments were advanced against the claims, still heard in some quarters, for the absolute character of a father's rights over his children. Duruy's aide, Charles Robert, who dedicated his book *De l'Instruction obligatoire* to the Société industrielle of Mulhouse, maintained that compulsory education was already implicit in the civil code: Partners in marriage were required to bring up their issue. Did this not imply the duty to educate them?[157]

The Havrais agreed in November of 1869 to petition their deputy to introduce legislation requiring compulsory primary education and invited other circles of the league to join them, but Macé discountenanced even this mild politicization.[158] In an earlier letter (April 22, 1867) to groups in formation, he had urged modest, noncoercive means: "One can, without entering a school, busy oneself with those children who remain outside, hunt out parents guilty of neglect and premature exploitation . . . support indigence according to its needs . . . in a word, decree compulsory education all around us by private decree in the absence of a public one."[159] Members did not cease to be citizens and could work individually for political measures. Moreover, local circles were already free to do what they judged appropriate. Nevertheless, Macé urged Siegfried to eschew *any* political action. Nothing, he agreed, could better accomplish the ends they both sought than a law requiring school attendance; but a united campaign for legislation would begin the descent of the league into politics and would inevitably compromise it. He predicted with foreboding that it might lead even to endorsements of candidates.[160]

Macé had deeper objections, however. More than any other civilized people, he said, "We can scarcely imagine social progress accomplished other than by executive fiat . . . [thus] it is supremely necessary for us to undertake an apprenticeship in personal initiative, in private effort . . . *We waste our time overthrowing governments. When will we learn that we must concern ourselves with the machinery of government?*"[161]

Thus, the league's founder reiterated the pointlessness of insurrection – or of premature insurrection. Earlier, in May 1868, Macé had characterized his group as a Ligue de la paix à l'intérieur.[162] This itself was, perhaps, a studied ambiguity, because besides the asseveration that they worked for social appeasement, Macé evoked the actual Ligue internationale de la paix, which had met the previous year in Geneva.

The international group's congress, organized by Jules Barni, a Kant scholar and *lycée* professor who took refuge in Switzerland after the coup, had attracted the irreconcilable exiles Victor Hugo, Blanc, and Quinet; progressives (who were active in France) Michel Chevalier, Vacherot, and Emile Littré, Comte's democratic disciple who so influenced Ferry; the past and future republican ministers of public instruction, Carnot and Simon; and the important provincials Dr. Guépin, Arlès-Dufour, Lavertujon, Auguste Scheurer-Kestner, Marie-Victor Chauffour-Kestner, Rousselle, Jean-Jules Clamageran, and Eugène Delattre – all supporters of Macé. Its Belgian correspondent was Charles Buls of the Belgian Ligue de l'enseignement. At the congress French republicans insisted upon an attack on "caesarism" as a primary cause of war, and the word was retained in a public statement by a vote of 18 to 17, with 4 abstentions.[163] Thus, anti-Bonapartists were able to obtain from the congress an implicit condemnation of the emperor.

In comparing the Ligue de l'enseignement with the International Peace League, Macé suggested the range of his group's appeal and hinted at the balance of tendencies within it. It was on religious issues, however, rather than in debates about the form of government, that Macé had to struggle to keep the league sounding reasonable without thereby alienating those who believed the time for conciliation long past. Individual *curés* probably did support popular libraries (Macé insisted that he knew of instances in which they had), but the hierarchy was unanimously, anathematically disapproving of his many projects. The *Monde maçonnique*, although defending Macé from Monsignor Dupanloup's accusation that his program, "to be born, live, and die without religion, is nothing but revolution against the whole social order,"[164] nevertheless urged him to abandon inoffensiveness and reveal himself a freethinker. Félix Faure warned in January 1869 that Macé would find himself without firm support unless he declared himself to be in one camp or the other. Nothing would be gained by moderation, he maintained: Clericals were already opposed, and others would begin to question his sincerity. What role, Faure asked, might freemasons play in this "motley League, composed of the most diverse, disparate and hostile elements?"[165]

Charles Sauvestre, a publicist who expressed himself most often in mocking responses to Dupanloup's pastoral letters and himself a freemason, defended Macé. How ridiculous, he said, to be excommunicated simultaneously by the ultramontanes[166] and the "fanatics of atheism." Furthermore, Macé had made clear in the third bulletin of the league that although he welcomed masonic support, he was independent of it: Among his adherents were many "brothers," but only fifteen or sixteen lodges had affiliated with the league between November of 1866 and the spring of 1868. (By 1870, more than fifty lodges had joined.) Although he willingly expressed himself, de facto, a secularist, he adamantly refused to exclude clerics from his league. In a letter to the *Opinion nationale* (January 13, 1869), which the *Monde maconnique* reprinted, he argued that the problem would never arise: "Science," he said,

> is neither lay nor clerical; it is science. Reading, writing, arithmetic, bookkeeping . . . might be the subjects of League courses; should an ecclesiastic present himself willing to teach these subjects, without making of them a pretext for polemic, he would be admitted . . . I cannot comprehend how any man seriously devoted to the interests of popular instruction could have any doubts on this score.[167]

As to schools, those established by the league would be open to students of every faith, and their religious upbringing would be left entirely to their parents. "These conditions, no religious congregation will be able to accept. That is abundantly clear. Therefore, it seems to me gratuitous to compromise, on that account, the principles of the league, which wishes to exclude no one." This seemed to satisfy the *Monde maçonnique*, which pronounced "effectively" irreligious any group that assumed that a priest could not accept its program, but the paper took exception to Macé's characterization of science as neutral. There were, it asserted, two antithetical methods of education: one based on supernatural faith, the other on direct experience.[168]

If doubts persisted about the league's politics and, among doctrinaire freethinkers, about the adequacy of its anticlericalism, deeper ambiguities clouded its class character. Macé was, moreover, careful to promote a degree of local autonomy that would be sufficient to prevent disruptive clarifications. Certainly, it was nowhere predominantly a working-class movement, although education was indisputably a popular issue.

In Lyon, where – as elsewhere – libraries and evening courses were crucial to workers' organization, the members of the Freethinking Laborers' Library "entered resolutely into the Ligue de l'enseignement so courageously undertaken in France by a handful of gallant men." Of the fifteen original members, eight listed their occupation as "weaver" and two were shoemakers. M. Rossigneux, a bookkeeper who served on the municipal council in the next decade, was probably their most bourgeois member. The police judged them "democrats but not men of disorder"[169] and considered their object to be praiseworthy but unattainable. The choice of books seemed to the commissioner the most difficult point: He doubted that any of the group was qualified to judge matters of science or philosophy but recommended, nonetheless, that the group be permitted to continue. It was, he concluded, neither more nor less dangerous than other cooperatives.

The Freethinking Workers explained their own purpose in these terms:

> To establish a society on the basis of mutuality and reciprocity, the members of that society must possess a greater [sum of] moral and intellectual capacity than the working class in general now possesses . . . We have no illusions about the grandeur of our enterprise, [and] success depends not upon our will alone but upon the number of sincere adherents we can reconcile [with our aims] . . . [,] because it is a truth painful to admit that the great majority of workers do not understand that ignorance is the principal cause of miseries of every kind.[170]

They continued, "Our program is to realize that ideal, to make of every citizen a free and moral being and of every producer a creative laborer" (*un travailleur synthétique*).[171]

The group insisted upon its popular character and, to maintain it, forbade honorary memberships, "pour prévenir toute influence étrangère" (Article 4 of its statutes). It emphasized, too, its appeal to workers of both sexes: Its members included eight women who requested that the library obtain the *Catéchisme de la morale universelle par une mère*. That book, written in a Piagetian series of ascendingly demanding moral stages, urged parents to develop progressively the sentiments that nature gave to every child, "a being good and estimable," and suggested that morality was contained in three words: liberty, fraternity, and equality:

Q. What is the purpose of your life?
A. To conform in all things with the laws of nature . . . to develop in

relations with others, RESPECT FOR PERSONS IN MYSELF
AND OTHERS.[172]

The chief duties of adults were to preserve their liberty of action, dignity, and independence of character and to participate capably in the work
of humanity.[173]

Skilled laborers and employees, like the Lyonnais freethinkers, were
often league members; but more frequently, adherents were manufacturers, merchants, doctors, lawyers, journalists, and in garrison towns,
officers (often from the corps of engineers) – men concerned about bridg-
ing the widening gulf between the people and the bourgeoisie and, perhaps, about securing their standing on the more dignified side. Curiously, although this would seem almost to describe schoolmasters, teachers
never joined in large numbers.[174]

Macé had written in 1867 that "there exists, today, in the absence of
intercourse between the groups, a mutual uneasiness between the people and the bourgeoisie." He recommended a "multitude of contacts, of
encounters today too rare."[175] League circles at Marseille, Roubaix,
Rouen, Metz, Mazamet, and LeHavre hoped to involve workers in their
civic apprenticeship. League members were aware, too, that relation-
ships between teachers and pupils often replicated those between economic classes. Indeed, one of the grievances alleged against the Ligue
marseillaise de l'enseignement by adherents of the more radical Association phocéenne was the unwillingness of their lecturers to fraternize
with their students.[176] In Nancy the league circle tried to organize meetings and classes in working-class *quartiers*, but municipal authorities refused to countenance that and offered instead an academic *grande salle* –
precisely the sort of intimidating location that members hoped to
avoid.[177] At Rouen, too, administrative harassment reduced the group's
activities to conventional philanthropy.

Elsewhere in the North and East, there was a vogue for classes taught
at home (*l'enseignement à domicile*). Vacca, an active freemason and a professor at the *lycée* of Metz, opened his house to members and students of
the league. Macé commended the remedial value of such informal set-
tings, where workers could glimpse something of the "propriety and
courtesy of well-bred people."[178]

At LeHavre Jules Siegfried – who, with his brother Jacques, had already contributed a hundred thousand francs to the Industrial Society
of Mulhouse for the promotion of workers' circles – sought to involve
workers in *la bonne cause*. Elwitt sees the Havrais circle as the "chief
means by which Siegfried and the big bourgeoisie of the city chose to
deal with the social question" and implies that the Commune fixed their
attention on this difficult issue.[179] In fact, Siegfried had been, through-

out the 1860s, a tireless promoter of interclass association.

André Siegfried has left an affectionate and penetrating sketch of his father, a man of little formal education and insatiable curiosity, of preternatural energy, charitable rather than fraternal.[180] Siegfried *père's* own writings reveal a self-portrait no less candid. His proposals for workingmen's clubs told much about the breadth, as well as the limitation, of his social vision. He dwelt at some length upon what he judged the failures of the British Mechanics' Institutes as well as those of F. W. Robertson's Workingmen's Institute at Brighton. The latter was – as the Mechanics' Institutes had ceased to be – usefully elementary and cheap; but it, too, failed to provide a place to meet and talk freely, perhaps subsequently to devote a few moments to study. He found a more useful model in the Saint Matthias Workingmens' Club, created by one Reverend Chalmers, who was concerned not only with the moral and intellectual well-being of members, but also with social and recreational needs. (To counter the baneful influences of gin, he served tea and cakes.)

It is not obvious from Siegfried's description, nor from subsequent British history, that Reverend Chalmers had entirely resolved the social question, but Siegfried's recommendations for France are nonetheless remarkable. His workingmen's circles were democratic: His first prerequisite for success was that the clubs be principally directed by the workers themselves. "Principally" meant that at the group's inception the workers' votes were to count not less than half in the group's direction, and eventually, for two-thirds.[181]

If this arrangement suggests a very qualified democracy, it must be contrasted with the statutes proposed for the Catholic Workers' Circle of Auxerre some eight years later. Auxerre, unlike Mulhouse or LeHavre, was a small city with virtually no proletariat. Most of its workers were artisans working fairly steadily.[182] There the by-laws provided for a committee drawn from *classes dirigeantes* (described as such) to survey the "moral and material interests of its members" and for the appointment by this committee of a director to watch more closely over these concerns. The only concession to the clamorous spirit of the times was a council of delegates elected by worker-members from a list drawn up by the director and approved by the committee.[183]

Siegfried, unsurprisingly, anticipated deference: The workers asked nothing more than the chance to educate themselves; "they are entirely disposed to enter into the views of persons who, by their education and instruction, know more than they; but they like to be treated with consideration, they want to be consulted . . ."[184] Further, he stressed that the chief aim of the group must be "to facilitate the social relations of workers": The clubs would provide "suitable recreations and distractions." He believed that there ought to be frequent lectures and readings, including many to which members' wives and daughters might be invited (Siegfried seems to have cherished quite Victorian hopes for the elevating influence of women).[185] Withal, the plan suggests the creation of a *foyer*. Although it would not bring about, as in *l'enseignement à domicile*, the actual introduction of workers into a bourgeois "interior," at least there would be the studied creation of a place – well-lit, suitably ventilated – where certain preferred social relations might come about: conversation, for example, including conversation between the sexes – not the febrile talk of the cabaret, but reasonable, large-minded discussion that would be as clean as the rooms and as wholesome as the refreshments.

Siegfried promised, too, a secondary but "immense advantage": The clubs would also facilitate relations between classes. "Honorary members" would be admitted, not to dominate the club, but for "the exchange of ideas"; and he foresaw therein an opportunity that would be especially valuable to young men in easy circumstances. These would be called upon to teach courses and thus put their learning to the service of the common good; they would learn how to speak in public and become accustomed to "directing the masses."[186]

Other industrialists, many in more modest circumstances than Siegfried, also worked in syndical chambers and workingmen's clubs. Charles Junker described himself in a letter to Macé as a "social intermediary," the owner of a small factory able thus to understand the situation of workers and entrepreneurs.[187] Junker and Emile Moreau, later mayor and deputy of Roubaix, were both active in secular educational societies: They lectured on nonviolent progress to be achieved through the schools and through peaceful association. Well into the 1890s Moreau attacked the Catholic Association des patrons du Nord and groups such as Notre-Dame de l'usine. Charging that workers were coerced by their employers into joining devotional circles, he demanded that the government protect the workers' "freedom of conscience and right to work."[188]

Macé responded to the concern of so many supporters for workers' education with the reminder that "there is also an education required for the bourgeoisie . . . Among these men – honest, decent, educated – many, it is true, are afflicted with a singular timidity; they appear egoist because they remain at home and people believe them incapable of taking the slightest action for the public good."[189]

It is easy to dismiss this. There appear to have been men wholly able to grasp and pursue interests, distinct from or in preference to the public good. What is remarkable, nonetheless, is the almost total unanimity among men of the Center and Left on educational issues. In 1870 Charles Delescluze, soon to die a *communard*, urged a negative vote in the last imperial plebiscite: The empire, he wrote, had condemned the children of the people to the "brutalizing lessons of the Ignorantines."[190] At the same time the league undertook its first national coordinated effort: a petition, such as Jules Siegfried had urged, for free, compulsory primary schooling. The signature campaign was begun in Alsace in the spring of 1870, interrupted by the outbreak of war, and resumed by the Paris circle of the league in 1871.[191] It was an unprecedented campaign. The petition, signed eventually by more than a million citizens, was formally accepted on behalf of the nation in June 1872 by a group of radical deputies – all league members – when the National Assembly itself refused, in a "revolting affront," to take notice of it.[192]

Although a subscription to a journal, like a signature on a petition, cannot be taken as evidence of profound commitment, the readers of the *Bulletin du mouvement de l'enseignement par l'initiative privée* composed, by the fall of 1871, the constellation that would become the Radical establishment.[193] Among these were Jules Ferry, Jules Siegfried, Léon Say, and Corbon. An intimation of *revanche* came with Henri Martin, Colonel Philippe Denfert-Rochereau, the defender of Belfort, and Macé's friend Zopff, aide to the late Mayor Kuss of Strasbourg. (Kuss, deputy of the Bas-Rhin, died at Bordeaux on the day the assembly ratified the loss of Alsace and Lorraine.) The next year brought the promise of final disestablishment in the names of two young lawyers, Léon Bourgeois and Emile Combes. Of greater significance for the struggle at hand were the many advocates of public education who would become majors, deputies, prefects, in the next decades; Drouot at Nancy, Thomas at Rheims, Emile Lebon at Dieppe, LeBastard at Rennes, Emmanuel Jardet in the Allier, Antonin Proust, cousin of the novelist, in the Deux-Sevres.[194]

The ideological sympathy that cooperation on the schools issue both presupposed and strengthened did much to secure the local ascendancy of secular democrats that Daniel Halévy recognized as the "revolution of the townhalls,"[195] a movement best understood in its local manifestations.

In all, the league's history is somewhat episodic, incoherent by necessity if not by design, made more fragmentary still by the ravages of war and persecution. Much league activity was concentrated in the departments of the north and east, fought over three times since its creation. Worse, in 1942, after the league was suppressed (for the last time) by the prefect of the Seine, acting under orders from Vichy, its offices were pillaged and its records burned. Jean Macé's own papers were lost, and the league archives today consist only of printed bulletins that it was possible to reassemble after the Liberation.[196]

The depredations of the French fascists confirm – more convincingly, perhaps, than the evidence they destroyed would have done – the acknowledged association of the league with republican France; yet it has been possible to reconstruct from published sources and from the almost inexhaustible *cartons* of the *Police politique* and the prefectures (one wonders if these are the *inépuisable* resources of which the Second Empire boasted) the activities, so ingenious and multifarious, into which the reformers' protean energy flowed.

The lamentable destruction of the league's own records forces a historian to distinguish – more sharply than one might wish to do if a more complete picture of its activity were available – between its political impact, which can be documented, and its philanthropic or pedagogic influence, which cannot. This is to be regretted, because it seems obvious that many league members believed the two aspects of their work to be inseparable.

The fragmentary nature of the evidence creates other problems. Educational societies were invariably and, it seems, almost *ipso facto* suspect: The Ministry of the Interior subjected them to unrelenting scrutiny. Much evidence remains, although some deals with the league rather obliquely. One must work from public records, from anxious and self-exculpatory administrative correspondence, and from accusations made about groups with overlapping memberships.[197] Inevitably, such reports tended to exaggerate it as a menace, whereas Macé's published writings would suggest a different, somewhat implausible impression of correct and cheerful calm. Unfortunately, the distortions do not cancel each other, because both friends and detractors shared an interest in establishing the league's significance. The national archives have provided, then, not an exhaustive or balanced account of the league's work, but rather some characteristic strategies and exemplary difficulties. If the account seems sometimes anecdotal, recall that an acquaintance with obscure, utterly sincere *types* is one of history's pleasures.

The character of the league can be inferred in part from biographies of its prominent members – although this perhaps exaggerates its importance as an element in political careers. The printed lists, so steadily lengthening, of adherents and subscribers, reveal little except names: There is no evidence, apart from their varying generosity, of the importance that any of them attached to the league. Did it affect the lives of any but its members? Did it successfully proselytize? Was it essential to the unity of the convinced? It is difficult to answer these questions satisfactorily. There can be no question, however, of the heightened confidence and self-assertion of the associated educational societies when, in the later 1860s, they became overtly democratic and secularist and also more public.

Fortunately, it has been possible to reconstruct for two very different departments, the Yonne in Burgundy and the Bouches-du-Rhône (with

Marseille as its capital), indisputable evidence drawn from rich municipal and departmental archives of the league's central importance in the
development of an opposition that became a governing cadre. In the
Yonne, a high-minded and ambitious provincial bourgeoisie, descendants of the intransigent Jansenists of Auxerre, associated themselves
with a Jacobin peasantry in more than a dozen rural centers. In the more
tumultuous politics of Marseille, a schism occurred early between the
philanthropic Ligue marseillaise de l'enseignement and the Association
phocéenne, whose membership (which included the Provençal contingent of the International) organized Gambetta's campaign in 1869 and
staffed the Commune, as well as the prefecture, after *le 4 septembre*. In
both departments the league produced groups of markedly indigenous
character that remained able, nonetheless, to enter into national alliance
with others equally expressive of regional cultures and local priorities.
Sanford J. Elwitt quite rightly notes its "careful attention to local sensibilities."[198]

The Ligue de l'enseignement early championed the paramount issue –
free, compulsory, secular primary education – common to virtually all
those who would come to power with the Third Republic. It was not, of
course, their only link, but it would prove in many ways their most
resilient and durable bond. Let us see, then, how that bond was forged
in two departments.

PROVINCIAL ORGANIZATION

To unite the deux pays: *the Society for the Propagation of Popular Instruction in the
department of the Yonne.* In Burgundy, in the departments of the Côte
d'or[199] and in the Yonne, provincial republicans, persistent moderates
who sensed that their day was coming, drew closer to a Jacobin peasantry. The Yonne had a long and remarkably consistent history of dissi-
dence: Huguenots had resisted slaughter there, and the diocese of
Auxerre had been for forty years after *Unigenitas* a defiant haven for
French Jansenists.

Charles de Caylus, bishop of Auxerre from 1705 until 1754, who was
first moved to consider Jansenist teachings seriously by the bull con-
demning them, became their exponent and protector. The exiles who
flocked to his see made it an intellectual center. They taught in its
seminary, in an enlarged system of primary schools, and in a curiously
modern-sounding free boys' school that taught, in addition to Latin and
French, English, science, mythology, banking, and accounting. The
bishop inaugurated in 1749 the first of the city's many literary societies,
the Society for Arts and Belles-Lettres, in which his clergy mingled with
the *noblesse de robe* and with a cultivated bourgeoisie.[200]

After the death of Caylus, his two successors before 1789 harried and replaced the priests he had protected. The clergy who felt the force of the Revolution were thus men whose trials aroused little sympathy. Furthermore, the attachment of the laity to Jansenist practice and Gallican organization made them peculiarly insusceptible to nineteenth-century Catholicism – both to the sacramentalism of the Gothic revival and to its ultramontane politics. The department of the Yonne became indisputably anticlerical,[201] and popular secularism could always be tapped by local republicans.

Even after 1848, bourgeois republicans could rely upon considerable rural radicalism. Police reports of 1849 found the Yonne "deeply penetrated with socialism through the efforts of the clubs and secret societies."[202] Later reports suggest that what was broadly painted as socialism was in fact rural republicanism. In May 1851 the republican secret society Marianne was believed to be attracting large numbers of country people, day laborers, woodcutters, the inevitable café owners, and "artisans."[203] After the coup, it was considered a troublesome department: The dossiers of 1,167 individuals were reviewed by the "mixed commission," and 443 suspects received the severe punishment of "Algeria plus," which condemned them to incarceration in North Africa, and not merely deportation there. Haussmann was prefect at Auxerre before he was sent on to cope with the Gironde.

Throughout the fifties close watch was kept for signs of renewed opposition. Persigny suspected that freemasons might attempt to "transform themselves into a revolutionary organization," and his queries brought reassuring though ill-documented replies from the Yonne. At Joigny, two lodges manifesting a "bad spirit" had already been dissolved. At Sens, freemasons were described as "men of order"; elsewhere –at Avallon, Tonnere, and Chablis – there was little activity. Indeed, the subprefect at Chablis thought it a weakness of the masons that they were unable to interest countryfolk in their movement.[204]

Town-dwelling freethinkers would soon develop more inclusive forms of sociability. Already in 1853 authorities complained that civil funerals were made occasions for political demonstrations,[205] and the subprefect as Sens believed that a Protestant school planned there would furnish a "pretext" for all who wished to reestablish "a state of things contrary to order, morals, and respect for authority."[206] Whether or not that deplorable "state of things" was a full-blown republic, he felt that it should not be allowed.

Sens, however circumspect its freemasons, seems to have been continuously lacking in respect for authority. In the 1830s it had welcomed Methodist missionaries; in 1855, its former mayor, an architect named Parent – "moral anarchy personified" – presided over meetings of the

Cercle du commerce, from which cries of Vive la République! A bas l'Empire! resounded.[207] Even so, elections did not go badly for the government: In 1857, official candidates were elected in the first and third districts of the Yonne, and only in the second constituency, which included Sens and Joigny, was an independent, Léopold Javal, returned.

The character of the first independent elected in the department after the coup told much about the path that successful opposition would take. A wealthy moderate, born in Mulhouse and educated in Paris and in England, Javal represented the Jews of the Haut-Rhin in the *Consistoire central*. He served on the general council of the Gironde from 1852 until 1861 and, even before accusations about "electoral maneuvers" in that department, had bought land in Burgundy and run for office there. Javal was not one of the Cinq; and although he voted with twenty-three other deputies against the draconian *loi de sûreté générale* of 1858, he was not an expressed opponent of the regime. His electoral posters in 1863 promised neither "blind devotion nor systematic opposition."[208]

An advocate of economic development, Javal was close to the Saint-Simonians, and especially to Michel Chevalier. As a youth he had spirited out of England a cloth-printing machine that enabled his father and uncle to expand greatly their production of *toiles peintes* at a period when the British themselves, little persuaded of the uses of competition, had made the export of patented machinery a capital crime.

Javal continued to urge industrializatoin and, as a model farmer and stockbreeder, also supported agricultural improvement societies. There had been only one such group, at Joigny, in 1847. By 1857 there were nine *comices agricoles* in the department, and Javal often spoke before them. A contemporary wrote that "he never feared to raise the thorniest problems of economic science before his audience of farmers." In his "causeries en plein air," he argued against protection for agricultural products. Quoting Montesquieu ("A land is cultivated not in measure of its fertility but by virtue of its freedom"), he recommended diversification and, to make this possible, education. It was, he said, "the most powerful means of progress . . . Let us augment the value of the producer. In increasing tenfold his productive powers, education makes him aware of his rights and his duties; it brings riches as well as morality."[209]

Javal was unbeatable. Neither official disapprobation nor the designation of "official candidate," offered him in 1863 and equivocatingly, perhaps never definitively accepted, affected his success.[210] He was reelected in 1869 and in 1871 and was succeeded after his death, in 1872, by Paul Bert. The elections of 1863 were contested by other men who would continue in public prominence. Edouard Charton, the editor of the *Magasin pittoresque*, whom Javal defeated, campaigned as a man "incapable of servility." He inveighed against centralization and called for an expansion of free education, "which alone can make citizens equals."[211]

Charton was elected deputy in February 1871. Other notables of the Second Republic who reentered politics in the 1860s – Guichard, Rampont-Lechin, Rathier, and Etienne Savatier-Laroche – all were returned to national office in 1871, and some even earlier. Rampont-Lechin, a former member of the Constituent Assembly and president of the *comice agricole*, defeated at Auxerre in 1863, regretted then that "the hour had not yet come for a general conciliation on the basis of liberty."[212] In 1869 he defeated the official candidate.

These men, who offered plain but nuanced opposition to the emperor, nonetheless received encouragement and support from Victor Duruy in their efforts for popular education. In the winter of 1864–5, the Société des sciences historiques et naturelles organized a series of lectures described as a "public course of higher education." In January of 1865 the prefect reported to Duruy "a success as decisive as one could wish" and attributed it to the minister's impetus. More than five hundred people, including "all classes of society and many ladies," had listened to Mayor Challe's talk on the first centuries of Auxerre. The audience had filled the Grand Hall of the Palais de Justice and overflowed into the vestibule. The society's effort was carried out almost wholly, the prefect noted, by members of the liberal professions, not (with the exception of two professors from the *collège*) by men attached to the University; yet this circumstance seems to have aroused no worry. Even before the creation of the Society for Popular Instruction, the administration was prepared to allow independent notables tolerably free address "to all classes of society." Surprisingly, too, when informed that the mayors of many rural communes wanted schoolmasters to undertake similar evenings, Duruy replied that he would view the profusion of such lectures with great pleasure. Disregarding the repeated insistence of the minister of the interior that each public meeting be investigated individually before authorization, he urged the prefect to carry on and trouble himself no more with "formalities."[213]

The lectures flourished, and Duruy (who, faced with a hostile Chamber of Deputies, had decided *faute de mieux* to "municipalize reform"[214]) found ready supporters in the general council of the Yonne, as well as in many municipal councils there. The general council had consistently resisted implementation of the loi Falloux and concerned itself, too, with free schooling. Auxerre and fifteen other communes – Joigny, Sens, Tonnere, Avallon, and Seignelay among them – had established full *gratuité* in twenty-seven schools before the law of April 10, 1867, and in the next years the movement became general. Moreover, in an action that could not have failed to please Duruy, six new girls' schools had been established in 1866, each one designated as secular by the municipal council that supported it.[215]

In the same year, Hippolyte Ribière, already a municipal councillor in Auxerre and a member of the *conseil d'arrondissement*, was named by the minister to the municipal library committee, there to preside over edifying books.[216] The pastor of the Reformed Church at Branches expatiated on "French civilization, letters, art, and science, and its relation with social and domestic life." Some difficulties did arise: Emile Deschanel was denied permission to lecture on literature at Sens after disquieting reports of him reached Paris; and the next year a Dr. Moreau of "exalted and notoriously familiar political opinions" was forbidden to offer a free public course on physics and chemistry at Véron. In general, however, relations were cordial between Duruy and the members of the learned societies.

In 1868, a popular library, distinct from the municipal library and intended to serve the needs of workers, was created at Auxerre, with Arthur Savatier-Laroche (the son of Etienne Savatier-Laroche, member of the Constituent Assembly in 1848–9) as its secretary. The library kept its reading room open from noon until midnight on Thursday and Friday and offered, in addition to elementary courses, a bracing and distinctly modernist selection of books. Its volumes included, of course, the department's notables (Charton, Paul Bert, Savatier-Laroche's fables and stories as well as his *Affirmations and Doubts*, and Challe's edifying history of the religious wars), many of Macé's works, Franklin, Voltaire's *Essays on the Mores of Nations* and *The Century of Louis XIV*, Montesquieu's *Considerations on the Causes of the Grandeur of the Romans and Their Decline*, and Michelet's *Jeanne d'Arc*. The political-economy section was wholly orthodox (e.g., Bastiat's *Harmonies économiques*): The emperor's early socialist writings, preserved by Savatier-Laroche *en bon sujet*, were by far its most subversive offerings. Novels there were in abundance, along with the anodyne Scott and Cooper, some more provocative works by Dickens and Balzac.[217]

In July of 1868 the Society for the Propagation of Popular Instruction in the Yonne (SPIP) was founded. Hippolyte Ribière and seven other men availed themselves of the newly enlarged liberty of association and asked permission for a "nonpolitical meeting" to consider "the best means by which popular education in the department might be improved."[218] All were men of local stature: Ribière himself, Paul Bert, Charles Lepère, Arthur Savatier-Laroche, Jules Challe, a judge on the Commercial Tribunal, the court's president, M. Mérat-Beugnon, and the printers Perriquet and Rouillé. The SPIP immediately associated itself with the Ligue de l'enseignement. It built upon the ongoing lecture program of the Society for Natural and Historical Sciences and upon the municipal and popular libraries. Indeed, except for a slight intensification of effort, the new group did not differ perceptibly from the old ones.

Rouillé recalled more harassment than his associates had actually experienced when he wrote in 1880 that the SPIP had "preserved a core of men attached to liberal ideas . . . The Administration viewed with scant benevolence the progress of an association founded by a group of men whose independent sentiments were so well known to it."[219] There seems no doubt that Duruy initially supported this venture as he had others undertaken by the same men. His aide, Charles Robert, wrote to Ribière in April of 1869, expressing sympathy for the group and recommending that they take care to observe administrative formalities.[220] In 1873 and 1874, when the regime of the "moral order" seriously attempted to destroy the group, Charles Moiset (who had been Ribière's secretary at the prefecture) lamented the loss of "the active intelligence and liberal heart of Victor Duruy."[221] Nevertheless, these men were, insofar as such a thing existed, the opposition. As liberal Bonapartism approached its dénouement, they gathered, prepared to cooperate with the regime and press their demands upon it, receiving support from progressives within the government and radicals outside it.

The society's especial care was to unite the *deux pays*. Their concern, like Disraeli's with Two Nations, dwelt upon cultural and moral as well as economic disparities. In France these sensibilities inescapably confronted differences not only between rich and poor, but also between pre-Revolutionary and modern mores. The SPIP undertook to bring more of the population into the society, which, in Ferry's words, "proceeded from the French Revolution." To that end its organizers directed their efforts to rural communes and the many small market towns. They kept alive consciousness of the Revolution and of the virtue required to defend *droits acquis*. Arthur Savatier-Laroche, for one, lectured on "Agriculture and the farmer before 1789" at Aillant, Saint-Florentin, and Seignelay in 1869 (Peasants elsewhere were not without fears concerning restoration of the tithe. In the spring of 1868, peasants in the Gironde, in the communes bordering on the Charente-Inférieure, destroyed fleurs-de-lis in churches as rumors circulated that the empress wished to reinstitute the tithe on the occasion of the prince-imperial's first communion.[222])

The statutes proposed for the society in January of 1869 explicitly foresaw its organization as a "departmental society" with headquarters at Auxerre fostering courses, libraries, readings, and popular lectures in outlying communes.[223] Initiative did not come only from the department's capital: Saint-Florentin and Branches had maintained, by popular subscription, libraries and public readings since 1866. The SPIP was, however, instrumental in supporting the creation of popular libraries in Fleury, Guerchy, and Neuilly in 1868.[224]

The new dispensations governing public meetings and the growing body of precedent authorizing adult courses and popular reading rooms permitted significant numbers of men – if not of "all classes," at least, of the politically active classes – to meet together. The verities they agreed upon, unexceptionable or even banal from many points of view, provided ritual formulas upon which republican solidarity would one day safely rest: a particular interpretation of French history, a certain appreciation of the Enlightenment and of the relation between secular and democratic institutions, a veneration for science, for labor, and, especially, for the self-made man – whose success evinced the utility of both. (Lectures on the lives of Benjamin Franklin and Bernard Palissy, the resolute Huguenot potter, abounded.)

In the Yonne, as in the acknowledged hotbeds of radical activity, Lyon and Marseille, citizens delivered and drank in lectures on political ideas that were soon to assume great importance. Ernest Denormandie, president of the chamber of *avoués* at the civil tribunal of the Seine, discussed "the history of the commune in France" at Appoigny, a village of some few hundred souls whose municipal council had attracted official attention the previous spring when it forbade agents of the mayor from distributing ballots in the general elections.[225] Throughout the winter of 1869–70, after the elections that had returned the *quarante-huitard* Rampont-Lechin from Auxerre, more than eighty lectures were presented in no fewer than ten towns: Auxerre, Branches, Aillant, Saint-Florentin, Seignelay, Joigny, Appoigny, Falguy, Courson, and Sens. The membership of the SPIP had doubled within a year, and by April of 1870 its circles met in twenty-four different communes.[226]

In the spring of 1870, the founders of the SPIP sponsored meetings urging a negative vote in the imperial plebiscite, the emperor's last appeal to the nation after his lack of success in the general elections of 1869. Ribière, Rathier, Lepère, Perriquet, and Savatier-Laroche assumed responsibility as sponsors of such meetings in Auxerre and promoted also similar gatherings in smaller towns: Toucy, Chablis, Courson, Carisey, Egleux, Vézelay, Branches, Appoigny, Tonnere, and Sens. The last mentioned was expected to become uproarious, because its organizers had asked for an open meeting and wished to admit all comers "recognized by those present to be electors *without cards or certificates of registration*." In general, both workers and members of the liberal professions sponsored these meetings: At Appoigny, a butcher and a carpenter were among the petitioners; at Chablis, the signatories were identified not by occupation but as members of the municipal council. Among the citizens asking permission to convoke at Toucy a meeting where Ribière and others would speak was the cobbler Félix Frémiot, whose name would head the list of the Society of Popular Instruction at Toucy four years later.[227]

Immediately after *le 4 septembre*, Gambetta named Ribière prefect of the Yonne and he chose as his aide the physiologist Paul Bert. The two *rapporteurs* of the lois Ferry – Ribière in the Senate and Bert in the Chamber – thus first shared office in Auxerre. Bert, who in the SPIP's 1869–70 lecture series challenged the mind-body dualism with talks on "involuntary motion," had already attained celebrity as an anticleric, a title that Javal, whom he succeeded in the assembly, could obviously not cultivate.[228] Early in his public career, Bert had brought suit successfully against the legitimist paper *La Bourgogne*, which had charged that his family fortune was founded upon a sacrilegious theft. His great-grandfather, Simon Boyer, it alleged, had been a servant of the Dominicans and, entrusted with their assets and charged to repurchase their confiscated property, had simply bought the *biens nationaux* for himself and kept them. Bert took action for libel and established that his calumniated ancestor, a timber merchant and *bourgeois d'Auxerre* who was allied by marriage with the petty nobility, had possessed a substantial fortune before the Revolution. Moreover, the Dominicans in Auxerre had employed in 1789 (or so a court held) only two servants, neither of whom was Boyer. With the damages that he was awarded, Bert established a *Prix Simon Boyer* at the free boys' schools of Auxerre.[229]

Ribière and Bert chose as secretary-general of the prefecture Charles Moiset, an SPIP lecturer whose specialty had been the careers of Franklin and Palissy. Moiset's organizational sense became increasingly important. As the society's officers became national figures, it was he who was immediately concerned with the survival of the SPIP. There remains a revealing letter from Moiset to the mayor and municipal council of Véron: Having decided that it was "the duty of every citizen to further the development of popular education," they hoped to sponsor in the council chamber of the town hall public readings and *soirées d'hiver*. They had designated Alexis Paul Moreau (whose "exalted opinions" so troubled the imperial governments) to receive subscriptions and draw up a catalogue for their library. Vacheron, the new subprefect at Sens, supported the project. Moiset's reply to this unexceptionable plan gives evidence of his foresight: He recommended that Dr. Moreau's committee be charged with the creation of a communal library but insisted that a circle of the SPIP maintain an existence distinct from the municipality.[230]

The society did, however, receive municipal and departmental subsidies and took steps to institutionalize itself. It settled, too, upon a practice that maintained ties with the countryside: Each year a different canton's chef-lieu was chosen as the scene of an "extraordinary meet-ing." In 1871 its petition for the status of "public utility" described lectures of general interest as well as free courses on commercial and civil law, history, and applied science. It reported also the support of fourteen popular libraries.[231] The designation of "public utility" was duly conferred upon the favorable recommendation of the prefect, its founder.

In 1872 the SPIP associated itself with two national campaigns, the subscription for the "liberation of the territory" and the Ligue de l'en-seignement's petition for free, compulsory, secular schooling. It main-tained contact with educational societies in the neighboring departments – the Saône-et-Loire and the Côte d'or – among them, the League's *cercle bourguignon* at Semur, an advanced group whose first bulletin would argue that compulsory schooling was "illusory" if poor families were not compensated for their children's foregone wages. The league's circle in the Côte d'or included Joseph Magnin, elected to the Chamber of Deputies in 1863 as an opponent of the regime, and a future president of the republic, Sadi Carnot. Despite unpleasant passages with the au-thorities, the winter of 1872–3 saw in Semur, as it would in the Yonne, considerable activity: lectures on economics and society, cooperative associations, freedom of labor and the right to property, and the origins of the French Revolution.[232]

By the end of 1872, however, the SPIP itself became subject to admin-istrative "vexations." Ribière forwarded to the society a letter from the minister of the interior announcing that henceforth no general authori-zations for public meetings would be issued to organizations: Each lec-ture must be investigated and judged individually. Legally, this had never ceased to be the case, but the requirement had been waived tacitly by Duruy and Jules Simon. The minister had evidently decided that the public temper could withstand Arthur Savatier-Laroche on "the condi-tions of labor under feudalism" and "intellectual and social progress at the time of the Renaissance," nor could he object to the printer Perri-quet's interpretation of political economy and the history of labor. He asked, nonetheless, that in the future Ribière provide him with "more detailed information about the antecedents and bearing of persons soli-citing authorizations."[233]

The government required this information, because disturbing police reports had reached Paris concerning a professor of law, M. Renaud, who had spoken at Sens in November about decentralization and the "influence of capitalism." He had dealt with the "moral bankruptcy" of monarchies but had not confined himself to historical examples, speak-ing of "contradictory elements" in the government of Thiers. A grand old man, he asssuredly is, Renaud was alleged to have said, but one whose "past career and affections can give us only meager assurance." Those few moderates present listened coldly; the rest enthusiastically applauded. The police added that some thirty children from the communal school had been permitted to attend this appalling performance.[234]

The minister of the interior enjoined Ribière to redouble his "circumspection and prudence." It would not suffice, he emphasized, to establish (as Ribière unfailingly did) that lecturers were honorable and qualified men: Their lectures must be exclusively educational, and not propaganda in support of one political idea or another.[235] Paradoxically, the insistence that lectures be authorized individually permitted Ribière to vouch for each speaker rather than defend the general tendency of the series. So long as he remained prefect, he filed punctilious reports emphasizing the moderation and good character of the society's lecturers. Charles Moiset, *licencié en droit* and councillor-general, was described as the son of an esteemed local family, an "educated and prudent man" who had voluntarily resigned his position at the prefecture in May of 1872. M. Lancôme, the mayor of Saint-Florentin, who wished to lecture on "The Prussians after Jéna," cooperatives, and American education, was held to be a man whose tact and reserve guaranteed that he would treat any topic without "insulting allusion." Another petitioner was introduced simply as a "victim of the coup of 1851" and a moderate republican.[236]

At first, surveillance and control over the activities of the SPIP were extended with guarded courtesy and its members responded, in turn, with good humor. Arthur Savatier-Laroche asked Ribière to second a request from a science professor at the college of Châtillon-sur-Seine who wanted to speak in favor of gas streetlights: "It seems to me that gas illumination could under no circumstances provoke turmoil in the land."[237] The lines were hardening, however, and with them the tenor of debate. Administrative reserve was turning to real disapproval, and the society moved from mocking compliance to resistance.

In March of 1873, two months before the fall of the conservative republican cabinet of Thiers and the ascendancy of a considerably more conservative Moral Order under Marshal MacMahon and the duc de Broglie, Jules Simon had been forced to surrender the education portfolio to Paul Batbie. The Conseil supérieure de l'instruction publique was reestablished, granting an important role in educational policy to members of the ecclesiastical hierarchy. Schools were once again charged to combat "sinister doctrines" with prayers, catechism, and the gospels: only sacred history – that is, the Old Testament – was not restored to the curriculum.

The minister of the interior reiterated in March of 1873 that lectures inspired by "political preoccupations" must not be permitted to profit from immunities reserved for "higher education."[238] Lectures on American history were, in general, felt to lend themselves too readily to abuse; and, in March also, a lawyer Hérold was forbidden to speak at Maligny on the life of the Venetian republican Daniel Manin, a subject that was productive elsewhere of "digressions."

Anticipating that harassment would be followed by dissolution, the general assembly of the SPIP undertook in April of 1873 to regroup. In a major reorganization, it decentralized itself into thirteen self-governing local circles, "each exercising its autonomy yet united to the society by a federal bond" and pledging one third of its receipts to the departmental society. By the end of 1873, twenty-seven local groups covered sixty-three communes.[239] Ribière approved the new statutes in one of his last acts as prefect. Savatier-Laroche resigned the presidency of the group in his favor, and Ribière undertook to defend it against his successors in the prefecture.

In 1874 the newly federated group declared open opposition to the government. In introducing Edouard Charton, Etienne Flandin, a law student, so far forgot himself as to express publicly the wish that the library might replace the cabaret. Charton, now a deputy, spoke of the Restoration – in republican code an obviously comparable period of reaction – as a time in which "culpable egoism" had attempted to preserve ignorance as "the guardian of morality and the safeguard of virtue." In our day, he rejoiced, obscurantism has neither armies nor generals; only a few fanatical soldiers remain loyal to it. Much remained to be done: Five hundred communes lacked boys' schools, and five thousand were without schools for girls. He allowed also that for the mass of people education had to be "cautiously presented" (alas, he did not go on to explain what was to be included or omitted) but foresaw an end to the division of the *deux pays*.[240]

The society had solicited permission to assemble to hear Charton and others on "literary subjects." The secretary-general of the prefecture reported to the minister of the interior that their declaration had been properly made, adding that the signatories' integrity gave reason to believe the meeting would be confined to the topics they stated. The deputy himself, he felt certain, "would not exceed the limits he has described." Nevertheless, with his letter is filed a different appreciation of the group, undated but written on the paper of the prefect's Cabinet: The group, although undertaken in a most unexceptionable way in 1864–5 (*sic*) by "educated men" offering evening courses, had changed since 1871. "Several of the most honorable men had resigned and had been replaced by 'orators,' more advanced and ardent but not better educated." The report mentioned that ex-prefect Ribière served as president, the "zealous and active" Moiset as vice-president; Paul Bert and

Charles Lepère are singled out as examples of the group's radical character. Membership was estimated at about eight hundred.[241]

There appear to have been biweekly meetings during the spring of 1874. On April 26, Deputy Guichard (by then mayor of Sens) delivered a "heated improvisation" on the inadequacy of the government's newly introduced education budget. He faulted official statistics that claimed that most French children received primary instruction. The government, he concluded, either spent ridiculously little per pupil or falsified attendance figures. (School attendance in this period was, however, so very casual that a great discrepancy between children *inscrits* on the rolls and actually in school need not suggest fraud.) He welcomed the presence of women in the audience and in the schools movement. Mothers, he said, understood what was at issue: They knew education to be the surest protector of the hearth.

The society also reported during that spring great success with circulating libraries, farm wagons piled with books and sent out into the most inaccessible hamlets. Moiset's report on libraries specified three sorts, classified as to their degree of independence: school libraries, which were subject to direct governmental control; municipal libraries under the authority of the mayor – who was himself revocable and thus subject ultimately to the prefect; and popular libraries created by individual initiative and operating under no strictures except, of course, the twenty-person rule. These last were to be preferred, and might, of course, receive public benevolence if officials were disposed to grant it. The general council of Yonne, on which Moiset and virtually everyone else who held office in the SPIP served, had voted four thousand francs for "popular communal libraries" in 1873.[242]

Charles Moiset, who even from the prefecture had insisted upon independence for local circles, announced in May of 1874 that the libraries supported by the SPIP would no longer accept books donated by the Ministry of Public Instruction. The conditions decreed by the minister's *arrêté* of January 6, 1874, "would modify the very nature of these associations, and diminish rather than augment their influence and their force of expansion."[243] The objectionable conditions were these: that the library's catalogue be submitted to the police each year, along with the names and addresses of members, and that the library itself be "inspected" annually to verify the accuracy of information provided. At Sens, a library established in the town hall while its founder and president was mayor was abruptly removed to a new location after his revocation.[244]

The Ligue de l'enseignement and the Société d'instruction élémentaire intensified their efforts to support libraries no longer sustained by the ministry. Thirty-two communes in the Yonne got collections of books through the good offices of the national societies.[245]

What books were sent? The library of Fleury, a village about fourteen kilometers from Auxerre whose market town was – and is – Joigny, contained 117 volumes, in addition to *Uncle Tom's Cabin* and *Don Quixote*, Simon's *L'Ouvrière*, Laboulaye's *Paris in America*, biographies of Cromwell, Franklin, and General Grant, three volumes of the *Almanac of Cooperation*, works of Balzac, Michelet, and Macé, and other suggestive titles like *The Action of the Clergy in Modern Society, Project for a Rural School*, and *Workingmen's Associations in England*. Available, too, were books of educational statistics with maps – presumably, Manier's famous "maps of ignorance," which were widely circulated by the league. The library's sixty members – it was constituted as a circle of the Society for Popular Instruction in the Yonne – were almost entirely self-described as "farmers, gardeners, or wine-growers." Twenty-seven, including the president, called themselves *cultivateurs*; nine, *jardiniers*. The vice-president was a doctor, and there was a veterinarian also, but they were largely working men.[246]

Popular libraries remained an important aspect of the struggle. In November of 1874 "adherents" maintained the public and confident action that distinguished their republicanism from the earlier forms, which had failed more often than any of them wished to recall. Above all, they persevered:

> Practical difficulties . . . cannot justify, in any degree, an inaction that might appear a desertion of our cause. We must put ourselves to the task, without apprehension and without defiance. Above all, local initiative must never hesitate to manifest itself. The time is ripe for local circles to show themselves worthy of the place of honor that the society has given them within its ranks.[247]

The local circles, whose autonomy had been established in the new statutes of 1873, were expected to carry on, and did so unflaggingly in a "mode of organization, broader, more flexible, more favorable to the play of local energies." As authorizations for lectures became almost impossible of attainment, they were replaced with readings. "Simple readings aloud, in the past too much neglected, might sow the *seeds of the future* better than the most brilliant lecture."[248] Mayor Guichard of Sens was to become an especially pertinacious reader aloud.

The subprefect at Sens signaled the prefect about impending danger in April of 1875 and complained of his impotence: Is Guichard dispensed from complying with the law governing meetings? Must we permit him to corrupt public morals at the outset of an electoral campaign? Might the government not at least demand prior knowledge of the books from which he planned to read? Guichard disavowed any other intention than to develop in his audience a taste for the pleasures of the mind, and he provided a very long list arranged by literary period.[249] On one occasion, the police reported that he read for two hours from Thiers' *History of the Consulate and Empire* to an "indifferent" group of cobblers, farmers, and *vignerons*, but they took a more relaxed view than the subprefect, confident that the "unemployed rabble" who, with the municipal councillors, formed Guichard's audience would soon tire of Bossuet.

The subprefect determined to rid himself of the popular library: It was, he insisted, "a political machine created for politics, employing political agents; there . . . radicals find their marching orders between *two materialist and socialist volumes of Jules Simon.*"[250] His peculiar interpretation of Simon apart, he did not, nonetheless, exceed his superior's zeal.

Ducrest de Villeneuve, the new prefect of the Yonne, had in one of his first acts of office made local circles of the SPIP subject to article 291 of the penal code, insisting that each *meeting* of more than twenty members be separately authorized and its agenda submitted to him eight days prior to the session. He further demanded membership lists, including address and occupation, and verbatim transcripts of meetings. The society's accounts and correspondence were to be made available upon request to any agent authorized by him or by the minister of public instruction, and no new books were to be shelved in any library without prior approval.[251]

In this Ducrest seemed to have been ready to act with greater ferocity than the cabinet wished to exercise or deemed necessary. In January of 1875 the minister of the interior, in response to a question about action to be taken if lectures resumed, cautioned that a blanket refusal was impolitic. He recommended great reserve in the use of the prefect's power to adjourn public meetings. So provocative an action would be justified only if public order was threatened. No direct measures were to be taken against the SPIP "before having established, with new evidence, that its ostensible purpose conceals projects of radical propaganda."[252]

Although the minister of the interior counselled a dignified prudence – perhaps because he miscalculated his strength vis-à-vis the radicals – the gendarmerie and local officials who would be held accountable kept watch over the SPIP and over other manifestations of the department's fractious spirit. Their preoccupation, for example, with the preaching of a Protestant cobbler in Avallon and Tonnere is intelligible only in a context of political and religious polarization. Since the fall of 1873, a "shoemaker foreign to the village" had addressed to the peasantry a message described by police reports as essentially irreligious. In the spring of 1875, a parish priest demanded that the man be silenced, charging that his "blasphemous lies" mixed "contempt for dogma with irritating political questions."[253] The *curé* may, of course, have had reasons of his own for painting the man as a political threat: The report of the gendarmerie gave a more narrowly religious interpretation to his talks. There was no denying the man's skeptical cheek. Although the preacher had recommended that one must "respect what is respectable, even the clergy when they deserve it,"[254] the prefect summed up Protestant proselytizing in the department thus: His predecessor (Ribière) had not been "helpful" to the government in failing to appreciate the "grave questions" raised by religious meetings. The so-called evangelists were manifestly freethinkers, which explained the solicitude of certain members of the National Assembly for them.[255]

The functionaries of the Moral Order had increasingly to contend with the *faits accomplis* of republican incumbents. Republican and secularist members of the SPIP represented the Yonne in Paris; they also controlled the general council of the department. Its members, in concert with elected municipal councils, greatly expanded free schooling: By 1872, the department had spent six thousand francs in support of ninety free schools,[256] and they seemed ready to propose innovations more dubious than *gratuité*. In 1875 general councillors commissioned a schoolmaster, a M. Frontier of Bonard, to study primary education in Switzerland and make recommendations to them on the basis of his research. The report was presented in two parts – one on administrative organization, the second on pedagogy. Frontier reported that everywhere in Switzerland education was compulsory, although begun at varying ages (six years in some places, seven in Neufchâtel and the Vaud), and was everywhere solicitous of the child's energy and activity. He preferred the freedom of Froebelian kindergartens to the discipline of the *salle d'asile*, but, not surprisingly, he dwelt more upon reason than upon spontaneity. Like the school committees of the Paris and Lyon communes, Frontier described rational pedagogy as the great advantage of republican education: "Nothing is artificial."[257] The inconsequential, contradictory, and frivolous were eliminated simply by following nature. True to Rousseau (whom he did not mention) and to Pestalozzi (whom he did), the schools cherished the active, curious nature of the child, who was encouraged first to observe and only later – but inevitably – began to reflect.

Faith in the capacity to learn from reality led Frontier, as it led others, to advocate coeducation. He implored "our legislators" attention to its moral, as well as its intellectual advantages. In German Switzerland he found children up to the age of fifteen taught together and teachers in unanimous support of the arrangement. "The diversity of moral and intellectual faculties in the two sexes neither requires nor justifies separation." Mixed schools did not foster debauchery, they prevented it, Frontier insisted, and he quoted at length the opinion of a M. Grob that coeducation gave children of both sexes an opportunity to study "the other half of humanity," not in books but in reality, so that when they became old enough to marry, young men and women would have learned to distinguish outer appearance from inner worth.[258]

The department's elected officials thus fostered and circulated rationalist homilies. In doing so they aroused the hostility of the administration, which determined to destroy their grass roots. On October 7, 1875, the prefect demanded that each local circle of the SPIP and each popular library submit its statutes and its membership lists for his approval. He threatened those that failed to comply with action under Articles 291 and 292 of the penal code. Ribière, who in 1873 had approved the by-law revision permitting decentralization, responded that each circle was an integral part of the society, animated by the same principles and statutes that governed the whole. The SPIP had been legally empowered to devolve some of its activities, but there could be no question of separate accountability. Ribière and local groups denied the prefect's right to impose new conditions and refused to comply with them. In response, he annulled Ribière's approval of the 1873 statutes. Some circles suspended meetings; others declared themselves reabsorbed into the departmental group.[259]

The prefect had been concerned, of course, with diminishing the influence of the SPIP over the parliamentary elections of 1876 – in which republicans everywhere in France did very well. Those victories marked another turning point for the group. A new, more benign prefect reexamined the ukases of the previous year. Action was taken against them, members affirmed, although "no guilty act was ever even imputed to any local group," and the society promised to continue upon the "calm and laborious path it has traced for itself." The prefect assured them of his full sympathy and promised to authorize any of their branches "as soon as the request reaches the prefecture." Nevertheless, he did ask their indulgence in establishing "uniform jurisdiction," reminding them that the existence of "groups of a different nature" made the matter a delicate one.[260]

With this understanding, thirty-eight SPIP circles or libraries were legally reconstituted by the spring of 1877, when the society and the young republic faced its most serious threat. The crisis of May 16, in which President MacMahon forced Premier Jules Simon to resign and created a new cabinet unacceptable and irresponsible to the parliamentary majority, was followed in June by the dissolution of the National Assembly.

The depredations of the ensuing campaign are impossible to document fully. The republicans, who triumphed decisively in the elections of October 14, 1877, began in November to investigate the extent of the summer's "administrative terror," but the prefect had already instructed his subordinates that the parliamentary commission of inquiry "could not impel, under any title, agents of authority or simple citizens to enter into communication with it, or furnish it evidence or information." They were further told to put no meeting places at its disposal, to furnish neither direct or indirect aid.[261]

During the summer of 1878, republican functionaries were still trying to document abuses of executive power and to "reintegrate" republicans discharged, demoted, or transferred during the campaign. In the arrondissement of Joigny, Robert Allain-Targé (nephew of the liberal publicist Henri Allain-Targé) found in the archives of his subprefecture the circular instructing noncompliance and nothing else. However, four municipal councils had been dissolved and replaced with appointed "commissions," and the mayors of the towns were removed from office. The inspector of primary schools had been peremptorily transferred to Châlon-sur-Marne, and eleven teachers punitively reassigned. The firmness of the academic administration had prevented the displacement of eighteen others. Two police commissioners and a justice of the peace had been "disgraced," and the inspector of weights and measures at Tulle had been judged too radical for his post. At Sens, where Guichard had defeated the conservative ex-mayor Provent (who was "patronized by the clergy"), all documents for the summer of 1877 had been "carefully removed and destroyed"; even the communal registers contained only entries prior to May 16.[262]

The SPIP had, of course, been dissolved during the electoral campaign, and its libraries closed. Press censorship often took this form, because court actions against newspapers were lengthy and unavoidably public procedures. The government found it simpler to attack the means of dissemination: libraries, bookstores, and book peddlers. At Sens, for example, a republican journal, *The Constitution*, was actually seized from the hands of its sellers. "All for nought, as you know," the subprefect exulted, "thanks to the patriotism and good sense of the enlightened citizens of Sens." During this difficult time, the SPIP members, recognizing, as one of them said, that education and music are sisters, had continued to meet as a choral society.[263]

By 1877 the founders of the society were national figures, thoroughly in command of the department they had organized for the republic. When Macé had written that the needful work was already begun and needed only to be made aware of itself, he might have been describing the efforts of the Yonne's *quarante-huitards* and their younger sympathizers who maintained a public life throughout the empire, in local office as well as in the increasingly partisan activities of the educational societies. They never ceased to propound a secular and democratic rationalism. They provided the citizenry with books through the municipal library and later through a popular library also. In free evening courses they lectured on the moral consequences of the Renaissance, on the condition of the peasantry before and after 1789, on the lives of Washington and Franklin, on human physiology and electricity, on agronomy and hygiene – though no one in Burgundy suggested, as Schrader of the Philomatique had at Bordeaux, *L'Eau envisagée comme boisson*.[264] Their efforts issued in a tightly organized departmental party virtually indistinguishable from the SPIP, which had affiliated with the Ligue de l'enseignement in 1868. The same men – Ribière, Bert, Charton, Guichard and others – campaigned for opposition candidates and fought the plebiscite. In the face of conservative harassment, they won repeated and eventually irresistible electoral victories culminating in the full success of the republicans in the crucial elections of October 14, 1877.

In 1864 A. Challe, an *érudit local* soon to be elected mayor of Auxerre, had published a history of the religious wars in the Yonne. It is not farfetched to see in his scholarly account of Calvinist organization a covert appeal for republican counterparts. Challe wrote in the *Bulletin de la Société des sciences de l'Yonne* that the support of "the most enlightened and elevated classes" (and did that not describe his readers?) was indispensable, regardless of whether their motives were pure or worldly. He argued also that the massacres of Huguenots at Vassy and Sens might have signaled a campaign of extermination but for the "rapidity with which their already advanced association, or as they said their churches, enabled them to rise en masse."[265] Events after 1864 suggest that many shared Challe's notion of moral progress. Once again, reform depended upon prominent supporters and upon extensive, prudent organization.

Dissension within the ranks of progress: the Ligue marseillaise de l'enseignement and the Association phocéenne pour l'instruction des deux sexes. The movement for popular education is rarely free from tension between two goals: between success within a prevailing order and sustained opposition to it; between vocational training for individual advancement and ideological instruction to strengthen a common identity and purpose. In 1848 the Association polytechnique and the Association philotechnique had split over this very issue, but these two ends are not everywhere and always contradictory. Indeed, the republican position was plausible in the 1860s and 1870s because they were *not* felt to be irreconcilable.

Even so, the conflict erupted within the Ligue de l'enseignement at Marseille. Insofar as anything is common knowledge about the league, it is the inability of its center to hold in Marseille. In 1868 its local circle was divided on curricular and political issues: The "moderates," chiefly lawyers and businessmen, became the *cercle marseillaise*; the "radicals," lawyers also, as well as employees, writers, and workers, constituted themselves as the Association phocéenne pour l'instruction des deux sexes.

It is significant that the Association phocéenne – politically, the more important group – gathered not only the leaders of the commune of Marseille (Bastelica, Rey, Royannez, and Gaston Crémieux, the *avocat des pauvres*), but also the future prefects of the republic, Alphonse Esquiros and Delpech. It included, too, the "bourgeois" democrats and free-masons Rouvier, Boucher, Brochier, Labadié, and Amat, who would serve on the municipal council throughout the 1870s, struggling to preserve the commune's secularization of schools with a variety of legal and extralegal devices. The differences between the two league affiliates did not, therefore, prefigure the battle between the commune and the republic; it expressed the conflict between men who saw education as vocational and quietistic and those who urged its emancipatory promise. The commitment to the political aims of secular schooling provided a bond strong enough to survive the shocks of the commune.

The politics of Marseille seem, by contrast with Burgundy, febrile, tumultuous, hyperbolic. A port without Bordeaux's serene urbanity or the solid Norman comfort of LeHavre, Marseille elected Léon Gambetta in 1868 in by-elections following the death of the legitimist Pierre-Antoine Berryer. Berryer, no reactionary, was a respected exemplar of the Liberal Union and an adherent of the Nancy Project; he had, a few years before his death, volunteered to defend striking typographers.[266]

However the alternations in electoral politics may be interpreted, in Marseille as elsewhere, the movement for popular instruction showed itself persistent and continuous. During the Second Republic, the Workers' Atheneum had offered practical courses that the authorities had felt "cannot fail to be useful" and other classes in morals, philosophy, and history that the police had deemed "very bad"; but the members of the Atheneum had believed in 1851 that self-improvement and solidarity could be complementary, and many continued in that conviction.[267]

When, in 1866, the freemason Royannez – publisher of a weekly paper, *Le Père tranquille* – called for the creation of a popular library "to be called the Library of the friends of study and morality," the municipal councillors Amat and Labadié, both members of the Atheneum in its successive forms ("republican," "popular," "meridional," and *"phocéen"*), welcomed the proposal. Endorsing both municipal libraries and those due to individual initiative, they obtained for Royannez's library a municipal subsidy of a thousand francs.[268]

The library prospered, with a large and consistent though eclectic catalogue modelled on the selection of the library of the "Friends of Instruction" of the Fifth Arrondissement of Paris, the *quartier* of the Pantheon: Michelet, Montesquieu, Laboulaye and Channing, Blanqui as well as Bastiat and Louis Reybaud, Jules Simon, Victor Duruy, Jean

Macé, and other contemporary publicists.[269] Evening courses were organized too, and in March of 1868 Royannez reported to *L'Action maçonnique* that freemasons had supported for eighteen months classes for young people, "all adults," without any official patronage or subsidy.[270] It is surely to these courses that the lawyer de Pleuc had referred when he wrote to Jean Macé in May of 1867 that the league would find in Marseille "support already organized in a compact group of progressive men" who in the previous September had established a primary school and adult courses meeting six nights a week.[271]

The "compact group of progressive men" stood united until the summer of 1868. Then, as de Pleuc himself complained in an unctuous letter to the prefect, "the eminent functionary who had so obligingly protected this endeavor," their unity was "compromised by the hostile attitude of a small and violent group." More than seven hundred members, who had separated themselves in order to "remain faithful to our motto of conciliation and peace," asked authorization for new by-laws that would enable them to exclude "any member who had disrupted meetings in a systematic manner or against whom there exist serious objections" (Article 6). "As a measure of prudence," they had posted guards at the doors to bar any save card-carrying members from their election meetings.[272]

Now styled the Ligue marseillaise de l'enseignement, with de Pleuc as president, the ice merchant Nugues and another businessman, Jean Léonce, as secretaries (both men would be moderate republican municipal councillors in the seventies), they offered, in the fall of 1868, a series of eminently practical courses: grammar, arithmetic, elementary botany, biology, anatomy, industrial chemistry, applied geometry, and commercial law.[273] They must have believed that the subject matter did not suffice to exclude troublemakers; they specified that no one was to be admitted to class without his membership card.

Jean Macé took cognizance of the split with his usual *sangfroid*: It offered, he wrote, the great advantage of "emulation" to the *Marseillais*. The conservative group claimed twice as much money and many fewer members – eight thousand francs and sixteen hundred adherents – than the radical group, now styled the Association phocéenne pour l'éducation et l'instruction des deux sexes, with some twenty-five hundred members but only four thousand francs.[274] Macé undoubtedly realized that he could not reconcile the groups and disdained to reveal the limits of his authority by exerting it in vain. The *Bulletin du mouvement d'enseignement par l'initiative privée* nevertheless did report that the value of courses given by the Ligue marseillaise de l'enseignement was said by some to be diminished by the unwillingness of the professors to "establish rapport with their classes."[275]

The Association phocéenne offered courses, too, including one by the future prefect Delpech, a bookkeeper, on his *métier*; and another future prefect, a donnish socialist, Alphonse Esquiros, author of admiring books on British and Dutch domestic habits as well as the more programmatic *Life in the Future from a Socialist Point of View*, lectured on French history. The Jewish lawyer Crémieux, the only bourgeois to be executed for his role in the Marseille Commune, taught moral philosophy. Instruction in law, grammar, and "the history of the wars of religion" was also available.[276]

The courses, however, were supplemented by mass meetings, duly transcribed by the police. On September 12, 1868, the engineer Brochier, one of sixteen members of an administrative commission elected that month,[277] presided over a meeting at which Antomarchi, who "affected the use of the word citizen," attacked the schools of the Christian Brothers. The Ignorantine schools only pretend to be free, he said, citing the many small charges, for example, for books, supplies, and contributions – each trifling in itself but burdensome to poor families. A contributor to the radical paper *Le Peuple*, Charles LeBalleur-Villiers, a "democrat, free-thinker, and materialist," roused himself to a pitch of "violent exaltation" in an attack on "black and hierarchical" monkish education. Crémieux was held to speak more decently and moderately: The police evidently found encouraging his proposal that the association create a new library to combat "bad literature" to which the people were exposed.[278]

Crémieux's library did not meet their expectations, and the prefect spent much of the fall attempting to secure its catalog. The *phocéens* at first refused to acknowledge his right to demand it. Their letters were couched in very different terms from those of de Pleuc. In October they protested that his request "profoundly outraged their dignity as citizens."[279] (This letter, which acknowledged the library to contain volumes drawn from the works of freethinkers, was signed by Rouvier, Delpech, and Boucher and also by Bastelica, a Blanquist socialist and an important leader of the Marseille Commune who with Amat had withdrawn from the Association phocéenne in the summer and had later rejoined.)[280] In November the group grudgingly complied: They produced the catalog, accompanied by a brief note that their acquiescence in "this formality cannot engage our conduct in the future."[281]

The Library of the Phocéen Association was at once the most complete and most incendiary of the popular libraries. Its religious works included Calvin, Fénélon, Lamennais, and Renan. All the philosophes were available: Montesquieu, Diderot, Rousseau, Voltaire, and Condorcet, as well as Proudhon and Fourier, Michelet and Quinet, Milton, Swift, and Harriet Beecher Stowe. Contemporary detractors of the regime, liberal as well as radical, were amply represented: Raspail, Hugo, Laboulaye, Eugène Ténot, Louis Blanc, and Esquiros himself.[282]

As 1869, the year of the general elections, approached, police surveillance increased. The minister of the interior asked the Prefect of the Bouches-du-Rhône for information about a political society promoting "ultrademocratic candidacies." Reports had reached him of a group connected with the paper *Le Peuple* that was said to correspond with members of the Internationale such as Henri Tolain and with other radicals and socialists – among them, Charles Delescluze and Eugène Ténot. Delpech, Labadié, and Taxile Delord, later a deputy of the Bouches-du-Rhône and republican historian of the Second Empire, were thought to be local organizers.[283] The group was all too real, the prefect replied. It took no pains to conceal its object and openly published its intentions as well as the names of its adherents. He thought it was modeled on the Democratic Union formed for the elections of 1863. The minister also assumed electoral intent and asked if prosecution would be "inopportune." Might it regain for radicals the support of liberals from whom they had dissociated themselves?[284]

The authorities took no action, although they were certain by February that the "committee of the Phocéen association" existed to promote the reelection of Léon Gambetta.[285] Gambetta was standing for parliament both at Marseille and in the Parisian working class stronghold of Belleville. His Belleville profession of faith, a perfect statement of radical democracy, committed him to the election of mayors and municipal councillors, legal accountability of functionaries, full liberty of meeting and association, press freedom with jury trial for press offenses, suppression of standing armies and the *budget des cultes*, free, compulsory, and secular education, and "constant study and research" on economic questions "in the name of the principles of justice and social equality."[286] He accepted at Belleville an "imperative mandate" by which he contracted to execute the wishes of his constituents. This was the reason, some detractors said, for his decision, after victory in both places, to represent Marseille.

Gambetta, however flawed an agent of social regeneration, enjoyed in 1869 the support of a united left, gathered, as the police correctly surmised, within the Ligue de l'enseignement's radical affiliate, the Association phocéenne, which now sheltered dispersed members of the International. As Bastelica wrote to the Lyonnais socialist Albert Richard in February, "The socialist movement is moving slowly at Marseille. The Association of Laborers inaugurated it too well; since the last congress [i.e., of the International] the better part of its members have been scattered, the Ligue de l'enseignement has served as a refuge for the greatest number of them."[287] Although Bastelica endorsed the resolution of the International to support only workers' candidacies, he wrote optimistically in May of the prospects for coalition with bourgeois republicans. Democrats, he regretted, had lost a "revolutionary sense . . . Nevertheless, elements are not lacking to constitute, on true and authentic grounds, the Revolutionary Union . . . There are many sorts of demands (*revendications*) that impose themselves. All must find their natural place . . . and form a sum, if not a synthesis . . . Tomorrow I shall vote for Gambetta!"[288]

Gambetta was, of course, elected; and, as elsewhere in France, the good showing of democrats in the spring elections heartened their supporters and spurred them on to even larger and more regular meetings in the fall and winter of 1869–70. In November fifteen hundred people attended a rally of the Association phocéenne at which Crémieux, Bastelica, Gustave Naquet, and Delpech called upon the municipal council to secularize its schools. Crémieux spoke of the Mortara kidnapping – of the church's indifference to family and national feelings and of an antagonism between religious and natural morality.[289]

In addition to the predictable *laïc* references, the Mortara affair and the charges of child molestation brought against clerical teachers at Beauvais,[290] orators of the Phocéen Association spoke in a new idiom, that of the commune. The municipal council, which had disregarded their petition, was described as the commune's emanation and agent: "To found communal and democratic education, the collectivity of men forming the Commune has the right to demand of its mandatories, the municipal councillors, to intervene to defend the moral aspect of education." The council, legally empowered to choose between religious and secular schools, had become the captive of a "clerical coterie" and could not be seen as the legitimate voice of the city. Another speaker, M. Aumine, argued that the municipal council had usurped the rights of the commune: "Since the middle ages the people have worked and fought to constitute the Commune and today the Municipal Council disposes of its funds. Nevertheless, *we have the force and our will shall be executed.*"[291]

Bastelica did not advocate violence but invoked the principle of the imperative mandate;[292] Delpech reminded him that such contracts must precede elections. Moreover, Delpech thought it obvious that the councillors were following the wishes of at least some of their constituents. Naquet felt that the council was not representative and insisted further upon the reasonable and liberal character of lay demands. He combated the familiar charge that freethinkers were themselves intolerant: The group did not ask expulsion of clerical teachers – just an end to their exclusive subsidy.

The freemasons of Marseille supported the efforts of the Phocéen

Association to end the "fatal monopoly" of clerical teachers. In October and November of 1869, *L'Action maçonnique* carried reported of their battles for secular education. Deputy Esquiros, another victor in the spring elections, and Brochier, president of the masonic school committee, both spoke at a prize-giving ceremony where a crowd estimated (by the masons) at fifteen hundred heard them attack obscurantism and promise that education alone could achieve both social equality and social peace: "Equality will be truly established only after a healthy morality and a solid primary education has raised somewhat higher the intellectual level of those placed too low in the social category."[293]

Brochier did not speak felicitously. He had the pretension as well as the condescension too often associated with radicalism: No classes existed in his world, only "categories." He believed, as he said on that occasion, that a meritocratic "equilibrium" would result from adequate schooling. Today, he said, those on top owe their position to the ignorance of the masses. "When education has restored balance to society, we shall no longer risk its being one day shaken at its base."[294] His speech made plain, nonetheless, the curious relation of the radicals to violence. They abhorred it and dissuaded others from it, but the strong, almost inevitable, likelihood that some would resort to it they all understood as essential to their appeal. Without an implicit threat of violence, they could not present themselves as an alternative to it. This position, although not wholly dishonest, was charged with a certain antinomy that the troubles of the commune left unresolved.

Police who attended the masonic prize giving reported that Esquiros had been warmly applauded, and their informers told them that "thousands of signatories" were claimed for the petition to secularize public schools. Those who spoke about the league in the stock exchange dismissed it as "imbeciles" led by "intriguers," and the police maintained, "Three quarters do not understand one word the leaders say."[295] Confiscated correspondence testified, however, to the immediately political character of its activities. The letters of a baker Faucon had been seized, among them, one from Esquiros that reported his pleasure at receiving from "citizen Crémieux" the transcripts of several public meetings and continued, "Remain always within these principles . . . Let me always know the plans of your Ligue d'enseignement." Another letter, signed illegibly, referred to a committee in Paris including Gambetta, Bancel, and Esquiros and promised, "We are advancing *à grands pas* toward a Revolution . . . Keep me always *au courant*, as you know so well how to do with your educational leagues. Perseverance! We are nearing an end." The letter ends with the republican closing, "Salut et fraternité."[296]

The *phocéens* hoped to involve workers in the struggle. Rouvier, a clerk, called for greater popular participation in the movement. "Intellectual emancipation leads to all other . . . If the 25,000 democratic electors who voted in May were to cast their vote also for the Ligue de l'enseignement," he said, education would take care of the future. He concluded prophetically, "barricades built by illiterates are overthrown on the morrow."[297]

Meetings continued during the fall of 1869. The Proudhonian Rey took part in several, demanding free and compulsory education for the laboring classes as the basis of social reorganization. The oratory of a man named Gaillet (or Gaillot) impressed police spies greatly: They commented on his "gestures and extraordinary energy" as he implored that education be freed from "fanaticism and egoism." Political and religious leaders, he had charged, deliberately "brutalized the people in order to reserve for themselves all grandeur and pleasure."[298]

In the next spring these sessions became indistinguishable from the campaign against the plebiscite, but already in October a distinctly antidynastic note had been struck: Gaillet had read an impudent verse about Monsignor Dupanloup by a worker-poet and then launched into a prose attack on the government. The Convention routed the Ignorantines, he said, and a Bonaparte restored them; the Second Republic tried again to free the schools, and another Bonaparte declared himself for the church. "The progress we have sought in vain" he foresaw accomplished in 1870: "From education and instruction, shall arise our rights and our liberties."[299]

Documentation is scanty for the events within Marseille during the "insurrectionary period"[300] that followed the emperor's abdication. Esquiros, whom Gambetta appointed prefect of the Bouches-du-Rhône in September of 1870, ratified many of the municipality's actions, including the secularization of its schools and the closing of a Jesuit institution, the Mission of France.[301] He and Delpech, who served after him, sympathized with at least some of the commune's aims, so that when an elected municipal council succeeded the self-constituted commune, it could invoke the authority of the prefecture when it chose to find its predecessors' actions legitimate and binding.

After the violence began in Paris on March 18, 1871, Gaston Crémieux either led or assumed leadership of a group that invaded the prefecture in Marseille and installed itself there. He and Boucher called upon citizens to help them form a "provisional administration" while republicans on the municipal council elected in November 1870 watched with dismay, unable to support either the *versaillais* or the *communards*. Alexander Labadié flatly refused to organize a demonstration of the Marseille National Guard in favor of the conservative National Assembly and recommended, rather, manifestations in support of the republic. At the same time, as spokesman of the municipal council, Labadié refused Crémieux the two thousand francs he had requested for provisioning "citizens occupying the prefecture" until they had lowered the red flag and replaced it with a tricolor. Crémieux responded with a call for the dissolution of the municipal council.[302] Neither side was able to extricate the city from this impasse, and the national government suppressed the revolt. Crémieux's subsequent execution horrified republicans who regarded it as a judicial murder, and the municipal council made controversial, if inadequate, protest in the form of a scholarship voted to his son.[303]

The municipal council elected in May 1871 contained, according to police appreciation of its character, six men who were merely "ambitious" or "without political convictions," eight "moderate republicans" – one said to have only recently become moderate – ten "advanced," "exaggerated," or "impetuous" ("fougueux") republicans, six "radical socialists," and five thought to be affiliated with the International.[304] These men, as might be expected of them, determined to give the city free and secular schools. In 1872 the departmental council – which, unlike the elected general council, was an appointive body on which academic officials and religious notables sat by right – annulled their ruling, permitting them to create *new* secular schools, but not to secularize existing religious ones.[305] The municipal council responded first by refusing to pay any religious teachers, then by withholding salaries from uncertified ones (those without the *brevet de compétence*), and lastly by reducing salaries to the legal minimum, a tactic adopted by the Lille municipal council in 1866.[306]

As a result of its schools policy, and also for its refusal to vote funds for the welfare bureau, the municipal council was dissolved and replaced with an appointed municipal commission in March 1874. The commission reversed secularization, restoring nuns to girls' schools, and discontinued the city's adult evening courses begun in 1871. In December of 1876, when the city was once again governed by an elected council, Rech, described by the police in 1871 as a pharmacist of "good morality, but a very dangerous radical socialist,"[307] urged that the evening courses be reestablished. The courses had been suppressed, he said, by those who sought "to reduce primary instruction to its simplest expressions," by men who ridiculed efforts to enlarge the scope of popular understanding. In addition, he could not fail to observe that *only* secular classes were suppressed, whereas those maintained by the teaching orders were actually augmented.[308]

Anxiety over the outcome of general elections, no less than the defense of clerical schools, led the police and other agents of the interior ministry to watch the freethinkers closely. Men elected to the Municipal Council in 1871 – and whose role in the public meetings of 1869–70 the police had not forgotten[309] – clamored for amnesty for the *communards*, the return of the National Assembly from Versailles to Paris, and free compulsory schooling. Freethinking funerals became at Marseille, as in Lyon, republican manifestations. Members of the six radical clubs – the Independence, the Atheneum, the Progress, the United Friends, the Bellevue, and the Chartreux – attended all civil burials,[310] and the republican press regularly invited citizens to pay their last respects to Brother X, who had died *en philosophe*. These obsequies, celebrated with defiance, enraged the authorities; but the prefect of the Bouches-du-Rhône, unlike the prefect of the Rhône, judged that he would make himself ludicrous by attempting to regulate them.

The police believed that three thousand freethinkers were organized in twenty-one sections in all quarters of the city and that their president corresponded with members of the International.[311] Somewhat more precise information, which pertains to the dissolution of the municipal council, was presented to the prefect in March 1874. The police requested then that he close the Chartreux circle. They said, as a matter of course, that odious proposals contrary to public order in general, and to the existing government and religion in particular, "were daily espoused within its precincts"; but they further reported that it was through this club that radicals had distributed, "in each quarter of the city," supplies and victuals intended by the government for the "victims" of September 4 and those of the insurrection in April 1871.[312]

The decree suppressing the municipal council singled out among its transgressions the misappropriations of funds for charity and the refusal to vote money for the welfare bureau.[313] The prefect alleged actual theft and personal misuse of funds, but these complaints about the Chartreux group suggest that the clubs dispensed patronage to the "undeserving" poor, whereas their elected representatives denied support to the welfare bureau upon which *curés* still sat. It seems plain that the radicals had, *de facto*, secularized the administration of charity as they had secularized the schools. Several municipal councillors, among them Brochier, Jean Léonce, and Rech, were among ninety members of the Chartreux in 1878.[314]

After republican circles – the Chartreux, Amat's Cercle du Paradis, the Cercle de l'Indépendance, and the Atheneum – were closed, radicals "took refuge" in masonic lodges, especially the Phare de la Renaissance, to which Boucher and Rouvier, both former municipal councillors, belonged. Nugues, supposedly a moderate and a former member of de Pleuc's Ligue marseillaise, was the director of their discussion group.[315]

As in the Yonne, administrative surveillance of radical groups eased in 1876. At that time, the deputy Amat and other members of the Athénée méridional, "industrialists, moderates, and the fathers of families," some of them general councillors of the Bouches-du-Rhône, asked the prefect to permit them to resume their thirty years of "literary and scientific endeavor."

Curiously, the police concurred in their request. Suppression had achieved nothing; the dangers they had hoped to avert had become more threatening. Within the Atheneum, which united all the democratic factions ("toutes les nuances du parti démocratique"), "the moderates calm the ardent ones and prevent them from actions hostile to authority." When the group was forbidden to meet, each element met separately in cafés: "The violent were left to themselves" and became increasingly irreconcilable and extreme. The police foresaw also irresistible economies in a reunification of the factions. Surveillance was much facilitated. The police emphasized that the same reasoning that supported the reopening of the bourgeois Atheneum applied also to the Independence whose members were workers ("L'Athénée ne recevait que des habits et l'Independance était en blouse"). The division between moderates and "exaltés" did not correspond to a class difference. The republican party was seeking to "withdraw itself from . . . despotic and dangerous direction," and circles like the Independence and the Atheneum were attempts to "develop institutions that would vitiate efforts of the violent element."[316]

The republican groups suppressed in 1874 were again attacked in 1877; but reprieves won for them throughout the seventies by the growing influence of their elected members, as well as by the resignation of the more worldly conservatives to their continued existence, permitted them to approach the elections of October 1877 once more "a compact group of progressive men." With other Provençal radicals in Aix and Arles, secularists in Marseille delivered the Bouches-du-Rhône to the republic.

3 Establishing the republic

Q. *And what did you teach them about morality?*
A. *[I] made them understand that they must act with*
   respect for themselves and with utility for
   their fellow men.

Adèle Mirouël, on trial, September 1873,
for violation of the loi Falloux[1]

[We demand] the most sacred of our rights, to have
our children educated by our equals, not by men [who are]
étrangers à nos moeurs.

La Société civile d'éducation libre et laïque des pères et mères
de famille du 6ᵉ arrondissement (Lyon)[2]

The undersigned . . . convinced that the Republic is the only form of government for their
country . . . convinced equally that there is moral disorder . . . and the permanent threat of
catastrophe so long as the mores and institutions of the monarchical regime create obstacles to
the regular establishment of the republican regime . . . declare their end to foster in France the
habits of mind and of public life of free countries.

La Société républicaine de Fère-en-Tardennois (Aisne)[3]

THE COMMUNES AND THEIR SCHOOLS, 1870–3

WHEN, AFTER NAPOLEON III had abdicated, the Third Republic was proclaimed on September 4, 1870, many municipalities asserted their authority over schools isolated from popular control during the Second
Empire. In some places insurgents formed communes, as in Paris, Lyon,
and Marseille. Elsewhere, as in Perpignan, men already in office were
free to accomplish the reforms that they had long advocated. In another
variation men forced from office at Arles for attempting earlier to secularize city schools returned in triumph. Everywhere, radicals were
elected, or reelected, to regularly constituted municipal councils.

Moreover, new prefects, themselves men of radical persuasion, approved the actions of revolutionary municipalities. For Gambetta, minister of the interior in the new Government of National Defense, had,
between September 4 and September 16, named eighty-five new prefects, many of them closely identified with the schools agitation. Jules
Ferry became prefect of the Seine, and Frédéric Morin, a member of the
Société d'instruction élémentaire, of the Saône-et-Loire. Adherents of
the Ligue de l'enseignement were placed in numerous prefectures:
Ernest Hendlé in the Creuse, Eugène Ténot in the Haute-Pyrénées,

Desseaux of Rouen in the Seine-Inférieure, Mestreau in the Charente-Inférieure, Delattre in the Mayenne, Chalamet in the Ardèche, Dr. Guépin in the Loire-Inférieure, and, of course, Ribière in the Yonne. Esquiros became "superior-administrator" of the Bouches-du-Rhône, and Lyon received Paul-Armand Challamel-Lacour, founder of the *Revue politique et littéraire*, as the "delegate" of the government in Paris.[4]

Subsequent events in the capital are well known: The Commune of Paris decreed the separation of church and state on April 2, 1871. Various *arrondissements* – among them the eighteenth, where Georges Clemenceau was mayor – had even earlier declared their schools secular. Citizens' school committees were established; and many *communards* hoped for "integral education," a synthesis of practical and theoretical subjects that would accustom every child to abstract reasoning and manual labor.[5]

Everywhere in France radicals were concerned with three aspects of republican education, moral, pedagogical, and social. They taught *la morale indépendante* or *effective*, ethics independent of revealed religion and "born," as the Lyonnais said, "of progressive experience and supported by universal assent."[6] They were committed to methods of instruction that cultivated observation, ratiocination, and judgment. They were determined, above all, that the experience of schooling itself be appeasing and uplifting. Education must be free, so that distinctions between paying and nonpaying pupils did not trouble the children's apprehension of equality. Children would not be subjected to indignities: Therefore, no invidious competition with other students and positively no corporal punishment would be allowed. Finally, in order to preserve this carefully defined republican character, schools were to be governed by popularly elected bodies closely associated with parent–teacher committees.

Iconoclastic – often literally so[7] – the free schools of Paris, Lyon, Marseille, Arles, Toulon, Montauban, Toulouse, and Vichy, and the masonic schools of Bordeaux, shared these commitments. It was, however, the Lyonnais, whose Committee of Public Safety had immediately "resumed possession of schools maintained at the expense of the municipality,"[8] whose schools most emphasized the exalted moral purpose of education, whose curriculum and administration were the most explicitly defiant.

The program of instruction at Lyon evoked the educational policies of the Revolution, quoting Condorcet's report to the National Assembly on April 20, 1792, which asked schooling "to render each capable of the social functions to which he has a right to be called . . . to develop the talents he has received from nature, and, by doing so, to establish among citizens an *equality of fact* and give reality to the *political equality* recognized by the law."[9]

The schools' statutes recalled to schoolmasters their sacred trust: The future of French society depended upon the health, intelligence (the "judgment as well as the memory"), and morality of the students they would form. Further, the statutes explained how republican mores would be instilled: It was the duty of teachers, "while abstaining from the discussion of any religious doctrine, to devote all our care to instruction in the principles of morality . . . Our solicitude shall be wholly given to . . . *effective morality*, distinct from any preconceived or exclusive system, born of progressive experience and resting upon universal assent."[10]

Lyon's schools remained neutral, also, before the "various religious theories" held by different elements of the population, recalling past intolerance, "experience long enough and dreadful enough and whose accumulated consequences we still suffer today." As always, however, secular moralists insisted that the new ethic of the republic was no less exigent than the old faith. It taught "the hope of the *Patrie* called to regenerate itself, the most rigorous notions of duties and rights of the individual, toward himself, toward the family, toward society."[11]

Among Michelet's many bitter reproaches against the church – perhaps the most damning in his contemporaries' eyes – was his charge that it was a "terrible pedagogue." Schooling predicated on the "atrocious" doctrine of infant damnation, he contended, could not cherish children's curiosity or their high spirits. It would subdue and terrify; its results would be the "annihilation of the personality" rather than self-realization.[12]

Teachers and supporters of the new schools agreed and relied upon the most advanced pedagogy. In *leçons des choses*, children were encouraged to handle and experiment with objects, to make comparisons, and to reach conclusions, gradually and by induction. Care was taken to make lessons intelligible: "Nothing will be taught that is not demonstrable."[13] Indeed, academic officers as well as republican militants had long protested that religious texts employed "rather too elevated a metaphysic."[14] Now a romantic fringe hoped to protect "spontaneity," and a great many more aspired to be reasonable.

The schools of the Third Arrondissement of Paris, among others, promised to require that nothing be accepted on faith. They stressed French grammar, logic, and argument: Every student "learns to express his ideas correctly, thus becoming eligible for all careers."[15] History, too, offered self-evident truths. The prefect of police who visited in 1874 reported: "A propos of the teaching of history, the director of the school has been heard to say to his pupils that 'all who fell on a barricade were heroes and martyrs.' "[16] They professed to teach gratitude and veneration for the "benefactors of humanity" and contempt for despots and popes and "that brigandage called conquest." Natural history, too, was "removed from all superstition," and the "fraternity of peoples" advanced by the study of foreign languages.[17]

As might be expected in education so concerned with solidarity, controversies over prizes were most revealing. Emulation, fierce and remunerated competition, was presented as the keystone of clerical education and, as such, deplored. Jesuit pairing of students taught rivals to subdue and denounce each other, an unfraternal relationship that was inappropriate for young republicans: It fostered jealousy, envy, and "contempt for the defeated."[18] In Paris, prize distributions were denounced as "pompous manifestations." The republicans of the First Arrondissement asked themselves: "Today, do we not have better motives to offer our children? Isn't work the source of human morality? Doesn't it have its own value and dignity?"[19]

The masonic schools of Bordeaux had done away entirely with individual awards publicly presented and, under pressure from parents and teachers to avoid "frivolous emulation," turned to "collective rewards" such as picnics and boatrides. Children would learn to despise notions of domination and preeminence. A more wholesome (and capitalistic) solution was suggested: an impersonal system of *bon points*, an accounting of credits and debits through which students might earn books or school materials.[20]

Inseparable from this high purpose was a rigorous prohibition of corporal punishment. Lyon forbade any discipline that was "brutal, injurious, vulgar . . . all allusion to families, or to the social position of the pupils' parents," any reproof "that could enfeeble the child's sense of his personal dignity."[21]

Similar aspirations were expressed in every republican precinct, but the curriculum at Lyon was conspicuously irreligious, and the organization of its schools radically autonomous. It was the schools of Lyon that conservatives were determined to shut down. The struggles of that city to preserve local control and to support republican teachers, "our free and virtuous men,"[22] displayed at its bitterest the conflict – soon to become general – between a republican municipality and an increasingly conservative national government. The rights of Lyon were upheld first by an insurrectionary commune (calling itself, in Jacobin fashion, The Committee of Public Safety) and later by the municipal council and by two mayors, both radicals of national reputation: Hénon, the only provincial member of the Cinq, and his successor Désiré Barodet.

Lyon was to be the test case determining the future of the irregular republican schools. Authorities at Bordeaux and elsewhere awaited a settlement there before taking action against secular schools.[23] In March of 1871 the inspector of the Academy of Lyon sent an alarmed note and a copy of the *Règlements et programme des écoles primaires municipales de la ville de*

Lyon to the minister of public instruction. It was in every respect a revolutionary document, and the inspector did not exaggerate its subversive significance.[24]

The academic administration seemed even more discomfited by the commune's disregard for regular procedures than by its unorthodox curriculum. The schools were independent of the academic hierarchy: The mayor named teachers on the recommendation of the schools' administrative councils, who, along with the mayor's appointees, supervised the staff. Teachers could not be fired without a hearing. Article 16 of the city's new rules required of teachers a "morality exempt from all reproach," a University diploma, and "proof of aptitude and acquaintance with pedagogical method." They were also to be "whenever possible mothers and fathers of families."[25] Worse still, the municipal council had taken it upon itself to increase the pay of teachers.

It was worrisome that members of the teaching staff should look to people other than their hierarchical superiors for professional advantages. The last straw seems to have been the decision of Mayor Hénon to create municipal school inspectors. This was received as an act of scandalous usurpation. The primary inspector Aubin believed that were he more adequately staffed, he might do much to undermine the city's pretension of administering its own schools. He reminded his chief reproachfully that such difficulties had been foreseen as early as 1858. In August of that year, the departmental council of the Rhône had urged that the arrondissement of the capital be split into two sections, *l'agglomération lyonnaise* and rural communes. Mayor Hénon had, in fact, justified the new inspectorates with an assertion that although the regular academic authorities visited each of the city's 110 schools only once a year, the municipal council felt that schools required more than perfunctory supervision.[26]

The Ministry of Public Instruction, with Jules Simon still at its head, took the position that the schools were clearly illegal in two essential points: inspection and curriculum. It noted, too, that the commune failed to achieve its goal of a single secular school system, because children were withdrawn from its schools and placed in newly reconstituted religious classes of the Christian Brothers, as well as in the older secular institutions supported by the comfortable skeptics of the Société d'instruction primaire du Rhône.[27]

The commune at Lyon had not much exerted itself to attract bourgeois liberals. Article 1 of the Règlements announced the intention of the city to create public schools "by necessity of population," without regard to existing independent schools.[28] The municipality declared its unwillingness to recognize or support either of the two existing school systems, yet the deputy LeRoyer, a masonic venerable and a member of

127

the Society for Primary Instruction, interceded for the commune, playing a role that would become typical of members of the Ligue de l'enseignement: first mediating between radical and liberal secularists and, when that failed, attempting to protect radicals from administrative violence.

The commune's slighting of the Société d'instruction primaire du Rhône, LeRoyer believed, had been a foolish and gratuitous one:[29] The commune had intended its schools to teach religion "distinct from preconceived systems," and this commitment, which his society shared, had been greeted differently by the several classes of the population. Workers as well as members of "dissident cults," Protestants and Jews, generally favored it,[30] but because much of the bourgeoisie was hostile, LeRoyer felt that the commune had been ill advised to provoke the animosity of the liberals.

Withal, LeRoyer urged the minister not to take abrupt action against the commune or its schools, because although it had alienated substantial elements of Lyonnais society and imprudently neglected to seek allies among the liberal bourgeoisie, every effort had been taken to involve the populace in the activities of the schools. Families were assured that no pupils would be privileged and that all were subject to the same discipline (Article 11). The teachers were protected from "administrative caprice" and put in close and regular contact with parents. There were obligatory monthly meetings for professors and also monthly meetings of faculty with parents to inform them of their children's "moral and intellectual progress." Parents were requested to exert all effort "to support the efforts of professors" (Article 49).[31]

The schools were joyfully celebrated at a great *fête* on the property of Arlès-Dufour. Quinet, hearing of the school celebrations, rejoiced that France once more had civic *fêtes*, like those that had so moved him during his exile in Switzerland.[32] Simon, instructing the prefect to restore order with "firmness and prudence," asked to be informed whether votes to assert municipal control over the previously independent schools had been taken by surprise or chicanery. The prefect replied that the votes were entirely regular and very popular, and, he believed, the administration should concentrate on "reintegrating" independent teachers.[33]

"Reintegration" meant two equally important changes. First, salaries of the ousted teachers would once more be paid by the city, and second, teachers would be subject to academic discipline: The city resumed the expense, and the bureaucracy regained control. The prefect had enjoined the municipal council to do these things; but he frankly advised the minister that neither the present council nor any probable successor would submit to his condition, the resumption of the *status quo ante* September 4. He preferred to concentrate his hopes on a reconciliation of the municipality with the Société d'instruction primaire du Rhône: Its members, moderate and *politique*, were desirous, in the main, of a conservative republic.[34]

In November of 1871 Simon ordered the mayor to dissolve the "administrative council" that directed the city's schools and to notify teachers that they would henceforth receive their instructions, not from the municipality, but from legally constituted academic authorities. Months passed. During the spring of 1872, temporizing letters continued to be exchanged by the prefect, the mayor, and the minister of public instruction: Prefect Pascal informed Paris that he had placed himself in "excellent rapport" with Garnier, the editor of *La Décentralisation*. Pascal felt confident that the "burlesque reforms" of the revolutionary period, the interlude of "effective morality," had been definitively rejected. The municipality had completely capitulated; the complexity and inertia of the school system alone prevented the administration from exercising full control.[35]

But Barodet, who became mayor after Hénon's death in April 1872, continued to uphold municipal, or popular, control of education. He insisted that his teachers omitted religious instruction because of their respect for the liberty of conscience. The Committee of Public Safety had put into practice reforms already generally admitted by "free intelligences," and irrevocably achieved in all countries "where religious despotism does not prevail." Furthermore, although there may have been initial irregularities in the nomination of teachers, all appointments had been sanctioned by the prefect of *le 4 septembre*, Paul-Armand Challamel-Lacour, and later by *Commissaire extraordinaire* Valentin.[36] Republicans, throughout the early 1870s, invoked this defense, the approval of the prefect of *le 4 septembre*. It became a common theme as successive functionaries of the "moral order" sought to undo secularist achievements of local elected bodies.

Pascal seemed to see some justice in the municipality's wish to share in the direction of its schools. He acknowledged that the city had never been regularly consulted and believed that this was doubly wrong. The least commune had a chance to express its preferences; moreover, the granting of such local voice would be appropriate to the "sincerely decentralist tendencies" of the National Assembly, whose wishes the prefect acknowledged to be sovereign. Nevertheless, he foresaw danger in complete local control.

When he was last in Versailles, Pascal had found the deputies of the Right determined to restore nomination of schoolmasters by municipal councils, as the loi Falloux had originally prescribed. (In 1854 that provision of the law was modified to selection by the prefect.) Should this become law once more, Pascal warned, the Christian Brothers would be dealt with all the more brutally, because municipal authorities would feel entitled to do what they pleased.

As to the religious orders, the prefect noted, they preferred to remain in the irregular position forced upon them by their ouster from public schools. He had hoped to conciliate immediately "the communal will with the respect due to minorities" but had been surprised to find the brothers averse to "too prompt and too radical" a reintegration. The vicar-general of the Christian Brothers, Thibaudier, preferred to await a new law on primary education. He wanted a temporary *modus vivendi* to alleviate the "crying injustices" of their present plight and to end certain unspecified "scandalous disorders"; but the prefect was convinced that the bishop and the superiors of the teaching orders were "as much terrified" by the ardor of their supporters as by the fury of the *communards*.[37] Pascal seemed ready, at least provisionally, to permit the teaching orders an independence that he would deny the elected representatives of the city of Lyon.

Finally, Pascal suggested a compromise: After an official census of enrollment, he would divide the city's schools between the Catholics and the radicals. A certain number of schools would retain permanently their confessional character, but the city would be allowed to maintain a number of secular schools. Each school would receive a municipal subsidy proportional to its enrollment. If the municipal council refused to support clerical schools, the prefect would mandate the expenditure.

While Barodet corresponded graciously with Pascal – the differences that remained between them were the "object of my continuing preoccupation,"[38] – the municipal council studied the loi Falloux. It found ample precedent for the administration of schools independent of the academic hierarchy and cited the example of the Society for Primary Instruction of the Rhône, which had enjoyed for many years the autonomy that the city now claimed. Its administrative commission and corps of inspectors managed their schools in almost unalloyed liberty; and although the prefect "named" their teachers, he invariably relied upon their recommendations.[39]

Nevertheless, on June 1, 1872, Pascal decreed that the city must maintain both secular and religious schools *as public schools*. The relative numbers were to be determined by a commission presided over by the inspector of the Academy of Lyon and including the vicar general of the Christian Brothers, the grand rabbi, a member of the Protestant Consistory (Protestant and Jewish schools had opted to join the city system after September 1870), several other notables, and two *curés*. Some members of the municipal council would serve in their capacity as general councillors of the department, but Richard was the only radical of note.[40]

The decision did not come as a surprise. Perhaps that is why Pascal risked issuing his decree in June rather than at a more inconvenient time, one closer to the opening of school. He may have hoped to resolve outstanding difficulties during the summer vacation; but, in effect, he gave the city time to organize its resistance. Barodet contended in August that Pascal had illegally "created" new communal schools: his "elevation" of the church schools to the status of public schools, with the stipulation that they, like the others, must be free, had added considerably to the city's expenses. There could be no such expenditure without the consent of the municipal council: A prefect could add items to a municipal budget by an administrative device, but here he had clearly exceeded his authority.

In September the metalworker A. Loenger, a republican militant and labor organizer, threatened at a public meeting that the decree would not be implemented without violence. "Such manifest progress has been accomplished [by the municipal schools] that the *gendarmerie* and soldiers will be required to execute that ignoble and absurd decree."[41] When the schools reopened the Christian Brothers were unable to obtain keys; and the deputy mayor Bouchon said he could not make available buildings or funds "without making myself an accomplice to movements which it is my duty to repudiate and condemn." After a week's lockout another assistant mayor, the deputy Dionys Ordinaire, intimated that the municipal council would never accede voluntarily but might comply if it were *visibly* constrained.[42] The keys were surrendered under protest.

Secular democrats determined to maintain independent schools. In several arrondissements of Lyon, they organized Les Sociétés pour les écoles libres et laïques (the ELL). The ELL drew upon a considerable and inclusive republican nexus. In 1869 and 1870 a group actually called the Société de l'enseignement libre et laïque had undertaken winter lecture series like those in Marseille and the Yonne. LeRoyer and Arlès-Dufour had attended at least some meetings. (Arlès-Dufour had also supplied books, at Loenger's request, to a popular library. Loenger had asked, on one occasion, for a good many rather incendiary works. His reliable patron sent him several and forwarded to Hetzel the orders he was unable to fill.)[43]

The principal organizers of the lectures were thought to be Rossigneux, the accountant who had helped found the library of the Travailleurs libre-penseurs in 1868 and would serve on the municipal council's school committee in 1870-2; Bonnardel, a republican important enough to figure on the police list of men to be arrested in times of trouble; Louis Andrieux, "a young, rich, ambitious man" whom the police foresaw no need to intern;[44] and Denis Brack, editor of *L'Excommunié*.

The minister of the interior had instructed the prefect of police in February of 1869 "to encourage that liberty in our customs that turns men from dangerous theories to discussion of things that prepare the way for legitimate progress"; accordingly, the lectures on Corneille, Molière, Washington ("We do not yet live under this regime [the universal republic] but everything gives us hope") continued until the spring of 1870. Free trade and trial by jury were advocated, and there was an incessant demand for popular education, education freed (as the future deputy Bancel foresaw) from the influence of "autocracies and castes who pervert religion and education in the service of their influence and ambition." The group agreed that education must be prior to liberty and proposed, therefore, that a man who neglected to educate his children be deprived of his civil rights.[45]

Again in 1872, Rossigneux (whom Mayor Barodet had known in the sixties at the Cercle de la Ruche[46]), with Loenger and Tony-Loup, a contributor to the *Petit-Lyonnais*, rallied the secularists. Tony-Loup proposed that funds to support the schools be collected centrally but that each quarter be left free to choose its own teachers.[47] The Civil Society of Mothers and Fathers of the Sixth Arrondissement for Free, Secular Education (la Société civile d'éducation libre et laïque des pères et mères de famille du 6ᵉ arrondissement) was established in February of 1873.[48] It was Loenger who advised the freethinkers of the Third Arrondissement (La Guillotière) in October that their society be given a commercial character: He told them that legislation of 1867 exempted "civil cooperatives" and profit-making groups from authorization requirements.[49] (Similarly, the *laïc* schools of the First and Third Arrondissements of Paris were "corporations," *les sociétés anonymes*.)

The Croix-Rousse and La Guillotière, the old artisanal quarters of the city, demanded "the most sacred of our rights, to have our children educated by our equals": They refused to deliver up their children to "men strangers to our ways."[50] The "civil society" declared its "complete adhesion to the program of the municipal schools of 1870–71" and maintained a very direct democracy. Only children of members were admitted to their schools: members with children attending the school paid one franc a month; others paid fifty centimes. Teachers were chosen by the general assembly upon presentation of the educational committee.[51]

During the spring of 1873, as the *conseil d'état* considered the conflict of jurisdiction that the city's protest had brought before it, the very integrity of Lyon was threatened.[52] Conservatives proposed its reorganization – that is, the dismemberment of the city into arrondissements and the suppression of the central mayoralty. Effectively, they sought the abolition of Barodet's office, and this was sufficient to assure his victory in a parliamentary by-election over Thiers's candidate Charles Rémusat. Barodet's platform called for the immediate dissolution of the National Assembly and its supersession by a new unicameral body empowered to grant amnesty (i.e., to *communards*) and end states of siege.[53] His defeat of Rémusat in April may have suggested to some Thiers's inability to check republican radicalism. The regime of "moral order" inaugurated after Thiers's expulsion from the cabinet in May continued his efforts with less suavity and no more success.

Throughout 1873 secular and democratic groups were watched closely. Collections for the ELL were taken up at civil weddings and funerals, and it was in June of that year that Ducros, who had replaced Pascal as prefect of the Rhône, attempted to restrict civil funerals to the predawn hours (before seven on winter mornings and before six in the summer). He imposed, simultaneously, a maximum on mourners. If no clergyman officiated, the bereaved must not exceed three hundred.[54] The defiance this invited may be imagined. Much heartened by the prefect's maladresse, the freethinkers flourished.

In August police reported a crowd of four thousand at the distribution of prizes for the schools of the Sixth Arrondissement. Little girls in white dresses with red sashes heard speeches from the deputies of the Rhône and messages from those unavoidably absent: "Faith is the daughter of idleness, science is the daughter of labor." A parent addressed the teachers: "We have entrusted you with our children and you have restored them to us citizens." It was, the special agent reported, a "perfect orgy of fizzy lemonade."[55]

The republican teachers celebrated at the fête were that same month charged with violation of the loi Falloux and brought before the departmental council. The prefect had decided to extirpate "the cancer of irreligion that poisoned the minds of children *of both sexes*." Louis Andrieux – young, rich, and ambitious still – prepared the teachers' defense.[56]

The council decided that teachers could not omit to give religious instruction on the grounds that they were deferring to wishes expressed by parents or founders of a school. (This was the defense that had been offered by the teachers who were dealt with the most severely.) Adèle Mirouël argued: "I am illegally charged . . . The society of the Sixth arrondissement, in founding the school I direct, stipulated that moral education was to be distinct from religious doctrine." Furthermore, statutes that made this explicit had been sanctioned by the prefect.[57]

Adèle Mirouël and fourteen of her colleagues were convicted: Six were suspended for a term; five, including Mlle Mirouël, whose reinstatement Jules Ferry effected in 1879, were barred from teaching in Lyon; and four were prohibited from the exercise of their profession anywhere in France. In October, however, Inspector Aubin discovered that the ELL schools had been reopened – some, with the same personnel, in a neighboring commune, and others, with a new staff, in the old location. These schools, he reported, were "incontestably the same."[58]

Attention turned to the schools' supporters. Tony-Loup was thought to have raised twenty-eight thousand francs for the free schools. A dyers' mutual aid and insurance society, whose adherents were all "politically notorious" and whose president was the *communard* Vindry, organized concerts and *fêtes* for the ELL. The police assumed (correctly, it would seem) a double motive: "They see in the results obtained not only the means of putting their educational principles on a level with their social ideas, but at the same time of *manifesting the efficacy of their resistance.*"[59]

Moreover, it was to be feared that other workers' groups were doing the same. Certainly, Loenger's metalworkers were. They raised money for the free schools and also for the families of political detainees. Furthermore, even before Loenger's union was suppressed in May of 1874,[60] the dissolution of the Lyonnaise Ladies' Literary Society – including Mme Rossigneux and a convicted schoolmistress, the "exalted" Mlle Bonnevial – was pronounced. Their efforts for the moral uplift of their sex, hailed by Garibaldi, Macé, Esquiros, Blanc, and Mme Ange Guépin, were declared a danger to public order in October of 1873.[61]

Republican and socialist groups were harried throughout 1874 and 1875. Their members frequently complained that municipal charity was withheld from them: The "fraternal circle of Pierre Scize" alleged that the *curé* recorded the names of children who took communion and those who did not and then refused bread, meat, and coals to freethinking families.

By the fall of 1875, the police assumed the existence of a "republican alliance" of freemasons and "workers who resist their bosses and support the ELL."[62]

Throughout France three devices were used to reinstate clerical education, and all of these were tried in Lyon. First, secularist prefects were dismissed or transferred and their decisions countermanded by conservative successors. Second, prefects, using their discretionary authority over town budgets, forced expenditures for church schools. Third, the departmental councils of education, which were nonelective and certain to be less popular in character than any municipal council, were made final arbiters in matters affecting education. These measures were taken whether or not an insurrection had preceded the ouster of clerics.

The suppression of the communes and the restraints imposed upon republican municipalities left the political future of France again in doubt, but the Third Republic, unlike the First and the Second, enjoyed the great advantage of extensive prior organization: In 1848 a revolution in Paris did not ensure a republic; in the 1870s, a republic could no longer be destroyed by quelling insurrection. Everywhere, republicans were able to regroup. They relied heavily upon voluntary associations developed under the empire, and educational societies, affiliated with the Ligue de l'enseignement, proved their most ineradicable means of action.

A network of clubs, libraries, and "corporations" found supporters in the National Assembly and on municipal and general councils. Radicals could also anticipate favorable rulings from an occasional secularist functionary. Often, a republican school was the object for which they fought; but whether or not education was the immediate preoccupation, an educational society was likely to be the vehicle.

THE DEFENSE OF REPUBLICAN SCHOOLS

The suppression of the communes by armed force at Paris and Marseille and the curbing of revolutionary municipalities by administrative action, as at Lyon, divided republicans and left them again suspect and under close surveillance. Even so, their unity was not wholly destroyed, nor was their appeal less compelling. Supporters of secular schools had found themselves on both sides of the barricades; the republican school survived the battle, although all of its defenders did not.

Questions will always be asked – certainly not one has received, to this day, a satisfactory answer – about the complicity of bourgeois republicans in the savage repression of the *communards*,[63] but it is well established that members of the Ligue de l'enseignement were prominent among those who attempted to mediate between the Paris Commune and the National Assembly. One of the founders of the Paris circle, Emile Brélay, along with Isambert, Floquet, and some recently ousted prefects (Frédéric Morin, Eugène Delattre, and Henri Allain-Targé) worked through the Ligue républicaine pour des droits de Paris[64] to avert violence. One of its members, Loiseau-Pinson, undertook to unite all republican groups, syndical chambers, free masonic lodges, and educational societies in this effort. The Société d'instruction élémentaire pledged its support.[65]

It is hard to imagine what hopes men might have had for this mission when only its failure remains apparent; but it should not be forgotten that even those radicals who acquiesced in the assaults on Paris and Marseille sought almost immediately to rehabilitate the *communards* as patriots, to mitigate their sentences, and to reintegrate them into political life. Amnesty for political crimes, which Barodet demanded in 1873, became part of the republican platform in 1877 and was voted by the National Assembly they controlled in 1879. More important, bourgeois republicans were determined to preserve the chief institutional legacy of the insurrectionary period, secular public schools.

To do this they resorted to many devices. There were as many tactical variations as there were towns in France, but the basic pattern was everywhere the same. Radical republicans would not be suppressed. They refused to be characterized as irresponsible or divisive. They never ceased to insist that republican mores alone could calm and reconcile France. Educational societies gathered in the Ligue de l'enseignement were, of course, committed to this view. They formed an infrastructure to which were quickly assimilated *ad hoc* groups organized to protect precarious school reforms and military charities whose members sought not *revanche* alone but regeneration.

"It was the German schoolmaster who has won the war." This account of the catastrophe was widely accepted and lent itself to conflicting interpretations. Monsignor Dupanloup thought that loyal and obedient troops had triumphed, as they necessarily must, over rebellious and insouciant ones. Others attributed the defeat to sheer ignorance, chiefly, scientific and technical insufficiencies. Jean Macé defended the army: Illiterate voters, not illiterate conscripts, had failed France. An informed electorate would not suffer a government foolish enough to be duped unready into war, nor would an enlightened people have permitted the prior squandering of national resources in, for example, the expedition to Mexico.[66]

Rupublicans took it upon themselves to heal all wounds, domestic and foreign. They organized in the capital an affecting symbol, the Orphélinat de la Seine, a home for children orphaned by the war or – and this was the preeminent concern – in the fratricidal violence that followed defeat. Children of every faith would be welcomed and taught there only those moral, social, and political doctrines expected to promote brotherly love. The project exemplified the radical conviction that in the absence of a secular state, conciliatory education must be the work of the citizens themselves. Various battalions of the national guard donated to the orphanage the balance of their funds.

In Paris and throughout France and North Africa, a shadow radical regime took shape as radicals organized to defend republican schools. Radicals exalted local autonomy and private initiative and in fact relied upon voluntary association so long as their triumph remained incomplete. In Paris, for example, "shareholders" in the communal school of the Third Arrondissement (organized, as in Lyon, with impunity as a profit-making enterprise) insisted upon equality. They had eliminated school fees "to remain faithful to our principles and to eliminate an unfortunate distinction of position among children seated on the same school benches." They added a prudent note: "Unity in school is certainly the *easiest* way to bring about the rapprochement of the different classes of society and to extinguish their differences." A letter to residents of the First Arrondissement asking support for its schools cited ignorance as the prime cause of foreign and domestic misfortunes and justified the continued existence of independent schools in a republic. In all free nations, it argued, voluntary associations second the efforts of the state, and in education they enjoy a greater liberty to experiment with new subjects and methods.[67]

In 1874 the police noted continuing support for free secular schools in the First, Third, Ninth, and Eighteenth Arrondissements of the capital. Rama, a "delegate" concerned with education under the commune – in which capacity he had insisted upon a scientific and "experimental" approach to all physical and moral phenomena – directed a school in the rue Blanche.[68] In the Eighteenth Arrondissement, where Georges Clemenceau had been mayor, secular instruction was perpetuated by a corporation that had issued, in 1871, 110 shares at fifty francs each. An "Appeal to Tradesmen" in the Third Arrondissement asked for funds to help twenty thousand Parisian children still denied schooling because of inadequate facilities. The sponsors of that appeal in 1872 had been Albert, the "worker" member of the provisional government in 1848; Courtney, sergeant-major of the Sixty-Eighth Battalion of the National Guard and a *communard*; and the radical Dr. Collineau, a former member of the Union républicaine pour les droits de Paris.[69] The police remarked carefully, too, the suspicious (or illustrious) patrons: Gambetta himself, Barodet of Lyon, Quinet, Scheurer-Kestner, Emile Brélay, Laboulaye, and Greppo. The prefect of police apparently had access to the correspondence of the schools' officers: He quoted from a letter written by Lassez, secretary-general of the "corporation" of the Third Arrondissement, to a friend in the provinces, claiming for the independent schools supporters of all social conditions, religious and philosophical persuasions, united by one aim: the complete separation of church and state. The police report acknowledged that in addition to republican notorieties, the group did command the allegiance of many *honnêtes gens* who were disinterestedly devoted to education.[70]

By 1878 the school of the First and Third Arrondissements had become the favorite charities of the radical establishment, second, perhaps, only to the Orphélinat de la Seine. Victor Hugo sent commemorative volumes to be given as prizes; and Eugène Spuller, Gambetta's secretary and companion of the famous balloon journey, predicted at their distribution "the emancipation of the individual by science, the rebuilding of the fatherland by new generations of Frenchmen, more enlightened and more free."[71]

Everywhere in France, in the *grandes villes* and in the provinces, republicans rallied around the schools as prefects of the "moral order" replaced those of *le 4 septembre*, threatening the secular and egalitarian character of public education. There were countless improvisations on the theme of perseverance.

Even before 1870 the municipal council of Arles, urged on by one of its members, Augustin Tardieu, had attempted to create secular schools for boys. Tardieu had paid homage to the Christian Brothers, "those modest men, the proletarians of the Church"; but he maintained that education, although it should inspire the children with "Christian sentiments," must not neglect "duties toward society and an appreciation of the dignity of man," nor must children be permitted to despise those institutions that they are destined to uphold as adults – the nation and the family.

Tardieu alleged, too, shameful discrimination in church schools. The municipality subsidized them as free public schools, yet the monks charged a fee for keeping children from eleven in the morning until noon, the hour when families usually dined, and he had found that they maintained separate classes for pupils who stayed until twelve. This segregation of fee-paying and nonpaying children he pronounced incompatible with the end that the city sought to achieve in offering free education.

Two thousand copies of Tardieu's report had been printed in 1866, and the subprefect proposed that their distribution be prohibited.[72] The authorities did more than suppress the pamphlet. They "brutally dissolved" the municipal council, Tardieu recollected when he resumed his seat in 1871, for its opposition "to the clerical monopoly of education so disastrous to the aspirations of democracy."[73]

When Tardieu returned, triumphant, to the municipal council, reminding all of his 1866 report, the schools were secularized. In consequence, Arles again enjoyed an appointed city government in 1872. Esquiros, while still prefect of the Bouches-du-Rhône, appeared in October promising that the republic would never cease to attack the root of inequality, ignorance. Thus encouraged, Tardieu and like-minded men persisted. By 1874, the subprefect had concluded that it would be futile to dissolve the municipal council again. Tardieu was certain to be reelected: He would probably head the ticket. In 1876 Tardieu, mayor and deputy of Arles, accepted a compromise. The city would foster "competition" between the types of education. *Pères de familles* could choose between a secular boys' school and two coeducational religious schools.

Because most devout Catholics opposed coeducation at least as much as they objected to secular education itself (Pius IX had expressly condemned it), the choice could not have been an easy one. Tardieu presided in August 1876 at the dedication of a new secular girls' school, expatiating upon the "serious advantages of education in harmony with the spirit of the century."[74]

At Toulon after *le 4 septembre*, Dutasta, a lycée professor of philosophy and another academic victim of the coup of *le 2 décembre* (whom the administration would later describe as the most dangerous *agent provocateur* in the Var),[75] headed a committee charged with advising the city on its schools. Dutasta found an earlier study, commissioned in 1847 and carried out by the town's librarian, Curel. Dutasta felt that he could not improve upon it and quoted it at length. Curel's criticism evokes all Michelet's loathing for frivolity, surface, lack of substance. Children, it was stated, were incapable of the degree of abstraction required to draw moral principles from complex and abstract dogmas. Mystified, they were left with "vain formulas," with a narrow religiosity, "all exterior," vulgar, lacking in sublimity, "too familiar with *le bon Dieu*, representing, in material and vulgar form, the Supreme Intelligence . . . in the hideous features of a holy card or a plaster figurine." Incredulity or fanaticism might result from such instruction, but one should not expect virtue. Dutasta himself particularly regretted clerical inattention to French history, from which less ambiguous moral lessons might be drawn. He charged, too, that religious teachers were simply unqualified. Of the forty-nine religious teachers in Toulon, only eight were certified, whereas all the lay teachers, except one female assistant, had proper academic credentials. The report included, too, complaints of brutal corporal punishments. It adduced a letter from one Auguste Roland, who said that his son had been partially crippled by the Christian Brothers. (These allegations were discounted by the *inspecteur primaire*, who said such reports had never reached his office.) Finally, clerical education could not be governed by laymen: "We [France] are an authority they detest and submit to."[76]

Dutasta's committee recommended, therefore, that all Toulon's schools be entrusted to qualified laymen after October 1, 1871. His advice was followed; but in 1873 the prefect, in concert with the academic inspector – who took his stand with those convinced that religion had to serve as a "counterweight to human passion" – reinstated the teaching orders. Dutasta rallied the *laïcs*. In the late 1870s he was elected mayor of Toulon.

Authorities believed that Dutasta was responsible, too, for the Association pour le développement de l'instruction et de l'éducation pour les deux sexes at La Valette, which they dissolved for "unauthorized change of location" and for affiliation with other societies.[77] Its lectures were not submitted for prior approval. Highly offensive political verses were said to be sung at its meetings and, in the streets, by processions of school children corrupted by its members:

> A la lanterne, les Jésuites
> Ces vauriens, ces fainéants
> Ces charlatans, ces hypocrites
> Qui se cachent dans les couvents[78]

The conservative mayor of La Valette had complained as early as December of 1871 that the group was nothing but the continuation in permanent form of an electoral committee, as its membership list attested. This committee included three day laborers at the arsenal, all scarcely able to read or sign their names but "animated by the most exalted opinions." Another member, Maurel, an assistant schoolmaster, served on the council of the arrondissement and was notorious for his "exaggerated radicalism."[79]

The "electoral committee" of La Valette did, however, maintain a school whose master, one M. Bretonville, received correspondence from Geneva. The mayor felt that this sufficed to establish his connection with the International (he was said also to have fought with Garibaldi). The school was supported by fees, dues, outright gifts, "balls and collections," and by "certain circles in Toulon, even within the *Conseil Général*."[80]

Such patronage the prefect found especially trying, although there was nothing out of the ordinary in it. For decades municipal and general councils had subsidized to some extent nearly every charitable enterprise in France. It was to be expected that republicans in office would continue selective patronage and favor republican or radical groups. At La Valette a conservative mayor was at odds with the radical departmental council of the Var, and political unevenness in almost every region ensured that this would be an increasingly general phenomenon. Cities and their departments, elected officials and bureaucrats were likely to find themselves increasingly out of phase. A republic had been proclaimed, but its political nature, its very existence, was not yet definitively established. Thus, the prefect of the Var complained that the Ligue de l'enseignement disturbed him, although he found it difficult to document its transgressions. The group did teach children to read and write while introducing certain political notions: It continued "to concern itself with political propaganda in an occult fashion difficult to put one's finger on."[81]

At Perpignan, the republic had not brought new men to power but had enabled the existing municipal council to fulfill long-pursued aims. During the Second Empire Perpignan had repeatedly sought control over its schools. In 1862 it petitioned the Senate for a voice in the selection of new teachers when vacancies arose. (At the time there was no question of ousting incumbent clericals.) Yearly since 1866, it had voted to support only lay teachers, and in each of the earlier years, the imperial prefect had added to the municipal budget an expenditure for religious schools.[82]

In 1870 an academic inspector predicted that Perpignan would again elect a majority hostile to the monks. Secularists won by a narrow majority, 15 to 12, and after *le 4 septembre* they expelled the congregations from the city's schools. The municipal council insisted that it was not suppressing religious schools, but merely executing a budgetary decision of the previous July that, as in the past, prescribed expenditures for secular schools only. In the fall of 1870, the republican prefect had not, like his predecessors, inscribed charges for church schools, but named secular masters in a "perfectly regular and authoritative manner."[83]

In 1873 a prefect of a different persuasion demanded funds for three congregational schools. Escarguel, mayor of Perpignan (later a member of the Ligue de l'enseignement and a Radical deputy), refused, with the support of his council, a return to the *status quo ante*. To accept this compromise would be to abjure the principle they had upheld for eight years "with the support of the population." The prefect acknowledged that the mayor and council were popular and cautioned the administration not to proceed against the secular teachers, all worthy men. This, the prefect feared, would lead to an "immediate and open war" with all local authorities. The Christian Brothers had departed in September 1870 in the face of "manifest popular hostility." The prefect regretted that "liberal conservatives" did not exist in his department, but hoped to unite the "reasonable people" and took care to include in his proclamation reinstating teaching orders a promise of promotion, wherever possible, for displaced secular teachers.[84]

At Vichy the struggle took yet a different form. The initiative for secular schools came in the late 1860s from the academic inspector, and there it had been repulsed by the mayor. In 1868 the inspector appealed to the prefect that the "moral and scholastic . . . as well as the political and social interests of Vichy" required some secular education. Such, the inspector maintained, were the wishes of the people; but the mayor had refused to discuss it. In December 1870 the inspector raised the question with a new mayor, Emmanuel Jardet, a member of the Ligue de l'enseignement; and in January 1871 the municipal council, dwelling upon military calamities just endured, decided on the basis of "academic inadequacies and deficient virility" to dispense with the services of the Christian Brothers.[85]

Jardet, like Tardieu and Dutasta, fought this battle for nearly a decade, combating hostile prefects through independent organization. In other cities and towns where a republican prefect remained in place, a different pattern emerged. In the Saône-et-Loire, for example, a moderate prefect tried to protect and enlarge the powers of the municipality while delaying the reinstatement of clerical schools. Voluntary activity here was less visible and intense, generally limited to petitions that enabled sympathetic functionaries to argue that reprisals against secular schools would enrage the population.

Frédéric Morin, who became prefect of the Saône-et-Loire in September 1870, already enjoyed an established position as an anticlerical publicist.[86] He dismissed teaching brothers and nuns in eight towns of the Saône-et-Loire: In each instance, however, he merely sanctioned action taken by municipal authorities. At Montcenis, at Semur, where mayor Hugot headed an active circle of the Ligue de l'enseignement, and at Cluny, the monks were dismissed as communal teachers by the existing municipal council. At Cuiseaux and Cuisery the ouster was among the first acts of the Comité de défense, the extraordinary commission that supplanted the municipal council after September 4.

By the spring of 1871, a more moderate but still republican prefect, Regnault, had been installed. He recommended against reinstating the teaching orders and noted with satisfaction that the bishop of Autun was willing to rely on the "jurisprudence" of the minister of public instruction until a new law might return to the clergy the preeminence assured by the loi Falloux. Regnault stressed in correspondence with the minister that whatever Frédéric Morin's reputation might lead one to suspect, his actions as prefect had been limited in every case to support of popular *faits accomplis*. He had always followed the "justified decisions of municipal commissions," and the men who had taken these actions had been reelected with large majorities. A reversal of his actions would do violence to popular opinion, "which has varied less on this point than Monsigneur d'Autun would appear to believe."

He reminded the minister that his predecessors, two prefects who briefly succeeded Morin, had both thought it impossible to recall the religious orders. Regnault emphasized the extraordinary unity of the Burgundian population on this matter and noted that the numerous petitions in support of lay teachers "have the exceptional character of including all classes of society." Mme la comtesse de Villeneuve had sent her son to a secular school, and another countess headed a delegation of "mothers of families" in support of the *laïcs*. The municipal council of

Cuisery was alone in protesting the ouster of nuns, and its mayor, a count, dissociated himself from the council's appeal and declared himself in favor of secular schooling. Regnault felt that because popular will consistently upheld secularizers and because the ousted religious were at liberty to open independent schools, no action should be taken. He succeeded in delaying resumption of funding for church schools until 1875, when the Conseil d'état decided in favor of the congregations.[87]

Regnault had recommended, too, that mayors be more closely associated with educational policy and, to that end, proposed a new law enabling mayors of *chefs-lieux* to sit by right on the departmental councils. Regnault thus gave voice cautiously to a growing radical demand to democratize and to broaden the departmental councils, which were often used in this period to overrule revolutionary municipalities.

Less temperate than Regnault was César Bertholon, ousted prefect of the Loire, whose actions in support of the municipal council of Roanne had been countermanded by the departmental council. Bertholon, then a candidate for the National Assembly, wrote in *L'Eclaireur de Saint-Etienne* on December 22, 1871, that although radicals might accept, in a spirit of conciliation, some fixed division of schools between Catholics and *laïcs*, they found intolerable the composition of departmental councils, which seemed to ensure the clerical supremacy.[88]

At Toulouse Jules Ferry's younger brother Charles, prefect of the Haute-Garonne, dissuaded the administration from a drastic suppression of the city's secularized schools. He asked for "leisure" in which to conciliate the municipality and avoid an arbitrary settlement that would help no one but the deposed prefect, Armand Duportal, a Radical candidate for the National Assembly. The intransigent municipality of Toulouse refused the compromise, which would have permitted them to keep secular schools for boys if they had agreed to let girls be taught by nuns.[89]

It was in general more difficult to secure administrative approval for the secular education of girls. A determination to provide *laïc* education for both sexes served as a touchstone for radicalism. Worldly men were, in general, happy to find in their boys a manly stoicism. One suspects they felt, too, that a touch of the raffish epicurean sat well in a masculine character. No such pagan glory attached to an unbelieving woman: She was, even for many sophisticates, a dreadful object. It took an especially earnest attachment to their cause to imagine that its women would not be faithless, to entrust *both* sexes – and thus all future generations – to the new morality.

That was precisely the issue at Algiers. There, the Ligue de l'enseignement noted, "it can escape no one that to be quick, useful, and certain, the reform of our education must begin with the education of women."[90]

The prefect at Algiers was disinclined to allow even a private secular girls' school, but the governor-general overruled him with the eminently conservative argument that fathers had a right to educate their children as they chose. The estimated costs of the girls' school were five thousand francs per annum; and the league was greatly helped by a donation of seven thousand francs from the now idle ambulance brigade.[91]

All the municipal schools of Algiers had been secularized immediately after the republic was proclaimed, but the political situation was precarious. League members wished "to affirm public sympathy for the municipality that had made the schools secular and free. [We must also] prepare a refuge for our children in case the schools of the commune succumb to clerical intrigues.[92] Succumb they did: Nuns were reinstated in 1875.[93]

Radicals prided themselves, nationally, on their resilience and they determined to strip conservatives of all devices with which secular projects could still be thwarted. In 1872 the SIE proposed major changes in the composition of the departmental councils – bodies called upon, unfailingly, to undo secularizations. The radicals believed that legislation revoking the loi Falloux should introduce new elements into these councils. Teachers, both men and women, elected by their colleagues as well as men of science, a doctor and an engineer from the *ponts-et-chaussées*, should be party to their deliberations. Catholics would be assured one seat only – for a representative from a Catholic faculté des lettres, or, if there was none such in the department, someone from a Catholic college.[94] Unfortunately for them, secularists, despite their growing strength, could not yet prevail at the national level.

In 1870 radicals had briefly taken possession of France. In 1871 insurrection and repression had put them on the defensive but could not destroy them. They preserved, if not the communes, the schools of the communes, and in every republican area they were committed to maintaining secular education. They were convinced that rational, egalitarian instruction was necessary to the survival of the republic. They found, too, that the schools issue reliably rallied a broader and more ardent coalition than any other cause. Thus, republicans drew together in mutually sustaining concert with radical deputies and moderate prefects. This republican nexus grew in strength and in consciousness between 1874 and 1877. In 1877 it would assure the triumph of the radical republic.

"AN ARM OF THE PARTY," 1873–7

The government of moral order had shown itself to be hostile to popular education as a cause and suspicious of its supporters. During the years from 1873 to 1877, educational societies, whatever their tendency in the 1860s, became overtly republican and were treated as such by the police and prefectures. The secularist network, sustained by republican officials, was correspondingly strengthened or threatened as republican fortunes rose and fell.[95]

There is ample evidence that conservative officials and the clergy, on the one hand, and the league members, on the other, recognized this polarization and deliberately exaggerated it by their actions. In the first months of its existence, the government of the moral order issued two circulars intended to harass and confine the league's activities: The circular of August 11, 1873, forbade competition for the Prix Ménier; that of December 24, 1873, requested detailed information about the activities of the league, the SIE, and any other educational society, in order to determine if they had "deviated from their original purpose."[96] Nevertheless, the schools movement persisted, and the "administrative terror"[97] wrought upon it in 1877 testified to the adversaries' sense of its power and centrality.

The political capacity implicit in the league was in these years made manifest. The league appears to have been considered a major arm of the emerging Radical party not only by the cabinet, but by the republicans themselves. This strengthens the contention that the character and, perhaps, the survival of the Third Republic was assured by a preexisting nexus of secular voluntary associations.

Macé in this period abandoned toleration and spoke openly of the church as the enemy. (*The Enemy* was indeed the title of his most combative book.) In 1874 Macé called for an organization of "republican societies to oppose the restoration of the Middle Ages." He was especially concerned to counter "Catholic circles, *soi-disant* workers' circles," established by the deputy M. le comte Albert de Mun ("knight of the Syllabus")[98] and by Charles-Emile Freppel, the contentious bishop of Angers.

A sympathetic modern account of Catholic organization argued that the outbreak of the communes made wealthy Catholics aware of the need for a Christian reorganization of society. The "new apostolate" took the form of the Oeuvre des cercles catholiques d'ouvriers, organized in 1871 under the sponsorship of the comte de Mun, Freppel, and the deputy Keller. Lille had in 1870 already established seven parish committees, and by 1874 twenty-one committees and thirty-three circles had been formed in the west and also in the north in the dioceses of Cambrai and Arras. The organizers denounced political and social "naturalism" and "rationalism" in science, industry, and labor. They insisted – as did the radicals – upon an incompatibility between the Christian position (which the Catholics, perhaps unwisely, took to be expressed by the *Syllabus of Errors*) and the principles of 1789.[99]

Macé ridiculed the count's pretension of speaking for workers. It was the Ligue de l'enseignement, he wrote in *L'Ennemi*, that was "par excellence a socialist work." Macé himself might have explored social issues more seriously; he said merely, we all have "something to clamor for . . . to the degree envy seizes us." Nevertheless, he implored workers not to hope for material improvements at the cost of "a submission of the mind against which everything rebels," not to trade the Revolution – their birthright as Frenchmen – for a mess of clerical pottage. The Catholic circles he dismissed as patronage societies. Had not the Capuchin Ludovic described them as such: "the Christian organization of workshops . . . a way of placing Christians in Christian establishments"?[100]

The social power of the church was manifest in selective hiring, in the distribution of charity, in clientele politics generally.[101] Republicans insisted that religious orthodoxy not be a condition of employment; moreover, the church had to be stripped of its power to bestow or withhold material benefits. All radicals were concerned with the near-monopoly of charity exercised by Catholics. The *mères de famille* of Chalon-sur-Saône sought to remedy this with female conscription. They suggested a three- or four-year period of service – the first years devoted to training *au sein de famille*, and the rest to work in schools, nurseries, and hospitals – so that services performed by nuns might be offered on a secular basis also.[102] Macé wrote: "Sad to say, but our service of public assistance may be considered almost entirely as a vast camp where the papal militia is entrenched."[103]

Faced with these pressures, Macé believed that only a countervailing organization of republicans could save the republic. He rejoiced that republicans were now in "the regions of power," but political power would not suffice: "CE SONT DES MOEURS NOUVELLES A FORMER."[104]

Republican deputies, senators, and mayors might be elected, but the republic could be assured only by republican ascendancy in every department, arrondissement, and canton. Macé urged as a model the responsibility undertaken by organizers of the Société républicaine du canton de Fère-en-Tardennois (Aisne), and the republican press took up Macé's plea for a network of self-consciously secular citizens' groups. M. Laisant, a deputy of Nantes, issued a similar appeal in the *Phare de la Loire* with the caution, "They are violent; be moderate."[105]

Macé reiterated the theme of his earlier writings: A reform had to become part of legitimate and habitual behavior, "the rooted habits" of a people, and legislation alone was impotent. Partisans of *l'école laïque* had to expect reactionary resistance to thwart all laws and decrees "until the patient and resolute action of citizens has conquered *sur place*."[106]

Active citizenship was required merely to preserve the republic; but Macé thought, too, that men would find psychological rewards in *civisme*. He advocated proportional representation because it more sensitively expressed the popular will. He thought it essential that political participation gratify the voters' conscience and reason. "This is a *matter of personal satisfaction*, not without its own importance in an infant Republic."[107]

Such contentment would elude republicans so long as elected officials took office only to be left powerless. The educational societies associated themselves increasingly, and more consciously, with the efforts of republican mayors and deputies. Municipal councils had strongly evinced their desire for free, compulsory, secular education in the actions they had taken after *le 4 septembre*: They acted in concert with local league circles, whose agendas mayors and deputies frequently set.

This coincidence had not escaped the notice of the government. In February 1874 its president, Marshal Patrice de MacMahon, tried to reintroduce executive nomination of mayors, and a list of elected mayors henceforth dismissed from their functions was printed in the *Journal officiel*. The project aroused furious protest and was abandoned;[108] but although the general purge of mayors was deferred until 1877, municipalities were closely supervised and their powers diminished. Municipal councils were frustrated even in their most customary and trivial actions. In 1873 the academic inspector at Orléans asked the advice of the vice-rector of the Academy of Paris: Might he allow schools to accept books bearing the *cachet* of the Ligue de l'enseignement? He was instructed to refuse, "even if it happens that a Municipal Council votes the acquisition of books stamped by the League and charges the teacher to serve as librarian." The vice-rector, who urged his subordinate not to identify himself or the academic establishment with the league, was commended by the minister of public instruction for his prudent reply.[109]

The government's conviction that municipal and general councils would do whatever they could for the league was shared by the league's officers. When its proposals were denied an adequate hearing at Versailles, it marshalled the municipal councils behind them. Emmanual Vauchez, a founder of the Paris circle and its secretary-general during this period, had undertaken in November of 1872 an inquiry to ascertain the wishes of the population on matters of education.[110] He addressed a letter to all members of municipal and general councils in France. He turned to these groups, confident of their response and in an effort to lend more effective and legitimate support to the league's proposals. Its citizens' petitions, bearing more than a million signatures, had been ignored by the National Assembly in June 1872, and the assembly had granted only slightly less perfunctory hearing to similar proposals presented by Jules Simon, minister of public instruction. Monsignor Dupanloup himself presided over the legislative committee to which the project was consigned.

Thus, Vauchez asked elected local officials to pronounce on free, compulsory, secular education and carefully explained "laïcité," the most controversial term of the three: "science at school, religious instruction at church . . . that is to say the neutrality of public schools subsidized by the state or the commune."[111]

Significantly, Vauchez defined a public school as a school receiving *any* subsidy from *any* level of government, a category into which fell nearly every Catholic school in France. The *patrie* required the "abnegation" of prejudice, Vauchez said, and although this could not be expected from his own generation, the schools of the republic would eventually accomplish it. He promised that this declaration for free, compulsory, secular education, a cause ever inseparable from the battle for the republic, "shall be in the future an historic document . . . Myriads of families will take pride in finding the names of their ancestors among the number who cooperated in the regeneration of French schools, in the foundation of the republican school in France, to call the thing by its proper name."[112]

Vauchez's investigation mapped both the strength of the republic and the progress of secularism in France in the decade of the seventies. The Conseil général de la Seine affirmed the need for free and obligatory primary education and emphasized that the state, which represents the interests of civil society, ought not to subsidize any teachers but those who "exclusively represent those interests." The declaration was signed by the entire council, including Dr. Marmottan, Emile Combes, Georges Clemenceau, Cadet, Henri Allain-Targé, Charles Loiseau, Loiseau-Pinson, Charles Floquet, and Edouard Lockroy.[113]

The municipal council of Bordeaux, its mayor, councillors-general, and deputies, agreed that legal compulsion was necessary to secure universal school attendance and, further, asked that schooling be completely free at every level, not just the primary, "as a right and the only means of ending the antagonism of castes." Many towns – among them, Rheims, LeHavre, Vichy, Moulins, Toulouse, and Marseille – replied simply that recent elections, "the manifestations of universal suffrage," left no doubt as to the wishes of the people in this matter. They viewed their election as a mandate for secularization.[114]

Secularization was not unanimously supported, however: At Cognac, in the Charente, the league members – "the notary, the lawyer, the doctor, and the businessman" – regretted that their fellow citizens misunderstood the nature of their insistence on secular education and feared it to be synonymous with the destruction of religion. From the Aisne Henri Martin reported enormous support for obligatory schooling and for free education without any preconditions as to lay control. Martin found that it was not "a very lively preoccupation" in his department because the clergy exercised little influence there. In the Dordogne anticlericalism was a purely bourgeois issue; while the population was united in support of free, compulsory education, secularization had partisans only among "those who possess an above average education."[115]

Dr. Brard *père*, who with his son – also a physician and a municipal councillor at La Rochelle – fought a lonely battle at Jonzac for modernity in the West, wrote that "among a population whose ill will systematically opposes us," it had been sufficient triumph to avoid succumbing to counterrevolution. Although the men of the countryside and the "independent workers" wished for free, compulsory, and secular education, in the towns, reactionary *bien-pensants* reigned, and "the worker endures the domination of the bourgeoisie." Another isolated republican, an engineer in the Basses-Pyrénées, deplored the unwillingness of the peasantry to accept compulsory education. This principle was accepted by the "enlightened" in the principal towns, but peasants persisted in seeing time spent in schools as "time stolen" from a child's parents.[116]

The investigation was interrupted by the two cabinet crises – those of May 24, 1873, and May 16, 1877 – but eventually the league's program received the support of the municipal councils of Paris, Lyon, Marseille, Algiers, Bordeaux, Lille, LeHavre, Roubaix, Rheims, Toulon, Angers, and Clermont-Ferrand, and of the general councils of the Seine, the Bouches-du-Rhône, the Var, the Yonne, and the Saône-et-Loire. The league members liked to say that adhesions had come from councils representing more than half the population of France.[117]

The 1870s revealed a continuing conflict, not just between elected officials and functionaries of the *soi-disant* moral order, but conflict also within the academic hierarchy between those willing to associate themselves with popular agitation for education and those who were not. Unanimity did not exist even on the basic issue of compulsory and free primary education. Some educators feared the disruptive presence in the classroom of children unwillingly schooled. The *voeux* of provincial academic hierarchy believed itself to be threatened. Academic inspectors Lyon thought that free education would enable families who were able to pay to evade their share of the cost.[118] Some radicals observed that progressive taxation might obviate the objection, but this was dismissed as utopian. Catholics agreed that the rich should assume part of the cost of educating the poor but preferred that alms be given freely – to which Henri Tolain replied, "Charity remains for us a private virtue but . . . it has demonstrated its powerlessness, its inefficacy for the elimination of misery as well as for the elimination of ignorance."[119]

The fear most often expressed by the academic administration, as well as by the minister of the interior, in connection with the schools issue, was that recurring horror, the politicization of teachers. This frightful prospect was the subject of a circular issued by the minister of public instruction, on August 11, 1873, forbidding any collaboration with or acceptance of the Prix Ménier.[120]

In 1872 Deputy Ménier, a wealthy chocolate-maker who had been involved with educational reform[121] during the Commune when he was associated with Rama in the "Society for New Education,"[122] offered a prize of 100 francs for the rural, *laïc*, communal teacher in each department who enrolled the largest percentage of school-aged children. Efforts were made to match funds for a similar award to schoolmistresses. Ménier had long been a member of the SIE and of the Ligue de l'enseignement; the prizes were to be awarded by a league affiliate, the Commission des sous contre l'ignorance, whose president was the priest-baiting Charles Sauvestre. The extraordinary measures taken to suppress competition for the Prix Ménier indicate how seriously the academic hierarchy believed itself to be threatened. Academic inspectors and rectors were forbidden to furnish information on the basis of which such awards might be made, and teachers were expressly prohibited from accepting "recompense." The academic inspector of Toulouse indignantly protested the Ligue de l'enseignement's attempt to establish a "protectorate" over his functionaries.[123]

This protectorate would be doubly dangerous: First, it would subvert the academic chain of command; and second, the teaching corps might serve as a powerful auxiliary of the Radical party. The schoolmasters' position was regarded as particularly suited for electioneering. Teachers, ill-paid and dependent but well-spoken men, made ideal election agents and had been so employed under the empire.[124] The close identification of the republican cause with popular secular schooling raised fears that teachers – no longer the grudging pawns of the administration – would become the eager tools of the opposition.

Some prefects did not fear the secularists, or, perhaps, preferred them to the alternative. In the Meurthe-et-Moselle, the question was sharply posed: Whose electoral interests were the teachers to serve – the republicans' or the baron's? In 1874 the prefect reported vigorous activity of educational societies in the department. He acknowledged that members of the League at Nancy were "scarcely moderates" but because their lectures were never attended by more than a hundred people, he felt that an attack on them would "confer an importance that they could not fail to turn to their political advantage."[125]

The prefect's restraint at Nancy became active protection at Pont-à-Mousson. He accepted as natural and appropriate the patronage of schools by the general council. The league circle at Pont-à-Mousson had been organized by men who were already elected officials. The impetus had come primarily from one M. Garnier, "much esteemed, much listened to," and the prefect believed it was a valuable undertaking intended mainly to support a *caisse des écoles*. The prefect stoutly defended their library, whose books had largely come from the ministers of public instruction and agriculture. In addition, these books were in any case at the disposal of workers – that is, adults, the prefect emphasized, not children, so one did not need to be overly fastidious about their contents.[126]

The minister was unable to comfort himself with these reassurances. He was receiving vociferous complaints from the Baron de la Coste. In February of 1874 the minister asked about new allegations that ecclesiastics who hoped to join had been rebuffed and that attempts had been made to intimidate, subvert, and bribe teachers:

> Our teachers must feel themselves to be sustained and encouraged by the administration in their modest and useful function . . . The Government, breaking with the tradition followed until the end of the Empire, had renounced their use as electoral agents, but *it does not intend that its moderation shall be turned to the profit of those who would make of them instruments of a politics hostile to society and to religion.*[127]

The prefect replied that his surveillance and the rector's sufficed to keep the group within its stated purpose; furthermore, there had already been so much harassment of these groups that each lived under implicit threat of dissolution. He continued, "I find myself in genuine distress" because he could not substantiate rumors of improper political activities. Obviously, it was impossible that the public-spirited actions of elected officials be without political consequence. Of the five-member league committee at Pont-à-Mousson, three were also members of the cantonal delegation that dealt with public education. They exercised no private largesse but put league funds at the disposal of the cantonal delegation, on which, of course, its views were not unrepresented. The prefect could see nothing wrong in this. "It has nothing to do with politics and looks forward to no electoral success." The only private and possibly self-serving approaches had been made by Baron de la Coste – who had offered schoolmasters two gold medals, inscribed with his name and valued at fifty francs each, in return for unspecified services.[128]

Elsewhere, different political assessments were made. There was reluctance in some administrative circles to permit teachers to assemble under any pretext. The prefect of the Aude tolerated the Comité Agricole de Narbonne, in consideration of the "high and honorable situation and the perfect harmlessness" of its sponsors, but forbade a proposed meeting of schoolmasters in the *chefs-lieux* of the cantons, under the very eyes of the primary inspectors. Such meetings, especially in a center so "agitated and populous" as Narbonne, could not be expected to proceed in good order. It was far better to leave "these gentlemen in their villages to distract themselves as little as possible from their modest habits and from their labors."[129]

Similar strictures were urged by the inspector of the Academy of Grenoble, who had on his own initiative banned competition for the Prix Ménier. He refused permission to three professors at the Collège de Vienne who had hoped to offer courses in morals, history, and grammar under the auspices of the *cercle viennais* of the Ligue de l'enseignement. He recalled these men to their primary business, advancement within the academic hierarchy, and paternally advised that time was better spent in pursuit of their *licence*.[130]

Some academic administrators, however, welcomed the generosity of educational societies and of the municipal and general councils. The inspector at Bordeaux, an unusually self-confident administrator, was disposed to cooperate with the awarding of the Prix Ménier. He insisted on the orthodoxy of his subordinates: "The sad events of September" had produced there "neither cabal nor petition of any sort." He vouched for the absence in the minds of his teachers of a single "wicked or even systematic thought" and saw no danger in private, philanthropic support for his feeble efforts and those of the general council to encourage school attendance. The inspector foresaw no trouble or expense in furnishing "the trifling information" that the league required in order to award its prizes because the data were already collected. He objected only to the distinction made between lay and clerical teachers: He would not wish to introduce that distinction between men working under his administration in perfect sympathy and solidarity.[131]

Other inspectors felt that the distinction was a thoroughly permissible one. Fleury, of the Academy of Douai, noted that lay teachers went alone into the countryside, whereas members of the teaching orders were never sent out separately but remained in the populous heart of the region. Catholics were well organized in the Nord, and perhaps Fleury feared that church schools in the cities might create an ultramontane proletariat.[132]

Most academic authorities tried to insulate the schools from electoral politics; but this was hard to do in an epoch when the character of education became the stuff of national politics. Provincial republicans were now closely associated with the Ligue de l'enseignement, and prefects and rectors were asked to document this alliance in December of 1873. A circular from the minister of public instruction asked that they investigate all societies of instruction – the league and the SIE are mentioned by name – within their jurisdictions and verify the dates and circumstances of their authorizations.[133] The responses give a comprehensive national account of the societies; they attest, and some lament, the groups' multiplicity of purpose and their intense vitality. Many of the groups had already been dissolved in 1873; most would be again after May 16.

It is evident that the prefects feared a republican nexus, capable of organizing an entire department and of communicating with several classes. "Purely local" meant innocuous. The prefect of the Aisne reported only one group, and that "very honorable." Its president was the Protestant deputy William Waddington. "The work is purely local and has no connection whatsoever with other societies that, under the same name, undertake not to moralize and instruct but to foster among the people certain political doctrines."[134]

Many prefects found it difficult to estimate the political importance of the league or the threat it posed. Their reports reflect this perplexity. Supporters are described as "advanced but honorable," "of excessive philanthropic sentiments," or, often, "exalted." The prefect of the Maine-et-Loire had unearthed nothing to substantiate fears that educational societies attempted political propaganda, yet "the men who compose them inspire no confidence in me." His most disquieting finding had been that, in the past year, for the first time, the league circle at Bauge had neglected to take the advice of the academic hierarchy in choosing teachers to honor.[135]

The prefect of Morbihan, too, sensed the league to be pernicious. He had suspended a mayor and his assistant, both members of the Ligue de l'enseignement. He was convinced that their committee, which he had also dissolved, continued to meet secretly and to produce the most deplorable effects but could adduce "no precise fact." The rector at Poitiers held the league responsible for all secularist activity in the west, in the departments of the Vienne, Deux-Sèvres, the Vendée, Charente, and Charente-Inférieure.[136]

Circles protected by deputies naturally received the closest scrutiny. The future premier René Goblet, a deputy of the Somme, presided, like Ribière, over a departmental association – to the great discomfiture of the prefect, who dissolved it in November of 1873. The decree of dissolution cited as particularly noisome the group's circulation of inflammatory and irreligious books, among them the Declaration of the Rights of Man and the Citizen. That document, the prefect stressed, if "thrown out among the popular classes," would produce "the most appalling consequences." The chief objection to the group, however, was to its very form: A departmental organization was *ipso facto* intolerable. The prefect sensed that it would furnish important links between the deputy and the Radical mayors, councillors, and teachers. Members in the Somme, in concert with the committee of the league in Paris, sought to establish groups in each arrondissement. This, the prefect believed, was manifestly "a school of radicalism opened in view of the elections." Happily, he was able to adduce their self-incriminating statement of purpose. They admitted it was not enough to instruct and moralize the electorate. Compulsory education alone would not suffice, they said, equally necessary were books that would initiate the people "to the incessant progress of the human mind and open their intelligence to an exact understanding of their rights and their duties."[137] What more needed to be said?

Deputy André Rousselle's support of the league in the Oise – and particularly his patronage of teachers – was held, too, to constitute a political danger (although it was later acknowledged that its "tendency" was more objectionable than its action). The circle at Saintes, whose president, Deputy Mestreau, had been the first republican prefect of the Charente-Inférieure, was thought to meddle in politics; similarly, Desseaux, president of the league at Rouen, a deputy and former prefect, did not respond to a "genuine" educational need, but rather posed a political danger.[138]

Burgundy continued to be unruly. An innocuous circle at Leurre was subsidized by the ministry as a *caisse des écoles*, and one at Beaune was led by an "advanced" but law-abiding banker. The Société pour la propagation de l'instruction primaire at Châtillon, authorized in December of 1867 and widely believed to be a branch of the Ligue de l'enseignement, was attacked as such by the clergy, who cited Macé's insistence that differences in name signified nothing. In the sixties, the society had busied itself with charitable work: free courses for adults and books and clothing for indigent children. After the war it began to display overtly political and irreligious tendencies. Several old members resigned, and the new bureau included "several notables of radical persuasion," including one who had just buried his father without the comforts of religion. Membership halved, and the prefect regretted that an enterprise capable of great service in honorable and disinterested hands should fall into the hands of "intriguers." He feared their distribution of largesse: These schemers might create for themselves, "outside of the municipalities, means of action that they promise to utilize for the success of their electoral interests."[139]

Worse, there was the circle at Semur, which plainly exasperated the prefect: It complicated his relations with the clergy and encouraged insubordination among his staff. He wanted it dissolved and reconstituted without its dangerous elements and had long recommended the dismissal as mayor of its president, Hugot, "chief of radicalism in the arrondissement of Montbard," a man who officiated at civil funerals. New provocations came from a lecture series: Public lectures on agriculture, engineering, history, and morals had been authorized for the spring of 1872. The lectures had been carried on in "a very bad spirit," and the prefect thought that public talks henceforth should be limited to the topics indicated as acceptable in the minister's list of May 7, 1872.[140]

Regrettably, the lectures and Hugot himself were championed by the subprefect at Semur, one Malherbe, who, accompanied by his family, always attended the lectures presented with his permission in the hall of the subprefecture. Malherbe had reported only that the lectures were "celebrated," and his superior suspected that he had failed to convey an adequate notion of the mayor's character to the minister when Hugot had requested permission to speak on the topic of political economy. That talk had left "the most unpleasant memories" and provoked an open break between the academic and parochial authorities. Priests refused to enter a school where they would be insulted by the students "under the eye of impassive teachers." It was thus, the prefect noted, that the league members "abstain[ed] from religious polemic," as they undertook to do in Article 4 of their statutes.

Their library, too, was a plague: a "means of action as dangerous as it is convenient." The prefect questioned whether its unexceptionable printed catalogue was a complete or an accurate one. Each Sunday the library took on the character of a public meeting, and the librarian, M. Paillard, "an inspiring man, active while appearing calm," worried the prefect considerably. In his continuing rounds to receive dues or distribute books, he went "from door to door, to workers' homes, to receive or give information . . . I expect he gives rather more than he receives." He concluded that the group, in the hands of men notorious for their immorality, their irreligious passion, and their radical political opinions, had become nothing but "an auxiliary of party."[141]

As the great dénouement of 1877 approached, republican deputies could rely upon a national alliance of secularists and radicals. This alliance, more deeply rooted in the countryside than republicanism had ever been, was also more self-confidently respectable than ever before. Republicans were committed to the return of 363 members of the National Assembly dissolved in June of 1877: Whatever their social or economic opinions, their seats would not be contested by other republicans.[142] The resignation of the moderate republican premier, Jules Simon, had been forced on May 16, 1877, by Marhsal MacMahon, who then named a cabinet that was plainly irresponsible to the parliament. The conservatives had thrown away their greatest advantage: their reputation for prudence. Republicans were able to portray them as subversives, reckless of liberty, destroyers of the constitution. Hippolyte Taine foresaw that the crisis would help radicals immeasurably.[143]

This time the republicans had prepared for themselves everything that they had lacked in 1851. Of course, in fairness to MacMahon and his advisor, the duc de Broglie, it must be said that after they dissolved the National Assembly, they called for new general elections – not a "plebiscite" in the manner of Louis Bonaparte. Like Napoleon III, though, MacMahon characterized the voters' choice as one between good and evil:

> Frenchmen –
>
> You are going to vote.
> The violence of the opposition
> has dispelled all illusions.
>
> No, the Republican Constitution
> is not in danger.
> No, the Government, however
> respectful of religion [does not follow]
> a policy compromising the peace.
>
> *The struggle is between order and disorder.*[144]

Thus was the battle perceived and fought; but for the first time in France, republicans could credibly present themselves as a legitimate established power persecuted by a usurping administration. Jules Grévy, president of the assembly, told his colleagues, when they were "adjourned" by MacMahon: "Remain within the law. Remain there with prudence, firmness, and confidence." John Lemoine, writing in the *Débats*, alleged an "administrative orgy" unmatched since the most shameful days of the empire.[145] In all, 1,383 functionaries – including 62 prefects – were dismissed and 4,779 transferred peremptorily; six hundred thirteen municipal councils were dissolved and 1,743 mayors and 1,344 assistant mayors were suspended or dismissed.[146]

The 363 incumbents of the Center and Left agreed upon a manifesto written by Eugène Spuller:

> France wants the Republic; she said it on February 20, 1876, she will say it again. We, your mandatories . . . call on you to protest against the policy of reaction and adventure that has abruptly called into question all that has been painfully won these past six years [and for] the prudent, firm, peaceful and progressive policy that you have already sanctioned . . . The Republic will emerge stronger than ever.[147]

Among the 363, the most prominent were men who had early support-
ed the Ligue de l'enseignement and the cause of secular education: Car-
not, Prince Napoleon Bonaparte, Léon Gambetta, Jules Ferry, Georges
Clemenceau, Paul Bert, Désiré Barodet, Louis Andrieux, Alfred Naquet,
Edouard Lockroy, Henri Germain, H. de Lacratelle, Henri Allain-Targé,
Henri Brisson, Philippe Denfert-Rochereau, Dionys Ordinaire, François
Raspail, Jules Barni, Benjamin Bardoux, Charles Floquet, Antonin
Proust, Louis Blanc, and Spuller himself. "L'Union des gauches d'abord!"
Ferry had urged the year before. The schools issue preserved the unity,
both ideological and organizational, of the Left. As Jean Macé said,
"Now there are only two parties in France."[148]

Later, in July of 1877, another ministerial circular similar to that issued
in December 1873 was sent to all departments: The cabinet required
information on the activities of all educational societies. On the basis of
the accounts it received, it began to dissolve league circles all over
France. Educational groups that included candidates among their members were, of course, suppressed, and radicals argued that this disruption of civic life proved the government not conservative, but destruc-
tive and fearful of liberty. Macé ridiculed the language of decrees
dissolving educational societies and libraries. Many were peremptory
decrees, but when the reasons were given, they were couched in terms
like "perverted from the purposes for which it was instituted" or "far
from its original end." Macé goaded his adversaries: Why not admit
frankly that you believe that "the development of instruction in the
lower classes constitutes a danger for society"?[149] To many it did seem
that learning itself was suspect: In the Hérault, for instance, all libraries
and bookstores were put under surveillance.[150]

Republicanism and support for secular education had become inseparable. In the Ardeche the incumbent deputy, Chalamet, planned to speak
at the Prize Day of the Société pour l'encouragement de l'instruction at
Vernoux. The prefect was certain that the ceremony would provide "an
occasion for a political manifestation." Chalamet had taken steps to
assure the attendance of all local notables, and the prefect read in his
request "the secret desire to protest a ban"[151] so that republicans could
portray the administration as inimical to popular instruction. The prefect, however, judged the danger of dissolving the society a lesser evil
than permitting its operation.

The league was well organized in the Charente-Inférieure at La Rochelle, Rochefort, and Saintes, and with determination – if less success –
at Jonzac. There, the "administrator terror" (as a republican whose candidacy it had undermined described it) was harshly applied. The
Charente-Inférieure was one of the departments to lose a prefect suspected of sympathy with the republicans. (Regnault, who had advised

that Frédéric Morin's secularizations be allowed to stand, was replaced in the Saône-et-Loire by a baron of "legitimate-Bonapartist tendencies.")[152] The four hundred members of the Ligue de l'enseignement at La Rochelle were, the new prefect reported, "young people, workers, the principal chiefs of the radical party."[153] Their main activity was the support of a popular library. Dr. Brard *fils* served as its president; Barbadette, the republican candidate, and the editor of the *Courrier de la Rochelle* were among its members. The prefect especially deplored the library's close association with the radical press (Brard was also the local correspondent of *La République française*). On September 10, the cooperative library and the circle itself were dissolved. Brard taunted the prefect: "Will you then declare that reading poses a public danger? We work exclusively for the intellectual uplift of the population." Soon after, the prefect felt compelled to dissolve also the Société philharmonique de Saint-Martin and an agricultural improvement society, the scene of "political manifestations and tumults."[154]

Barbadette lost a close election at La Rochelle: He received 9,430 votes; the conservative, Fournier, was elected with only 9,957. He protested, in addition to the harrying of his supporters, the systematic defamation of his character by the clergy. Priests had spoken to him as "the devil's candidate" and had circulated rumors that he refused to baptize his children. At Pontivy (Morbihan), where the count Albert de Mun was running against a radical doctor, public prayers were offered for the nobleman, and a novena begun that was to end on the day of the election with plenary indulgences for those who fulfilled their civic duties in accordance with "Christian" principles. The count's victory, like Fournier's, was one that the newly elected republican Chamber of Deputies would invalidate. Dr. Malguet – described by the prefecture as a "doctor of insurgents" – decisively defeated de Mun in new elections held on February 2, 1878.[155]

The workers' library at Rochefort, which was allied with the league, united the "chiefs of radicalism at Rochefort and all the workers' societies."[156] This group, also dissolved, included among its members the entire municipal council and three judges. These memberships were, curiously, put forward by the league as "strong presumption that the society has undertaken no political propaganda."[157] Their commitment to educate the people so that the republic might be firmly established was not, they said, a partisan one. They defended, they believed, the legitimate and necessary government of France and felt themselves to be invincibly impelled by *la force des choses*, which they understood to be a progressive force. It was intolerable that they be treated as intriguers and demagogues.

In addition, the society at Saintes, whose president was Deputy Mestreau, included academics "closely linked with advanced republicans whose opinions they share." At Jonzac its adherents, including many members of the administration, were radicals; and although the prefect was unable to verify his suspicions – he complained that police agents were not assigned to him in sufficient numbers – he wanted to dissolve the group and felt confident that conservative opinion, which found the league members objectionable, would welcome such action.[158]

The prefect of the Marne similarly deplored the Ligue de l'enseignement, so rashly authorized on the advice of Jules Simon in 1872. One of the groups in his department had been established by a carpenter named Blériot, who was condemned in 1848 for membership in a secret society. The police had found a copy of a letter he had written that, they felt, left no doubt that his intention was to unite all organizations with "radical nuances." He attended meetings of the republican committees of Châlon and of Rheims, committees of the bourgeoisie as well as of workers and debtors. Brochures that emanated from these groups contained "germs of the most detestable theories." Nevertheless, at Rheims the 568 members of the league felt no need to suspend their activities after *le 16 mai* and continued their lecture series and adult courses within the precincts of the Société industrielle,[159] whose protection had been extended to them a decade before.

About Ribière's network of societies, libraries, and courses in the Yonne, the prefect believed, there could be no doubt: "Its real aim is obviously to create everywhere political committees obedient to the direction of the central society in Auxerre and to flood the countryside with republican books and pamphlets . . . These societies are nothing other than the Ligue de l'enseignement."[160]

In the Seine-Inférieure, too – where most prominent republicans had organized circles of the league – dissolutions were pronounced at LeHavre, where Jules Siegfried stood for parliament, and at Dieppe, where Emile Lebon, who was successful in October, served as the group's secretary. The president of the Dieppois protested that the group had never acted as a center of propaganda. Some members, undeniably, were not strangers to the political struggles of the period; but their actions were entirely independent of the their support of the league, whose sphere was that of pure philanthropy.[161] The group at Rouen, whose president was the deputy Desseaux,

> is composed of industrialists, businessmen, lawyers, doctors, and landowners, nearly all part of the republican party in its most reprehensible aspects . . . The tendencies of the Ligue de l'enseignement are certainly most dangerous, its doctrines are those of free thought, thus it counts a fair number of Protestants among its adherents.[162]

Pascal Duprat, a Radical deputy and a league member, asked permission to speak at Rouen on the topic "Instruction and Its Influence." The prefect refused because the last public lecture of that sort, given by a M. Besselièvre, vice-president of the league circle, had produced "serious inconvenience" for the authorities.

In the Côte d'or, Pierre Joigneaux, who had been convicted in 1839 of "inciting class hatred,"[163] was reelected, as was Sadi Carnot (later president of the republic), the son of Hippolyte Carnot, minister of education in 1848; reelected, too, were Leroy and Levêque. All were members of the Ligue de l'enseignement. Mayor Hugot, whose conduct so pained the prefect of the moral order in 1874, was returned as deputy for Semur.

Three hundred twenty-three republicans were elected on October 14, 1877, and in the second ballot on October 28, assuring republican control of the Chamber of Deputies.[164] More would be returned in 1878 from constituencies where contested elections had been invalidated. The Third Republic was irrevocably in the hands of the republicans. Jean Macé expressed a sentiment shared by virtually all the victors: They had earned the victory; they were (who could now deny it?) the "best people in the country."[165]

Conclusion: The Republic *enracinée*: secularism and solidarity

A century of heroism . . . the most incontestable, the most authentic heroism. And I would say, the most French . . . and when we see what the reactionaries have done with saintliness how can we be surprised by what the revolutionaries have done with heroism?
Charles Péguy, *Notre Jeunesse*

The ideal society is not outside the real society, it is a part of it . . . We cannot hold to one without holding to the other.
Emile Durkheim, *The Elementary Forms of Religious Life*[1]

REPUBLICANS MOVED QUICKLY to consolidate their victory and to execute the mandate that none could now deny was theirs. They undertook simultaneously three measures designed to enracinate republican mores and to restrict the political power of the Catholic Church: First, they passed the lois Ferry, which established free, compulsory, secular primary education in France; second, they withdrew subsidies from clerical institutions and dismissed functionaries who were unsympathetic to secularist goals; and third, they markedly increased government patronage of radical organizations, many of which would soon unite in a federated Ligue française de l'enseignement.

The major legislative accomplishment of the republican majority – indeed, the only social legislation upon which they could agree – were the lois Ferry. The first, the law of June 16, 1881, assured free attendance in all public primary schools. The second law, passed on March 28, 1882, established a legal obligation to educate children of both sexes between the ages of six and thirteen and presented as a corollary the "neutrality" of public instruction. Citizens of various persuasions, by choice or in default of an affordable alternative, would place their children in state schools; doctrinal teaching must be avoided, therefore, to protect the liberty of conscience.

Paul Bert, whom Macé had wished to make president of the new Ligue française de l'enseignement served as *rapporteur* for Ferry's bills in the Chamber of Deputies. His committee included Lockroy, Lacretelle, Chalamet, Barodet, Spuller, Cantagrel, Floquet, and Blanc, all members of the league. Ribière, organizer of the SPIP in the Yonne, acted as *rapporteur* in the Senate. Bert had called for a new, organic law, *une réforme d'ensemble*, that would supplant all provisions of the loi Falloux with "equally logical legislation of absolutely different principles."[2] Bert, and the radicals for whom he spoke, were not satisfied in this wish; but Ferry did accomplish the essential reforms they had so long demanded.

Primary education became free and compulsory for all children. Parents could choose public or private schools, and children might even be educated at home – although public authorities had to examine them in order to verify that they were indeed receiving instruction. Bert had asked that departmental councils be authorized to determine whether private schools met minimal educational requirements;[3] he had urged, too, that towns be prohibited from substituting partly subsidized private (i.e., religious) schools for public schools. The lois Ferry included no such provisions, but in 1886 the October 30 Law on the Organization of Primary Education required public inspection of private schools in order to ascertain, among other things, that nothing was taught that was contrary to morality or to the constitution and laws of France.[4]

Radical concern for "independent morality," based upon human experience and accessible through the study of history, was manifest in Article 1 of the law of March 28, 1882.

Primary education includes:

> Moral and civic instruction
> Reading and writing
> Language and elements of French literature
> Geography, particularly that of France
> History, particularly that of France *up to the present time*[5]

Ferry insisted upon teaching the history of the Revolution and of the nineteenth century, which some wished to exclude as too controversial, but he promised that children would not be subject to partisan polemic. Civic education would "prepare the accord of citizens under the regime of the French Revolution . . . and of the Republic that is its definitive and necessary culmination."[6] These essentials of French history would be taught not as "articles of faith," Ferry explained, but as human approximations of moral truths.

Republicans sought also to destroy the temporal power of the church. The famous Article 7 was but the most drastic of a series of measures taken to diminish its social authority. Ferry's decree required all unauthorized religious orders to "regularize" their position and permitted them three months in which to arrange compliance with the laws of France. He also attempted to dissolve the Society of Jesus, and Jean Macé defended him: "The liberty to conspire against his existence, no person has ever granted another."[7] "The society born of '89," Macé believed, did not have to allow it to the Jesuits.

In 1878 Macé traveled throughout France, organizing republican societies of instruction. Generations of revolutionary struggle had secured the republic. In the face of this triumph, Macé said, reactionaries had become nothing but a "band of wreckers." Nevertheless, republicans had to be vigilant against a resurgence of clerical power. The first of Macé's lectures on this theme was given at Dôle with the assistance of the subprefect, Léon Bourgeois. Macé spoke at the end of 1878 in Count de Mun's old constituency at Pontivy (Morbihan): He brought greetings from the republican East to that "other frontier." Macé emphasized the need for continuous Radical effort. An educational society must do more than campaign; its role is to work in "the intervals between elections which are no less important."[8]

Impelled by fears much like those that troubled Macé, the cabinet moved against Catholic organization. There was a large and prompt shift in public subsidy of charities. Much of this, of course, can be dismissed as spoils, but the actions were dictated by fear of the entrenched (and hitherto nearly invincible) power of the church. The government was also anxious to remove conservative functionaries. Earlier, in August 1876 – after republican victories in by-elections had strengthened their position within the cabinet – the minister of public instruction had asked the SIE to inform him about functionaries who had shown themselves to be hostile to progress "in refusing to cooperate in the awarding of prizes to schoolteachers."[9] Subsequently, every effort was made – although records had often been destroyed – to track down those complicitous with the May 16 purges.

After 1877 republicans investigated Catholic charities and workers' circles. In the process they often expressed their conclusions in the same words that past regimes had used to justify suppressing them. Catholic philanthropies, they found, were "far from their original goal." The Oeuvre des apprentis et jeunes ouvriers patronized twenty different youth groups and ninety regular Sunday meetings. These had offered "wholesome diversions" to children who were neglected by their laboring parents and undoubtedly had been praiseworthy and useful,

> Unhappily, the committee over which the count de Mun presides does not appear to have limited its actions to this modest task . . . Originally instituted with a purely charitable aim, it has become an instrument of propaganda in the service of a party that does not conceal its hostility to modern ideas and republican institutions.[10]

This report was signed by Hérold: senator, league member, prefect of the Seine. He did not, however – unlike some of his predecessors – insist upon dissolution but urged an end to subsidy.

The municipal council of Paris had ceased in 1871 to support the Oeuvre des faubourgs, a society founded by Catholics to bring to the outlying sections of the city, those working-class suburbs that lacked schools and social services of every kind, "a spirit of order" and some material comforts. Regrettably, this group, too, had become "above all a work of religious propaganda."[11]

Subsidies were accordingly withdrawn, and the funds were transferred to republican and secular charities. The SIE which had been consistently, but less generously, patronized by the minister of public instruction in the past, received three thousand francs in 1878 and 1879 and four thousand in 1884; and in 1881 the Société d'enseignement professionnel du Rhône got three thousand francs. The Société philomatique of Bordeaux was given eight thousand francs from the Ministry of Agriculture; and the agriculture school and cooperative at Mettray, long a correspondent of the league, three thousand francs. Grants of one thousand or two thousand francs went to scores of "societies for the encouragement of independent and secular schools," and the Orphélinat de la Seine was awarded five thousand francs.[12]

The political aims of the Ligue de l'enseignement had become law, its opponents routed if not destroyed. The league sought in the 1880s to unite its manifold circles into one federation. Only by ceaseless effort, Macé thought, could the forces of "obscurantism" be kept at bay. Groups organized in lay strongholds in cities and in the securely republican departments turned their efforts to the unenlightened countryside. "One village is nothing. All the villages are France."[13]

In 1881 Gambetta exhorted, "Let us get out of the cities." Macé had proved that given the opportunity for education, "the interest of the workers draws incessantly closer to the life-giving sources of instruction."[14] Now the same fraternal appeal would be addressed to the peasantry. The league planned rural bookstores, first spoken of in the late 1870s: "Newspaper sellers, cobblers, barbers, watchmakers . . . turned themselves into booksellers."[15] The league would provide a moral rather than a financial guarantee for these enterprises, and it foresaw extensive *colportage*, peddling of republican books and pamphlets. It planned also a traveling corps of republican lecturers.[16]

Before undertaking the conversion of the peasantry, Macé hoped to consolidate in a new Ligue française de l'enseignement the various activities that had long been loosely grouped under its aegis. He therefore summoned to Paris delegates from all circles of the league, from the republican societies, from the *sociétés des sous des écoles laïques*, popular libraries, mutual benefit groups, and *amis d'instruction*.[17] It was to be a great celebration: The railways promised delegates reduced fares; Gambetta himself would give the oration.

The new federation, Macé assured those assembled, did not seek to regiment their activities. A new constitution would not subordinate local societies to a single direction, but would ensure that their "regular representation" and provide each group with "a central support," the Parisian circle.[18] Macé's project was not unanimously approved, but by 1882 there were nearly four hundred adherent societies. League circles or corresponding members could be found almost everywhere in France, and they flourished in the staunchly republican areas.[19]

Federation did not bring unity, nor did it fire members to the achievement of new goals. When Jean Macé began the league in the sixties, it gathered, sustained, and in some measure reconciled the nation's secular democrats. In the seventies it helped these men to prevail; and its members saw in the triumph of the radical republic a more ample fulfillment than history permits to most. The league would take up other causes but it would never again call forth, never again unite and express the progressive energies of France.

After the passage of the lois Ferry, the league could not find a new direction, nor, indeed, could French radicalism. Within the new Ligue de l'enseignement, nationalist members – especially Emmanuel Vauchez and Henri Martin, who had become involved with Paul Déroulède – tried to ally the group with the League of Patriots. These men urged compulsory military training in the years between the time that a boy left school and his conscription. Macé opposed this effectively, although he – who had lived twenty years in Alsace – also invoked the theme of *revanche*. The lost provinces had to be restored to France, he declared, and for that reason Macé opposed colonial adventures that, he thought, misdirected national energies.[20]

Many of his former associates were ardent expansionists. Jules Ferry is thought of, of course, as the father of the French empire, and Paul Bert died on a civilizing mission in Hanoi; but Mace's last vote in the French Senate was cast against imperialism. He died in December 1894, an old man of seventy-nine, exhausted by his pleading against the Madagascar expedition.[21]

Macé's coalition did not agree on domestic issues, either. By 1881 socialists attacked the league for concerning itself with primary education only, and some Radical republicans, too, wanted to press for free secondary education for all, accessible through competitive examination.[22] Jean Jaurès, who believed popular secular education to be the century's greatest triumph,[23] regretted that Radicals could not go beyond "a policy of religious vexation, without daring or grandeur,"[24] and see in socialism the logical and just development of their own principles.

In 1885 amid much questioning of the adequacy of free and compulsory primary schooling as a social policy, Macé said simply that he had always worked to enlighten the lower ranks of society and to rekindle social feelings among the higher,[25] *d'éclairer en bas, de réchauffer en haut.*

That relation between light and warmth, like Michelet's complementarity of bourgeois reason and popular instinct, was compatible with, if not actually predicated upon considerable difference.[26] The equality and solidarity that Macé valued were moral and intellectual, founded in the common cultural patrimony that he had explicitly contrasted in the sixties with material wealth.

Recently, historians have trivialized the radicals' achievement and impugned their egalitarianism. Jules Ferry is said to have "contented himself with providing free primary education." He is judged to have differed from Guizot – whose legislation required only that communes of a certain size establish schools where attendance was neither compulsory nor free, and who confined his solicitude entirely to the education of boys – simply "in the use he made of the egalitarian mystique that infused the popular movement in favor of primary education."[27]

Modern scholars have argued that the Radical program was irredeemably class biased. Edmond Goblot's suggestive book *La Barrière et le niveau* (1925) argued that the *bachot* had legitimated the status honor of the French bourgeoisie and had made of it a caste – closed, self-conscious, and recognized. More recently, Pierre Bourdieu's *Les Héritiers* (1964) confirms that in education, as in other spheres, to him that hath much is given. John E. Talbott and D. R. Watson have amply proven, moreover, that two tracks existed in French education: the free primary schools, which, save for promotion to provincial normal schools,[28] were "terminal" and the fee-paying "primary classes" of the *lycées* and *collèges*, which prepared sons of the bourgeoisie for a costly classical education and professional careers. Watson and Talbott, however, adduce no statistics earlier than 1899 and admit to a "regrettable absence of data about the social origins of French school children in the nineteenth century."[29]

Statistics alone will not settle this argument, because it is a question of historical sympathy and judgment. Secondary schooling was undoubtedly denied to many, but universal primary education itself was by no means assured by the passage of the lois Ferry. The social and political consequences of that triumph – and its costs, including the cost of securing compliance – were almost incalculable. Much remained to be done to establish the most minimal common culture.[30] Might not the Radicals, accepting the need *sérialiser la réforme*, have wished to generalize one level of schooling before proposing another?

Furthermore, there exists evidence that peasant children accounted in the eighties for more than half the enrollment in the provincial normal school.[31] *Lycée* scholarships in the next generation went preeminently to the children of schoolteachers and functionaries – and very likely, therefore, to the grandchildren of peasants. Radicals may have thought that it took two generations to make a bourgeois or *universitaire*. Indeed, so it may. There is, at any rate, something to be said for the sincerity and plausibility of the measures they proposed. They have been attacked chiefly for failing to anticipate the inadequacy of their reforms.

This century may rightly criticize the social realities that vitiate equal opportunity, and it is well to question the ethical premises of meritocracy; but in doubting the immense and liberating power of these ideas at the moment when their time had come, historians are guilty of anachronism. One cannot, without presumption, dismiss the faith of generations of republicans and socialists as false consciousness or as the homage that opportunist vice paid to republican virtue.

In fact, popular, primary education was not an obviously fraudulent program. Hope for careers open to talent was long kept alive in France – in part, because of the peculiar nature of French industrialization; in part, because the initial impact of capitalism is everywhere genuinely ambiguous. France remained in the nineteenth century, and well into the twentieth, a nation of small-holding farmers. Small shopkeepers and an artisanry persisted, too: If property is theft, Michelet had warned Proudhon, there are 25 million thieves in France.[32]

Even within the factory the process of "proletarianization" was obscured by a proliferation of *petites fonctions* – clerical and supervisory posts – and by the institution of the *équipe*, or work gang, "little cells within giant industrial organisms that preserved the personality of the workers."[33] The real ambiguity of the work task combined with the plenitude of consumer goods, made *embourgeoisement* as likely an experience as proletarianization. Although industrialization brought speechless misery to many, for others economic development meant elation and opportunity, the certainty of progress, the conviction of competence, and above all, a hunger for schooling, for the knowledge that made this future possible.

A modern economist, Albert Hirschman, has written with much insight about this. Whereas economists in general assume that increasing disparities of wealth exacerbate envy, he understood that they may have the opposite effect. Early capitalism can shatter the image of the fixed good: The good fortune of one man may be seen as a harbinger of good fortune for another, rather than as an injury to him. The optimistic, or non-zero sum interpretation of another's success depends upon the likelihood that one man will see another as his analogue, his *semblable*.[34]

In France such fellowship did in large measure exist. *Le self-made man*, an anglicism that began to replace *le fils de ses oeuvres*, was much in evidence. A man who owned thirty looms might still call himself a "weaver" and pride himself both on his ownership of them and his skill – or his boyhood skill or his father's remembered skill – in using them. Management and property were not yet entirely separate, physically or psychologically, from labor. This was manifest in the politics of the socialist movement when, at the Congress of the Internationale in Lausanne in 1867, English and German delegates called for an abolition of private property, whereas the French and Italians hoped to safeguard and generalize it.[35] French workers and artisans were thus not a proletariat in the mid–nineteenth century; instead, with the commercial and industrial *nouvelles couches*,[36] they formed the "productive classes," opposed as they had been in 1789 to the *fait-néants*. It is upon this common identity as worker and citizen that the Radical vision depends.

Their social program was, it is true, the one that Marx caricatured in *Eighteenth Brumaire* as the "petty bourgeois myth of the people": Everyone would work, according to his abilities, justly recompensed, and at reasonably dignified jobs; and respect would, fittingly, be accorded all essential tasks. Education and fairness, with perhaps more readily available credit, would enable talents to sort themselves out and to exercise themselves for the common good. These notions, Marx said, represented the fantasies of a "transitional class," the petty bourgeoisie, soon to be subsumed into the universal class, the proletariat.[37]

But which was really the "transitional class"? The industrial proletariat as Marx described it or the clerical, supervisory, shopkeeping, service-providing, examination-passing, intergenerationally mobile petty bourgeoisie whose virtues the Radicals extolled and sought to generalize? One might well argue that it was the Radicals who were betting on the "universal class" that actually emerged.

Marx himself expressed doubt about the class position of functionaries and professionals. In the noteworthy, unfinished Chapter 52 of *Capital* – a work that depends heavily upon factory inspectors and physicians to document the horrors of mechanized labor – Marx questioned whether officials and doctors should be considered capitalists. He speculated upon the emergence of an "infinite fragmentation of interest and rank" within the educated classes.[38] This seems to suggest alliances that French Radicals and solidarists, no less than democratic socialists, foresaw and relied upon.

Indeed, the Third Republic was unthinkable and unworkable without a durable Center–Left alliance, a coalition that was established prior to 1870 in institutions independent of the government and the church. Its supporters, who ultimately did take over the instruments of government, were first organized on a voluntary basis: Their organization could not have been sustained without a common moral passion, a revulsion against the religion of the old regime, with its "edifice of regrets," and a determination to live, at last, within the "society that follows from the French Revolution."[39]

In the introduction it was argued that French radicalism should not be dismissed as a mass of prejudices issuing in fitful expedients. In conclusion, it shall be maintained that radicalism, with its dual commitment to secular rationalism and social solidarity, provided honest and intelligent citizens with an idiom in which their common problems could be usefully discussed. Michelet had warned that one cannot with impunity isolate himself from his fellows. Tocqueville had seen egoism as the meanest vice and individualism as a grave error. Both believed that liberty teaches people their interdependence, that freedom delivers them from isolation.

Insofar as the Ligue de l'enseignement preserved, in the disarray of success, a common cause, its tendencies are best represented by the "solidarists" associated with Léon Bourgeois,[40] in whose presence Macé had first publicly urged the necessity of continuous political activity. Solidarism recalled at the *fin de siècle* an earlier concern for sympathy and *civisme* and carried into the twentieth century the Jacobin call for political action against "remediable depradations"[41] in the economic sphere. It presented itself as an alternative to collectivism certainly, but also to *laissez faire*: "Laissez faire[,] where the strong destroy the weak ... the spectacle of indifferent nature ... Is it for this we enter into societies?" Bourgeois asked.[42]

French solidarists wished to subject the economy to principled and scientific regulation. The academics, professionals, and functionaries who made the case for state action – and to whom also, it would seem, the appeal was chiefly addressed – were men who believed it possible to articulate the common good and, further, felt themselves to be capable of the disinterested exercise of power. Like radicals of an earlier generation, they had counterparts abroad;[43] and the arguments they made for adequate education, accident and unemployment insurance, and old-age pensions much resemble notions of guaranteed "social minimums" or "positive liberties" advanced elsewhere. They called, too, for some redistribution. (The solidarist Darlu, an inspector-general of public instruction, contributed an article on progressive taxation to the *Revue de la métaphysique* in 1894.)[44] French solidarists were rather less paternalist than some others, urging self-regulation through syndicates such as those that Durkheim proposed in his 1902 preface to *The Division of Labor in Society*.[45]

One can, of course (as Zeldin does) judge their recommendations an inadequate response to the social question. "Solidarism did not produce the radical change it could have done. This, rather than the lack of social legislation, was the great failure of the nineties."[46] The crises precipitated by General Georges Boulanger in the eighties, and later by the Dreyfus affair, disturbed republicans profoundly. It is hard to know even now whether there had been serious attempts to overthrow the republic, but it can be said with certainty that many were convinced that such plans were afoot. It seems, therefore, to be asking a great deal to wonder why, amidst this turmoil, the French could not agree on more audacious social programs. Can British or American progressives, faced with no plausible threats to their constitutional orders, be credited with more solid achievements? Is it not, for every Western society, difficult to assess movements cut short by the Great War? Moreover, solidarism, or the social conscience that informed it, seems to have evolved predictably into "Radical Socialism,"[47] with its endorsement of planning and its acceptance of the welfare state.

It was, of course, Emile Durkheim who gave the most ramified and suggestive account of the civic morality of solidarism. He urged compellingly that Frenchmen consciously assume the responsibilities that solidarity imposed upon them. His work, as a whole, vindicated Radical politics – and was so intended. Insofar as a triumphant radicalism was able to give a coherent, theoretical account of itself, that account was provided by Durkheim. Much as Michelet's writings had suggested to republicans what they must understand in order to take power, Durkheim's sociology told them what they must understand in order to hold it. Neither *laissez faire* nor collectivist, neither materialist nor spiritualist, neither atomist nor holist, Durkheim's work transcended many quarrels of the nineteenth century. To understand it is essential to a historical interpretation of French radicalism. Durkheim had always maintained that philosophical speculation was, inescapably, reflection about one's own society. Certainly, that is true of his theorizing, a lifework shaped by the partisan contests that he so candidly joined.

The son of a rabbi, Durkheim was born in 1858 at Epinal in the Vosges. The town of his birth, curiously, had long provided France with revolutionary iconography, the polychrome *images d'Epinal* that depict scenes from the Revolution and the revolutionary wars. His works, like these popular graphics, fostered republican spirit. He would explicitly acknowledge the reliance of a rationalist tradition upon imagery and ritual and see in that dependence, as he would in every other, not antagonism but completion. Ritual was not, for Durkheim, an alternative to reason: "Men cannot celebrate ceremonies for which they see no reason, nor can they accept a faith they in no way understand . . . merely to maintain itself it must be justified, that is to say, a theory must be made of it."[48]

Moreover, although the mature Durkheim became a thorough *laïc* of startling urbanity ("Between God and society lies the choice [of the source of moral authority] . . . Both [explanations] are coherent. I can only add that I myself am quite indifferent to this choice, since I see in Divinity only society transfigured and symbolically expressed"),[49] his early experience of Judaism, a religious practice grounded in the study of history and law, evidently prepared him to describe a civic religion. He readily imagined holidays as commemorations of historical events rather than of miracles and conceived of rituals as rites of solidarity rather than as sacraments.[50]

Durkheim's intellectual formation soon ceased to be rabbinic; he became preeminently a *normalien*; he was a principal spokesman of the Radical academic establishment and a beneficiary of their administrative patronage. After receiving one of the first French government scholarships to study in Germany, he taught at Sens, a Radical stronghold in the Yonne, where, in a speech to his students, he echoed the proselytizing spirit of Mayor Guichard: "To wish for the truth only the restricted cult of a few initiates is to diminish it."[51] Louis Liard, the national director of higher education, soon found him a desirable post in free-thinking Bordeaux. There, Durkheim occupied a new chair of pedagogy and social science and became president of the Jeunesse laïque. His distinguished career within the republican University culminated in 1906 with the creation for him of the first chair of sociology at the Sorbonne.[52]

Few of Durkheim's ideas were original. All his deepest beliefs were fundamental elements of the republican vision: that progress made men at once more united and more free; that authority must have a human, and thus an intelligible and responsible foundation; that the exercise of critical reason was itself a moral activity. Durkheim made of these convictions a powerful and coherent theory. His synthesis vindicated the uses of reason in ethical controversy and posited society itself as the source of moral obligation. Above all, Durkheim and the Radicals saw complementarity where others saw conflict: in the industrial division of labor but, more generally, also in relations between individuals and society, between duty and desire, between reason and faith, between the real and the ideal.[53]

At every point, in method and substance, Durkheim's work upheld Radical principles. His determination to "treat the facts of the moral life according to the methods of the positive sciences"[54] supported their optimistic rationalism. His arguments about the interdependence of the real and the ideal lent plausibility to opportunist incrementalism as a political strategy. His criticism of Herbert Spencer distinguished Radicals from free-market liberals while repudiating Catholic characterization of modern democracy as amoral, egoistic, and rootless. His conviction that *a priori* categories were not innate, but grounded in social experience, confirmed their emphasis on education. Lastly, his anthropological account of certain historic events as rites of collective self-definition gave substance to their cult of the Revolution.

Steven Lukes has noted, in a scholarly and sympathetic biography, that Durkheim was continually "preoccupied" with the "threat of irrationalism."[55] Certainly, Durkheim and the Radicals did not live in an age that permitted them to dismiss attacks on reason as fanciful anachronism. Therefore, they deliberately repudiated "that antithesis between science and ethics with which mystics of all times have wished to cloud human reason . . . " Durkheim demanded a large role of science, "conscience carried to its highest point of clarity,"[56] because he believed that the alternative was civil war: Between irreconcilable values, force decides. He relied also, as did other solidarists, upon the prestige of science to countervail the force of capital: "The growth of the economic life is such that the scientific function alone is able to dispute its ground."[57]

Durkheim recognized that reasonable men differed. He insisted, however, that political discourse rest upon "social facts" and experiences accessible to all.[58] Moreover, some "facts" about society were demonstrable: Indeed, the fact most strikingly apparent to Durkheim was that moral codes changed. "[Ethics] does develop in history and in the realm of historical causes . . . Whatever it is at any given moment, the conditions in which men live do not permit it to be otherwise, and the proof is that it changes as conditions change, and only then."[59]

Does this compel intelligent men to accept the imperfections of their society? No, Durkheim believed, it was not necessary to be an "indifferent or resigned spectator," but a person must train himself to treat reality with "extreme prudence."[60] He inveighed – as did all republicans after 1848 – against hopes for a social "miracle." Political reform could not be achieved arbitrarily, without its social prerequisites: In this, republican edict was as powerless as imperial *bon plaisir*.

He always spoke of progress in terms of growth, unfolding, immanence. "For the ideal rests on nothing if it does not keep its roots in reality." (In a later formulation he wrote, "The ideal society is not outside the real society, it is a part of it . . . We cannot hold to one without holding to the other.")[61] These statements can be read in very different ways. They can suggest that what ought to be differs so trivially from what exists that not much effort should be expended to bring it about. Or (and I think this was Durkheim's meaning, as it was the Radicals') they may promise that a society that is able to imagine liberty and fraternity is capable of realizing them.

His political intent was clear: to preserve and perfect the republic. His philosophical feat was to define an idealism grounded in shared social experience. He proceeded phenomenologically: Logical necessity is experienced differently from probability; moral obligation cannot be reduced to prudence. Nevertheless, neither the concepts that form the basis of logical reasoning nor the values that govern moral deliberation can possibly be innate. That hypothesis fails to explain the actually existing variety of categories, but the suggestion that these categories are arrived at *a posteriori* cannot account either for their general (if not positively universal) character or (and this he believed to be a more serious shortcoming) for the authority they exercise over the intelligences they pattern.[62] He concluded that there must be a social *a priori* – general truths rooted in social experience. Individuals experienced a force superior to themselves, a constraint that emanated from society. Speculating – a bit before Freud did – about the ways in which people might imagine society external to them, Durkheim described projection:[63]

> Assuredly, this representation [of a sanction superior to us] is illusory . . . Since these sentiments have exceptional force because of their collective origin . . . they appear to us as an echo in us of a force which is foreign to us . . . We are thus forced to project them outside ourselves, to attribute what concerns them to some exterior object. We know today how partial alienations of personality thus come about.[64]

Nevertheless, Durkheim did not believe society to be merely hallucinatory. It existed for him as palpably as France, the nation, did for the Radicals. Significantly, he used the same arguments to establish the autonomy of the social realm as he did to dignify the mental or spiritual one. He much resented the "accusations of materialism levelled against us."[65] Adopting arguments developed by French physiologists to describe living tissue without recourse to immaterial or supernatural forces, Durkheim insisted that social phenomena were no more adequately explained in terms of the society's component individuals than individual consciousness itself by bodily organs or living cells by molecules. The whole is composed of nothing but its parts, but organization has made it qualitatively different from its parts.

At the same time Durkheim insisted upon the significance of the individual; heightened individuation defined what he called "organic solidarity." Moreover, he believed that culture was important preeminently because it created personalities: "Society cannot exist except in and through individual consciousness, this force must also penetrate us and organize itself within us." Society was, above all, composed of "ideas, beliefs and sentiments . . . which realized themselves through individuals."[66] Although there may be conceptual problems with this formulation, it precisely captures that union of perfervid patriotism and ebullient individuality at which the Radicals excelled. History had made them French. It was a responsibility, of course, but what a glorious chance!

Durkheim shared the Radicals' historic self-consciousness; and it was this awareness of the social origins of particular sorts of personalities that gave Durkheim his compelling insight into revolutionary moments, the notion of "collective effervescence."[67] In explaining revolution he was not concerned with underlying socioeconomic change, which he simply assumed ("It is true that we take as self-evident that social life depends upon its material foundation"),[68] but with the collective *prise de conscience*. Of course, feudalism had been undermined in France by myriad forces, but Durkheim's account of the night of August 4, situated significantly within a discussion of the ecstatic *corrobboris* of aborigines, addressed not the process of change, but the final trancelike moment when cognizance is taken of it: When "changes are not merely of shades and degrees[,] men become different."[69]

This is the authentic voice of radicalism: Everything has changed; nothing is the same. Above all, Frenchmen have changed: they have called themselves citizens and held themselves to be equals. Durkheim recognized that these moments are fleeting. The assembly – like the *corrobbori* – disperses, and life resumes, "languishing and dull."[70] Nevertheless, the ideal self-definition, which the rite of solidarity expressed, remains part of the common culture and of every consciousness shaped by it.

This conception of history, the persistence of the apotheosis once glimpsed, entailed the notion of a progressively more just social order approaching and refining its ideals. Durkheim was the most systematic of the solidarists in celebrating evolution while denouncing Social Darwinism, in affirming individual freedom while rejecting *laissez faire* as inadequate to secure it. Much of Durkheim's criticism of liberalism is couched in attacks on its ahistoricism; and although Durkheim's moral polemic was undertaken against the irrationalist right, his professional scorn was reserved for the utilitarians – especially Herbert Spencer, whom he seems to have regarded as the latest and least convincing in a series of contractarian madmen.

Durkheim seized upon the concept of contract to describe the ways in which his social science separated him from the utilitarians. In so doing he used Radical principles that had sometimes been invoked to defend classical liberalism to argue for a more interventionist social policy. First, he pointed out the requisite "precontractual elements of contract." How could men make a compact without a common language? This seemed an obviously minimal condition. As for promise keeping and truth telling being natural to men as men, that premise was too preposterous even for Englishmen to defend. These considerations aside, was not trust in fact prior to the division of labor? Exchanges of goods were not merely sporadic encounters; they presumed a relationship, a willingness to accept dependency. The state should not – and historically did not – confine itself to the enforcing of contracts.

Durkheim held it to be a symptom of social pathology that the economy, now the most significant sphere of social life, should be "anomic," literally lawless. He saw grounds for optimism in the closer scrutiny given the content of contracts, and particularly in the increasingly refined notion of what constituted duress. At one time, if both parties were conscious and neither armed, consent was deemed adequate; but more and more, the state had to be satisfied that the parties were in sufficiently "equivalent" positions, to guarantee that equals were exchanged for equals.[71] As Léon Bourgeois had said, men do not enter into society so that the strong can oppress the weak.

With the solidarists, Durkheim imagined a broader role for the state than arbitration: It was to provide a "milieu in which the individual could develop his faculties in freedom."[72] In accordance with Radical hopes for autonomy, this milieu had to permit participatory liberty. The "professional groups" proposed in the famous 1902 preface to *The Division of Labor* are spheres for self-regulation, not "corporatist" cells in the fascist manner.[73] Above all, his concern for deliberative assemblies was a rationalist's solicitude. Assemblies, Durkheim said, were to the state what reason was to the self: "the sole instrument the collectivity has to prevent any action that is ill-considered or automatic or blind." He likened them, in an uncharacteristically utopian passage, to the conscious mind, which, as it takes control of obscure processes, enlarges the realm of light. Thinking cannot be done for the people, however: "From the moment that the people set themselves the same questions as the state, the state in solving them can no longer disregard what the people are saying."[74] Popular sovereignty, thus conceived, characterizes the modern era as irrefutably as servility defined the old.

Radicals knew that power, however circumscribed, would take forms that eluded democratic control: The state, they believed, was forced to intervene continually against the authoritarian and oligarchic tendencies that they saw as endemic in society. Solidarists proposed political measures to countervail persistent inequalities. Durkheim advocated a large role for the state. Rights have to be won from opposing forces that deny them: "the state must deploy energies equal to those for which it has to provide a counter-balance." And Durkheim anticipated victory. "It is society, we find, that is coming to exercise complete dominion over nature, to lay down the law for it and to set this moral equality over physical inequality which is, in fact, inherent in the nature of things."[75]

Whither was this evolution tending? The Radicals, attacked for their lack of social program, could not describe a perfect society because they did not expect history to end. "What kinds of subordination are legitimate and which unlawful? There is no final answer to this problem."[76]

It has been common to ridicule the Radicals' celebration of revolution in the eighteenth century and of meliorism in the nineteenth. George Sorel, for example, wrote, "The optimist passes with remarkable facility from revolutionary anger to the most ridiculous social pacifism . . . It is not always self-interest that suggests these expressions of satisfaction, as people have often believed: self-interest is strongly aided by vanity and by the illusions of philosophy."[77] The Radicals had accomplished one major and far-reaching reform. If their vision ended with secular rationalism and solidarity, it was because they believed that there was a logic in history – a coherence of ideas and institutions within every epoch and every society. They believed themselves to be in systematic antagonism to the Old Regime. When the moral and social basis of the old order had been destroyed and the new order legitimated, they believed, social problems would sort themselves out according to the new principles.

As Matthew Arnold said, France believed her society to be governed by reason rather than custom, by right rather than by fact, and "in this belief there is a part of truth and a part of delusion."[78] Arnold suggested that it would be more profitable for the French to concern themselves with the delusions and for others to reflect upon the truth.

Let us then consider the truth. From their failures republicans had learned the need to enracinate political power. "The school of decentralization," they believed, had to teach reason, disinterestedness, and generosity. The multifarious efforts of the 1860s, which continued in the associations of the seventies – the schools, lectures, and libraries – were instrumental and, I would argue, crucial to republican political success. The Radical republicans unquestionably campaigned and distributed patronage but they had a wider purpose: to preach and exemplify republican mores. The circles of the Ligue de l'enseignement and the myriad groups related to it gave social and political, if not economic content to the idea of equality. Within the league, people felt themselves to be citizens. They knew that they were acting as citizens should act and derived from this consciousness a certain dignity.

This feeling of moral worth was what equality had always meant. Arnold, no lover of unrest, had recognized it, even in 1860, as the imperishable legacy of the Revolution. Equality had given

> to the body of the common people, a self-respect, an enlargement of spirit, a consciousness of counting for something in their country's

action, which had raised them in the scale of humanity. The common people, in France, seems to me the soundest part of the French nation. They seem to be more free from the two opposite degradations of multitudes, brutality and servility, to have a more developed human life, more of what distinguishes everywhere the cultured classes from the vulgar than the common people in any other country with which I am acquainted.[79]

Unlike the successive governments that had proclaimed the principles of 1789, the members of the Ligue de l'enseignement understood that political principles had to be ratified in experience. They uttered republican homilies and made them part of the curriculum; and their organization, which established the principles of the Revolution as the national orthodoxy, gave those principles sense and authenticity. As the indirect but necessary consequence of these efforts, Radicals developed an account of secular ethics that was genuinely post-Enlightenment: They saw reason unfolding in history within an organic social order and defined its progressive movement. Their achievement was themselves, a lucid and self-respecting political class.

Notes

Introduction

1. Jean Macé, *Les Origines de la Ligue de l'enseignement, 1861–1870*, p. 12. "Nous avons affaire à un peuple acquis jusque dans ses moelles à la Révolution, et mariant par tradition la peur du mot à l'amour profond de la chose."
2. Marx wrote of the "shamelessly simple domination of the sabre and the cowl . . . Society now seems to have fallen back behind its point of departure." Karl Marx, *The Eighteenth Brumaire of Louis Napoleon*, pp. 18–19; Alexis de Tocqueville, *Souvenirs, Oeuvres Complètes*, p. 75, "une vilaine tragédie jouée par des histrions de province"; Jules Michelet, *Le Peuple*, p. 150.
3. Theodore Zeldin, *France 1848–1945*, vol. 1, p. 388.
4. Nicholas Wahl, "The French Political System," in *Patterns of Government*, Samuel H. Beer and Adam B. Ulam, (eds.), p. 238.
5. "Heureux les héros morts avant 1804!" Stendhal, *Lucien Leuwen*, p. 22.
6. Georges Lefebvre, *The Coming of the French Revolution*, p. 122.
7. Jules Michelet, *The History of the French Revolution*, pp. 19–27.
8. Emile Durkheim, *The Division of Labor in Society*, passim.
9. In *Feudal Society*, Marc Bloch brilliantly evoked a world without coins, clocks or legal codes. It is not a place of idyllic harmony, but a chaos wherein man cannot marshal his faculties to stave off cold, famine, wolves, or marauders, a culture unable to distinguish between natural and social catastrophes and defenseless before both. Marc Bloch, *Feudal Society*, vol. 1, pp. 59–87.
10. Cf., for example, Karl Popper, *The Enemies of the Open Society*, or J. L. Talmon's attack on Rousseau in *The Origins of Totalitarian Democracy*.
11. Alexis de Tocqueville, *Democracy in America*, vol. 1, pp. 408–9.
12. Denis W. Brogan, *The Development of Modern France*, pp. 147–8.
13. Maurice Agulhon, *Le Cercle dans la France bourgeoise, 1810–1848*, pp. 70–85.
14. Macé, *Les Origines*, pp. 203, 212–215. Jean Macé began to organize the league in the fall of 1866 with two articles in a Left Bonapartist newspaper, *L'Opinion nationale*. The first, appearing on October 25, described the Belgian Ligue de l'enseignement. Then, on November 15, Macé issued his "First Appeal for Adherents," answered by three almost mythical Frenchmen: a railway conductor, a stonecutter, and a policeman.
15. Prescient Frenchmen feared, after Sadowa, some catastrophe for France. Cf. Mme Edgar Quinet's account in *Edgar Quinet, Depuis l'Exil*, pp. 303–6, of renewed interest in Quinet's "clairvoyant" book *France et Allemagne*, which had appeared in 1831.
16. Karl Marx, *Capital*, vol. 1, p. 718.
17. Zeldin, *France 1848–1945*, vol. 2, p. 1123.
18. Ibid., vol. I, p. 683.
19. Ibid., vol. 2 pp. 1119–53.
20. Ibid., vol. 2, p. 1129.
21. Edmund Burke, *Reflections on the Revolution in France*, p. 76.
22. Alexis de Tocqueville, *The Old Regime and the French Revolution*, p. 13. In an earlier period the idea of one law for all estates was almost incomprehensible, "but there are other periods when it suffices to show them the image of

such a law, however distantly and confusedly, for all to recognize it and rush to embrace it."

23. Zeldin, *France 1848–1945*, vol. 2, p. 1123.
24. Isser Woloch, *The Jacobin Legacy*, p. 100.
25. Zeldin, *France 1848–1945*, vol. 1, p. 467.
26. Pierre Barral, *Les Fondateurs de la Troisième République*, pp. 69–70.
27. Erckmann-Chatrian's *Waterloo* captures, as their novels generally do, the popular republican feeling. After the coup of Brumaire (November 9, 1799), many Jacobins rallied to Bonaparte. Some were even reconciled to the empire when it was proclaimed in 1804, believing that Napoleon might salvage something of the Revolution – chiefly, the careers open to talent and the modernized civil and penal codes. Erckmann-Chatrian's republican watchmaker, le père Goulden, however, opposed him resolutely until, having glimpsed the Restoration, he opts for the emperor: "Do you believe that these processions, these expiations, [for the "sacrilege" of regicide], these fulminations against the sale of the *biens nationaux* and the 'twenty-five years of rebellion,' the continual menace of reestablishing the old regime . . . these could continue? . . . I am and shall remain for the Republic and the Rights of Man. And it is because of this I prefer Napoleon to the comte d'Artois, the émigrés, the missionaries, and the miracle mongers; he, at least, is forced to retain something of our revolution." Erckmann-Chatrian, *Waterloo, Contes et romans nationaux*, vol. 4, pp. 315–16.
28. I am grateful to Professor Laurence Wylie for teaching me the significance of *droits, places,* and *vérités acquis* (or *acquises*). One sees, for example, in Jean Barois' description of evolution as a "scientific truth definitely established" frequent evocation of the parallel cumulative progress of reason and justice. Roger Martin du Gard, *Jean Barois*, p. 24.
29. Quotation is from Peter Stearns, *Paths to Authority*, p. 9.
30. Jules Michelet, *Jeanne D'Arc*, pp. 172–6.
31. Elizabeth Eisenstein, "The Evolution of the Jacobin Tradition in France," p. 16, cites August Dide, writing in this vein about work of the sculptor Dalou in *Chronicle de la république française*. Mrs. Eisenstein, a student of Crane Brinton, wrote most sensitively, long before family history had become fashionable, about the political links between generations and about the nonverbal transmission of political ideas: Edgar Quinet's mother read him Voltaire; Renan's mother sang the "Chant du Départ." Mrs. Eisenstein noted, too, that many who had been taught to sympathize with the Revolution believed in their childhood that theirs was the only family that approved of it. Ibid., pp. 90–1.
32. Sanford J. Elwitt, *The Making of the Third Republic*, p. 182. Elwitt faults the radicals' commitment to liberty on the basis of statements like Jules Ferry's that "individualism . . . can neither explain nor master the complex of social relations . . . [it is] the fundamental negation of all social life" (ibid., p. 184). Had this appeared – as it easily might have done – in the writings of the young Marx, one imagines that Elwitt would acknowledge its force.
33. The Law of Association, legalizing trade unions, was proposed in 1881 by Henri Allain-Targé and passed by a Radical assembly. Elwitt, p. 258. Elwitt cites only one instance of strike breaking before 1906, admittedly, an astounding one: In October 1871, radical lawyers in Roanne informed police about a strike meeting and then rushed to offer themselves as counsel for the accused. Elwitt, pp. 86–93.

34. Indeed, his characterization of the French economy in 1870 as an "advanced industrial" one is questionable. Ibid., p. 26.
35. Ibid., p. 257.
36. Tocqueville, *Souvenirs*, pp. 34, 49–50.
37. Jules Ferry, *Les Luttes électorales en 1863*, pp. 6–7. V. F. de Persigny, later styled "duc de Persigny," served Louis Bonaparte as minister of the interior in the critical months following the coup d'état from January 1852 until July 1854, and again from November 1860 until June 1863, presiding over the early years of the "Liberal Empire." His "chivalrous attachment" to the emperor, his indifference to the authoritarian or liberal character of the regime, led Ferry to dismiss him as a man "outside his times," incapable of "systematic politics." The quotation is from ibid., p. 65: "cette classe raisonneuse qui se croient indépendante."
38. Marx, *The Eighteenth Brumaire*, p. 122, pp. 31–3. These appointed municipal commissions were no hypothetical danger: Hundreds of municipal councils were dissolved in the early years of the empire, and municipal self-government, including the right to elect mayors, remained an important popular grievance until the collapse of the empire. Ibid., p. 62.
39. Tocqueville, *Souvenirs*, p. 75.
40. René Rémond has emphasized that universal suffrage meant an electorate increased *fifty* times over the narrow *pays légal* of the July Monarchy. René Rémond, *The Right Wing in France from 1815 to de Gaulle*, p. 127. Under the Orleanist constitution there was 1 elector for every 170 people, as compared with 1 for every 26 in Britain after 1832. Jean Lhomme, *La Grande Bourgeoisie au pouvoir, 1830–1880*, p. 73.
41. Marx, *The Eighteenth Brumaire*, p. 54. Among those who remained republican, however, there was an effort to portray the rising as a tragically wrongheaded attempt to preserve the republic from the monarchists in the assembly. Corbon, a printer and a founder of the "press of the proletariat" and one of the few "workers" elected to the Constituent Assembly in 1848, wrote in 1863 that the June Days had been a product of a "frightful misunderstanding." He recalled that a delegation of workers from the Faubourg Saint-Antoine came to the assembly on the night of June 23 to assure themselves that its members supported the republic. Seeing his "pained astonishment," Corbon said, they told him that the city was full of rumors that the republic was in danger. A. Corbon, *Le Secret du peuple de Paris*, p. 198. At the time of writing, Corbon was active in support of "workers' candidacies" and insistent that "blame not be cast upon the people for the diminution of our liberties." Ibid., p. 6.
42. The three-year residency requirement demanded by the law of May 31, 1850, effectively disenfranchised a highly mobile work force, which in good times travelled seasonally between agricultural and urban work. In hard times labor was virtually nomadic. Furthermore, the *livret*, a sort of internal passport for workers, was retained by the employer. Georges Duveau described the effect of the law as a decrease of 28 percent in the number of voters, an electorate of 9.6 million reduced to 6,809,000. The reduction was far more drastic in democratic strongholds: In the department of the Seine (Paris and its environs) the electorate was diminished by 63 percent; in the Rhône, by 40 percent; in the Loire and the Seine-Inférieure, by 43 percent; in the Nord, by 51 percent. Georges Duveau, *La Vie ouvrière en France sous le Second Empire*, p. 59.

43. Georges Duveau, *Les Instituteurs*, p. 86.
44. Michelet and his close friend Edgar Quinet had taught a joint course on the Jesuits that had been banned at the Collège de France in the early 1840s: The two were probably the most eminent and notorious anticlericals in France. Charton, a republican and a sentimental Christian, was an important *vulgarisateur*, founder of the *Magasin pittoresque*, an early and immensely popular illustrated paper, and in the sixties, an opposition candidate in the Yonne. Renouvier and Martin, later an enthusiastic member of the Ligue de l'enseignement, wrote "Republican Catechisms" for Carnot. Cf. Duveau, *Les Instituteurs*, pp. 73–5; Edward K. Kaplan, *Michelet's Poetic Vision*, p. 5.
45. Duveau, *Les Instituteurs*, pp. 76–7. *Obligatoire, gratuit, libre: Gratuit* is always translated as "free," and *libre* as "independent," in this book in order to avoid confusion between those two very different objects. Carnot did not yet use the word *laïc*, which became part of the radical formula, "free, compulsory, and secular," in the sixties, when it was used by Victor Duruy, minister of public instruction from 1863–9, and by opposition candidates in their *professions de foi*. Condorcet's *Rapport et projet du décret sur l'organisation générale de l'instruction publique*, presented to the National Assembly on April 20 and 21, 1792, included a provision for adult education: "Each Sunday, the teacher will conduct a public lecture attended by citizens of all ages . . . He will develop therein those moral rules and principles, as well as those national laws, the ignorance of which would inhibit the citizen from understanding and exercising his rights." Condorcet, *Rapport*, pp. 6–7.
46. Duveau, *Les Instituteurs*, p. 84. Corbon was one of only three workers elected to the Constituent Assembly. Corbon, *Le Secret du peuple de Paris*, p. 4. It was with the greatest reluctance that workers stood for election in 1848 and with the greatest trepidation that votes were cast for them.
47. Antoine Prost, *L'Enseignement en France, 1800–1967*, p. 173.
48. A good summary of the law's effects is found in Prost, *L'Enseignement*, pp. 173–7. Communes with more than 800 inhabitants were required to maintain girls' schools; and, to provide them with teachers, the empire authorized 923 new congregations of nuns between 1852 and 1859. Ibid., p. 103.
49. Adolphe Robert, *Statistique pour servir à l'histoire du 2 décembre, 1851*, pp. 263–4. Cf. also Eugène Tenot, *Paris en décembre 1851* and *La Province en décembre 1851*, two works appearing in 1868.
50. Tocqueville, *Souvenirs*, p. 39, "incapable et indigne."
51. Cf. Jean Lhomme's useful distinctions in *La Grande Bourgeoisie*, p. 3.
52. Michelet, *Le Peuple*, p. 174.
53. Indeed, sociability was considered the most valuable trait of national character during this period. Michelet spoke of "l'amitié," as a fitting French social goal. He believed French people to be incapable of cooperation on utilitarian grounds merely: They must unite in sympathy, in an "union des esprits." Michelet, *Le Peuple*, pp. 229 and 249. Laboulaye thought that the French were the sociable race *par excellence*. Laboulaye, *Le Parti libéral, son programme et son avenir*, p. 42. Positivists, too, began to emphasize a social instinct or "affective principle": Jules Ferry acknowledged as the source of his positivism Auguste Comte's *Discours sur l'ensemble du positivisme*, the formulation that most stressed sentiment. Louis Legrand, *L'Influence du positivisme dans l'oeuvre scolaire de Jules Ferry*, pp. 32–3.
54. For example, *La Société anonyme des école laïques de la Troisième arrondissement de Paris*, Archives nationales, F[17] 12529.

55. This concern was not confined to priest-baiting journalists and village atheists. For example, Tocqueville violated his characteristic chivalry to deplore his sister-in-law's "pious egoism." In a moment of national crisis, she was incapable of including in her lamentations any concern for her country. He believed her to be "the most respectable woman and the worst citizen one could encounter." Tocqueville, *Souvenirs*, p. 62.

56. Quoted in positive form in J. B. Bury, *History of the Papacy in the Nineteenth Century*, p. 40. Bury noted, too, that the fifth thesis explicitly condemned the notion that revealed truth is imperfect and "therefore subject to a continuous and indefinite progress corresponding to the advance of human reason." Ibid., p. 12.

57. Religious papers were not deemed "political" and therefore were dispensed from the requirement to seek authorization and to post "caution money." Religious orders were subject to the authorization requirements, but the basic diocesan and parochial structure was unconstrained. Jean Maurain, *La Politique ecclésiastique du Second Empire, 1852–1869*, p. 156.

58. Edgar Quinet, *L'Enseignement du peuple, Oeuvres complètes*, p. 13. Quinet, professor at the Collège de France and representative of the Seine in 1848, disdained the general amnesty of 1859 and lived in intransigent exile until 1870.

59. Cf. Richard Cobb's remarkably concrete and evocative essay, "The Revolutionary Mentality in France," in Cobb, *A Second Identity*, pp. 122–41.

1. Defining the alternative society

1. Montesquieu, *Considerations on the Causes of the Greatness of the Romans and Their Decline*, p. 205. Montesquieu's chapters on the decline of the Eastern Empire are rich with hints about the "revitalizing" public effects of iconoclasm and with cautions as to the manner in which religious passions should be assuaged: "One should pay great attention to the disputes of theologians but as covertly as possible. The trouble one seems to take in pacifying them adds to their prestige; it shows them that their thinking is so important that it determines the tranquillity of the state and the security of the prince." Ibid., p. 209. He suggested, too, an interesting distinction between fanaticism, which invigorates, and bigotry, which enfeebles: "We see this in a famous revolution of modern times, when Cromwell's army was like the Arabs', and the armies of Ireland and Scotland were like the Greeks'." Ibid., p. 203.

2. "Modern Man, victim of the division of labor, often condemned to a narrow specialty, where he loses the sentiment of the general life and where he himself atrophies, needs to find at home a young and serene spirit, less specialized, better balanced, who can draw him out of his *métier* and reawaken in him a feeling for the great and sweet harmony." Jules Michelet, *Du Prêtre, de la femme, de la famille*, p. 272; "le triste loisir," ibid., p. 39.

3. The French bourgeoisie had not unanimously embraced Louis Napoleon as the "savior of society." In the general elections of 1852, government candidates got 83 percent of the vote cast, but this figure amounted to only 53 percent of the eligible electorate; moreover, departmental results often obscure large margins of defeat in traditionally republican cities. Official candidates lost badly, for example, in Brest, Saint-Etienne, Marseille, and the Burgundian towns of Beaune and Auxerre, and 70 percent of the voters in

Bordeaux *intra muros* refused to vote at all. Theodore Zeldin, *The Political System of Napoleon III*, pp. 39–40.

4. Charles Bigot, *Les Classes dirigeantes*, pp. 305–6. Bigot has been presented as a critic of the republicans on the strength of his demand for free secondary education and for a better sense than was common among republicans of his period for the social obstacles to equality of opportunity; but his conclusion that hierarchy is inevitable and proper so long as it is "nature's own hierarchy of talent," (ibid., pp. 6–7), taken along with a full endorsement of the government's educational initiatives in his introduction to the 1881 edition ("France has shown a political will of which many thought her incapable." Ibid., pp. I–II), reveal him to be a classic radical. His curiously cerebral notion of social progress also supports this characterization. Bigot steadfastly and in principle defended the rights of the poor and expected the ruling classes to recognize these rights when *leisure* permitted their intelligence a freer play.

5. Emile Durkheim, *The Division of Labor in Society*, p. 3.

6. Gustave Flaubert, *Dictionnaire des idées reçues*, Oeuvres, vol. 2, p. 1021.

7. This division between the Catholic and radical bourgeoisie has been a long-standing one. In the 1930s, Paul Nizan bitterly remarked on the *bien-pensant* horror of the "common." The word suggested disgraceful things: an unsanctified common-law marriage, the pauper's communal grave, the Paris Commune itself. Paul Nizan, *Antoine Bloyé*, p. 203.

8. Quoted by André Lavertujon, *Gambetta inconnu*, pp. 58–9.

9. Alexis de Tocqueville, *Democracy in America*, vol. 1, p. 7.

10. Pierre-Joseph Proudhon, *De la Justice dans la révolution et dans l'église*, p. 5.

11. Michelet despised *Les Paysans* for Balzac's picture of a savage and deceitful peasantry (Michelet, *Le Peuple*, pp. 57–8): "Under this hideous sketch he has brashly written a word that is the name of most of the inhabitants of France." Michelet was angered by "neo-Catholic writer[s], that impotent race, mourners for the Middle Ages who can only lament and copy . . . the peasant, because that world is only a destroyer." Ibid., p. 90.

12. Prévost-Paradol, *La France nouvelle*, pp. 9–10; ibid., pp. 238–9; ibid., p. 243; ibid., p. 233. I have added the emphasis. Prévost-Paradol further predicted that disestablishment, although inevitable, would have a baleful effect on the government that finally accomplished it.

13. Compare their relative acceptance in France with the furor over Catholic (1829) and Jewish (1858) emancipation in Britain and the exclusion from Oxford and Cambridge of Dissenters. (They were admitted as undergraduates in 1854 and 1856, respectively, but fellowships remained closed to all but Anglicans until 1871.) Brian Simon, *Studies in the History of Education, 1780–1870*, p. 296.

14. Albert Mathiez "Les Philosophes et la séparation de l'église et de l'état" (first published in the *Revue historique* in 1910) in *La Révolution et l'église*, pp. 1–25. Mathiez argued that a "neutral" state was not one of the possibilities imagined in 1789. None of the philosophes ever imagined that religious and civil authority might be separated. Most were thoroughgoing Erastians and Mathiez saw the Civil Constitution of the Clergy as the best effort of their disciples to organize a Gallican church allowing ample dignity to the *citoyen-curé* who preached passages from the gospels that were compatible with fraternity and *civisme*. In his study of the controversy surrounding the promulgation of revolutionary decrees from the pulpit ("La Lecture des décrets

au prône," in *La Revolution et l'église*, pp. 26–65, first published in *Les Annales révolutionnaires*, 1908), Mathiez found much evidence of country priests who were willing to expound the programs of the new government. Some were, no doubt, vicars of Bray, eager to clothe themselves with whatever dignity the age offered; others seemed to be ardent reformers. One asked that decrees be sent in duplicate so that priests might rally support for revolutionary measures if the civil authorities flagged. Only among priests described by contemporaries as "instruit" or "zélé" did Mathiez find refusals based on a discrimination between sacred and profane.

15. Prévost-Paradol suggested that both Catholics and freethinkers feared an end to the *budget des cultes*, but for mutually contradictory reasons: Churchmen dreaded a loss of funds, and their opponents feared that an independent church would be more influential. He recommended a gradual removal of the subsidy, leaving the church free to seek out and employ other resources, with the sole exception of land. This restriction he presented as being in the church's best interest: Ownership of landed property, he said, was the only practice that could make the church odious to the people. Prévost-Paradol, *La France nouvelle*, p. 249.

16. In 1853 a decree of the minister of public instruction ordered prefects to set for each commune the maximum number of pupils who might be admitted free. Victor Duruy abolished the maximum (May 28, 1866) and ordered that no indigent child be refused schooling. Victor Duruy, *Notes et souvenirs, 1811–1894*, vol. 1, p. 209.

17. An example from Britain recalls that disestablishmentarian concerns of this sort were not felt by the French alone. In the 1890s the left wing of the Liberal Party (often members of the National Education Association, a group not unlike the Ligue de l'enseignement) demanded that Church of England schools, the so-called "voluntary schools," receive no public moneys unless they agreed to accept elected members on their governing boards as well as Her Majesty's Inspectors sitting *ex officio*. No one spoke of abolishing the gentry or banishing the vicar, but, it was felt, they were not entitled to *govern*. Gillian Sutherland, *Policy-Making in Elementary Education, 1870–1895*, pp. 284, 293, 303–5.

18. Balzac, *Lost Illusions*, p. 17.

19. "Agissements Cléricaux," *Archives Nationales*, F[19] 5610; Jacques Ozouf, *Nous les maîtres d'école*, p. 34: "des représailles féroces sur certains commerçants."

20. Maurain, *La politique écclésiastique*, p. 5.

21. Charles de Montalembert in *L'Univers* of December 14, 1851, quoted by Maurain, *La politique écclésiastique*, p. 6.

22. Michelet and Quinet were purged from the Collège de France in 1852. Etienne Vacherot, a philosopher who became mayor of the Fifth Arrondissement of Paris in 1870, was forced from the Ecole Normale Supérieure. Paul Hazard, *Michelet, Quinet, Mickiewicz, et la vie intérieure du Collège de France de 1838 à 1852*, p. 275, and Léon Ollé-Laprune, *Etienne Vacherot*, pp. 1–2.

   Physiologists like Ange Guépin, a prolific writer (*Traité d'economie sociale*, 1833; *Philosophie du socialisme*, 1850; *Philosophie du XIXe siècle*, 1854; *Esquisse d'une philosophie maçonnique*, 1868) and an ardent freemason, were ousted from faculties of medicine for republicanism and "materialism." Many lost minor government posts at the same time. Guépin, for example, ceased to serve as medical inspector at the port of Nantes.

23. The works drew upon courses taught jointly at the Collège de France,

which led to the suspension of both men. All were reprinted numerous times; *The Jesuits* was in its tenth printing in 1873; Edgar Quinet, *Les Jésuites*, *Oeuvres complètes*, vol. 2, p. i. (the set of the collected works given to Harvard by Madame Quinet is inscribed June first, 1899); *The People* reappeared in 1866, and *Du Prêtre*, interestingly, in 1861, a year in which several ecclesiastics were brought to trial on morals charges. Maurain, *La Politique ecclésiastique* pp. 535–6. Maurain noted that for the first time in the Second Empire, relations between the civil authority and the church hierarchy were insufficiently cordial to permit out-of-court settlements. Michelet's new preface paid tribute to the "reawakening" of French justice and to the light that it shed on clerical celibacy.

24. Quinet, *L'Enseignement*, p. 5.
25. Ibid., p. 4. Quinet mistakenly attributed to Montesquieu the notion – most pernicious, he felt, for France – that religion is a discrete element that develops independently of other social institutions. Montesquieu had written, Quinet thought, paradoxically, that harsh religious doctrine permitted mild civil law and political absolutism accorded with easy absolution. Montesquieu had certainly seen these as complementarities. Ibid., p. 152.
26. Charles Sauvestre, *Monita secreta*, pp. 23–9, and Sauvestre, *Sur les genoux de l'église*, p. 51: ". . . les rêveries malsaines . . . détourner du travail."
    Gustave Lefrançais, a communist of strict personal rectitude, dismissed Sauvestre as a *mangeur du prêtre* in his discussion of orators of the sixties. Lefrançais, *Souvenirs d'un révolutionnaire*, pp. 304–5. Nonetheless, during this period Lefrançais himself wrote for a militantly anticlerical paper, *L'Action maçonnique*, which strongly supported freemasonic initiatives for secular education.
27. Gustave Flaubert, *Madame Bovary*, *Oeuvres*, vol. 1, p. 361. "Moi, si j'étais le gouvernement, je voudrais qu'on saignât les prêtres une fois par mois . . . tous les mois, une large phlébotomie, dans l'intérêt de la police et des moeurs."
28. Ibid., p. 323. "Les comparaisons de fiancé, d'époux, d'amant céleste et de mariage éternel qui reviennent dans les sermons lui soulevaient au fond de l'âme des douceurs inattendues"; "le plus grand baiser d'amour qu'elle eut jamais donné." Ibid., pp. 587–8.
29. Marie-Antoine-Jules Sénard's defense of Flaubert, printed as the appendix to the novel, ibid., p. 677.
30. Tocqueville, *Democracy in America*, vol. 2, pp. 25–6; Tocqueville, *The Old Regime*, pp. 112–13. Earlier in his argument he had stressed that it was as landed proprietors rather than as Christian ministers that priests were attacked during the Revolution. Ibid., pp. 6–7.
31. Pierre Sorlin, *Waldeck-Rousseau*, p. 220. And, here again, Erckmann-Chatrian's novels reflect this republican characterization faithfully. Mendicancy is detested as a form of unearned income. An actively charitable parish priest, the protagonist's schoolmaster, is snubbed by a bishop, representative of a hierarchy as insouciant of his dignity as they are of the welfare of his flock. Erckmann-Chatrian, *Histoire d'un paysan, Contes et romans nationaux*, vol. 1, pp. 76–80.
32. Michael Andrew Screech, *The Rabelaisian Marriage*, p. 27. Screech sees the Renaissance *Querrelle des femmes* as an argument about marriage and celibacy. Ibid., p. 2.
33. Edouard Lockroy, Chamber of Deputies, December 17, 1880, *Official Journal*,

p. 12481, cited in Prost, *L'Enseignement en France*, p. 213.

34. Maria Deraismes, *Une Lettre au clergé français*, p. 75; Erckmann-Chatrian, *L'Ami Fritz, Contes et romans*, vol. 5, p. 3.
35. Balzac, *Le Médecin de campagne*, p. 148.
36. Proudhon, *De la justice*, p. 93; Quinet, *La République*, p. 192.
37. Weber's definition of a religious *Wirtschaftsethik* is found in Max Weber, "The Social Psychology of World Religions," in *From Max Weber*, H. H. Gerth and C. Wright Mills (eds.), p. 267. In the same essay Weber also developed a distinction between "ethical" and "ritual" religious orientations.
38. Michelet, *Du Prêtre*, p. 174.
39. Ibid., pp. 50–1.
40. Quinet, *La République*, p. 253. "Les guerres sociales désorganisent une nation; les guerres religieuses ne font rien de semblable.

    Dans les luttes de religion, chaque parti contient tous les éléments de la société, grands et petits, riches et pauvres, c'est-à-dire, que la masse entière de la nation est représentée dans chaque faction religieuse."
41. Police report, February 9, 1869, on Denis Gros, editor of *L'Excommunié*, *Archives municipales de la ville de Lyon*, AM Lyon I² 61.
42. Ernest Renan, *Souvenirs d'enfance et de jeunesse*, p. 263.
43. "Sache les comprendre et les utiliser." Corbon, *Le Secret*, p. 50. Corbon regretted that the writings of Fourier, perhaps because they were in some respects "bizarre," remained insufficiently appreciated. It was useless, Corbon said, for bourgeois moralists to preach thrift and self-control: Economists ought to pay more attention to the producer than the product, to concern themselves with the "fecund appropriation of the energies that develop in us." Ibid., pp. 41–5.
44. Michelet, *Le Peuple*, pp. 107–8. Michelet's distress recalls that of the young Marx: "The worker feels that he is acting freely only in his animal functions – eating, drinking, and procreating, or at most in his dwelling and adornment – while in his human functions he is nothing but an animal. . . . The worker experiences activity as passivity, power as impotence, procreation as emasculation." Karl Marx, "Alienated Labor," in *Early Writings*, p. 327.
45. Tocqueville, *Souvenirs*, p. 169.
46. "Il gaspillera sa généreuse sève." Corbon, *Le Secret*, p. 89.
47. As Theodore Zeldin has repeatedly argued. Zeldin, *France 1848–1945*, passim.
48. Proudhon, *De la Justice*, p. 8: "Le malheur du temps et la faiblesse des âmes n'en eût retardé la glorieuse et définitive manifestation . . . et [que] c'est cette infidelité à nous-mêmes qui fait notre misère morale et notre servitude."
49. "Puissant en actes, fécond en oeuvres, qui veuille, et qui puisse, et qui crée . . . " Michelet, *Du Prêtre*, p. 294.
50. Significantly, it was with this proverb that Jean Barois's father, a skeptical doctor, concluded his advice to his devout and sickly son. Roger Martin du Gard, *Jean Barois*, p. 21.
51. Cited in Louis Girard, *Les Elections de 1869*, p. 11. Léon Gambetta first used the expression "nouvelles couches" in a speech at Grenoble in September of 1872 announcing the advent of a new social group, "upright in business, loving justice, solicitous of general rights." He spoke of them as part of "the world of labor to which the future belongs," new men who could overwhelm and displace all that was "uncertain, indecisive, and unwholesome" in the bourgeoisie.

52. Macé, "La Vérité sur le suffrage universel," *Les Idées de Jean François*, pp. 16–17.
53. Ibid., p. 20.
54. The Risorgimento was of immense interest to them – perhaps even more than the plight of the Irish and Polish "oppressed nationalities" – because Italian democrats were themselves struggling to establish a secular state grounded in *la cultura laica*. Cf. Clara Lovett, *Guiseppe Ferrari and the Italian Revolution*.
55. Eric Foner, *Free Soil, Free Labor, Free Men*, p. 65.
56. Georges Clemenceau, *American Reconstruction 1865–1870*, p. 24.
57. Foner, *Free Soil*, p. 109.
58. Vacherot, *La Démocratie*, p. viii; Alexander-Thomas Marie, soon to be a deputy and president of the Society for Elementary Instruction, appealed Vacherot's case, and the sentence was reduced from one year to three months (Ollé-Laprune, *Etienne Vacherot*, p. 47); Ange Guépin, *La Philosophie du socialisme*, pp. 269–70.
59. Ange Guépin, *Esquisse d'une philosophie maçonnique*, p. 7.
60. "trop méprisés et trop inconnus." Meyer Schapiro, "Courbet and Popular Imagery: An Essay in Realism and Naïveté," *The Journal of the Warburg and Courtauld Institute,* pp. 164–191.
61. Michelet, *Du Prêtre*, p. ix.
62. Cf. Eric J. Hobsbawm, *Primitive Rebels*, p. 112; Corbon, *Le Secret*, p. 29.
63. Vacherot, *La Démocratie*, p. 112; Ernest Renan, "Conférence faite dans l'ancien Cirque du Prince Imperial," 19 April 1869, in *La Réforme intellectuelle et morale*, pp. 307–8.
64. Stephen Lukes, *Emile Durkheim*, pp. 90–1. Like Kant, Renouvier was concerned with the progressive dignity and autonomy of the individual, but he broached criticisms of Kant's *a priorism* which Durkheim later developed in *Elementary Forms of Religious Life* and in *Primitive Classification*, written with Marcel Mauss. Lukes also noted Durkheim's debt to Wundt, who saw history moving away from groupings, by affinity, of like to like, toward the free union of dissimilar individuals. Alfred Naquet, *Religion, Propriété, Famille*, pp. 284–5.
65. Alain, *Eléments d'une doctrine radicale*, pp. 148–9.
66. Naquet, *Religion*, p. 192. Jules Ferry, "Egalité d'éducation," speech, April 10, 1870, reprinted by the Société d'instruction élémentaire, Paris, 1874, p. 9.
67. Elwitt, *Making of the Third Republic*, p. 198.
68. Charles Robert, *De l'Ignorance*, p. 15.
69. Celestin Hippeau, *L'Instruction publique aux Etats-Units*, pp. 2–9. The report was prepared in 1867 and sold out its first edition in book form in 1870.
70. Ange Guépin, *La Philosophie*, pp. 504–5.
71. Clemenceau, *American Reconstruction*, pp. 40, 62.
72. Peter Gay, *The Enlightenment*, pp. 33, 102–3; Alain, *Eléments*, pp. 285–6.
73. Quinet, *La République*, p. 113; Vacherot, *La Démocratie*, p. 130.
74. This is the thesis, for example, of a work by Victor Schoelcher, *La Famille, la propriété et le christianisme* (1873) cited by Georges Weill, *Histoire de l'Idée laïque en France*, p. 243. Schoelcher, who became a senator-for-life in the Third Republic, began his political career campaigning for the abolition of slavery in the French Antilles.
75. Michelet, *Du Prêtre*, p. 200.
76. Ibid., p. 201.

77. An excellent account is given in Theodore Zeldin's *Conflicts in French Society*. Zeldin returned to the theme in his attention to "love" in *France, 1848–1945*. I agree with Zeldin that the quarrel reflected basic unresolved tensions in French society but differ with him, as I shall argue here, in insisting that the political dimensions of the quarrel were identified and held capable of solution at a particular moment in history.

78. *Epanchement*, complete candor and self-revelation, occurs in French novels only between young men – Frédéric and Deslauriers in Flaubert's *Sentimental Education*, Jean and the abbé Scherz in *Jean Barois* – never between lovers. Flaubert himself wrote to Louise Colet that he hoped to have with her an entirely new kind of relation; "with a friend one does not love enough; with a mistress one is too stupid."

79. "Mais comment seraient-elles indifférentes aux grandes questions de la politique, qui sont toutes les questions de justice, de patriotisme, et de liberté?" Jules Simon, *L'Ecole*, p. 179. Quinet, *La République*, p. 190.

80. Michelet, *Du Prêtre*, pp. v–vi: "Nos femmes, et nos filles, sont élevées, gouvernées, *par nos ennemis*, ennemis de l'esprit moderne, de la liberté, de l'avenir," and "Il y a dans la famille un grave dissentiment, et le plus grave de tous. Nous pouvons parler à nos mères, à nos femmes, à nos filles, des sujets dont nous parlons aux indifférents . . . nullement des choses qui touchent le coeur et la vie morale."

81. The marital struggles of the French bourgeoisie are thus aptly characterized by J. Pommier, "Les Idées de Michelet et de Renan sur la confession," p. 522. Ten days after the book's publication, Mme Dumesnil's confessor cautioned his Sorbonne classes against it: Coeur's warning did not prevent the book from selling out three times between January and March 1845.

82. Quinet developed this argument in the fascinating Chapter 38, "Have Women Anything to Regret in the Past?" Quinet, *La République*, pp. 202 ff. "Le corps à l'époux; l'âme à l'aimant; voilà toute la chevalerie." Michelet, *Du Prêtre*, p. 199.

83. Martin du Gard, *Jean Barois*, p. 112.

84. The Assembly declined to act on this suggestion, but a basilica was erected on the heights of Montmartre, where the insurrection had begun.

85. Michelet, *Du Prêtre*, pp. 150–3.

86. Indeed, had he not been as anglophobe as he was anticlerical, he might have learned of British distaste for similar religious enthusiasms. E. P. Thompson, noting a confusion of maternal and sadoerotic imagery in Wesleyan hymns ("O precious Side-hole's cavity/I want to spend my life in thee"), quoted Leigh Hunt's disdainful question: "If God must be addressed in the language of earthly affection why not address him as a parent rather than as a lover?" (E. P. Thompson, *The Making of the English Working Class*, p. 371 ff. Hunt's essay was entitled "On the Indecencies and Profane Rapture of Methodism.")

87. Taine, *Notes sur l'Angleterre*, pp. 118–19. Although in general he admired English family life, Taine was not uncritical of it. He was appalled by the discourtesy shown to educated servants, tutors and governesses, and distressed by the rigid hierarchy that, he felt, ruled private as well as public life. The slang usage of "Governor" for father struck him as apposite and regrettable.

88. Vacherot, *La Démocratie*, p. 130.

89. Barois's father, a physician and skeptic, explained his wife's death to his young son: "She was much younger than I . . . excessively pious . . . I never

had the least influence over her . . . She saw me every day advising people, curing them; nevertheless, she had no confidence . . . I repeat, your mother died because she had no confidence." Martin du Gard, *Jean Barois*, pp. 19–21.

90. Louis Legrand, *Le Mariage et les moeurs en France*, pp. 10, 55–6. The work, a prize winner in 1870, did not appear until 1879.

91. Jules Ferry, "L'Egalité d'éducation," p. 28. "Le foyer éclairé, animé par la causerie, embelli par la lecture." Jules Simon's work had been published by Hachette in 1867.

92. Quinet, *La République*, p. 197; Naquet, *Religion*, pp. 208–27.

93. Maurain, *La politique écclésiastique*, p. 677.

94. Félix Dupanloup, *La Femme chrétienne et française*, p. 46.

95. Dupanloup's inquiry has been reprinted and analyzed by Christianne Marcilhary, *Le Diocèse d'Orléans sous l'épiscopat de Dupanloup*, p. ii.

   The figure of 67 percent is especially striking when compared with the lowest participation, 3.8 percent for men over twenty, and surprising, too, in comparison with the 20 percent cited for women over twenty.

96. Maurain, *La Politique écclésiastique*, pp. 845–7: "le terrain de leurs vrais devoirs." Maurain suggested that liberal Catholics seized upon this issue as an opportunity to vindicate, at little cost, their fidelity while fighting what they regarded as the more important battle against the proclamation of infallibility in Rome. Dupanloup, who was never made a cardinal, was regarded as Manning's ablest antagonist, but on this occasion Pius IX publicly congratulated him, and *l'Osservatore romano* called for Duruy's ouster from the cabinet.

97. Duruy, *Notes et souvenirs*, pp. 276–7. The letter is as good of its kind as anything Disraeli wrote to Queen Victoria. Cf. also Maurain, *La Politique écclésiastique*, p. 842.

98. Quoted in ibid., p. 840.

99. Ferry, "L'Egalité d'éducation," p. 25.

100. Ibid., p. 28.

101. Macé, *Les Origines*, p. 6; Marx, *The Eighteenth Brumaire*, p. 21.

102. Ibid., p. 24. Ferry might well indulge in good-humored self-criticism. His own marriage in 1876, a happy and immensely advantageous union with Eugénie Rissler-Kestner, granddaughter of the republican industrialist Charles Kestner, would be a civil ceremony at the insistence of the bride's grandmother and against the advice of Thiers. Maurice Reclus, *Jules Ferry*, p. 129.

103. J. S. Mill, *On the Subjection of Women*, pp. 170–1.

104. Zeldin, *France 1848–1945*, vol. 2, p. 992.

105. Michelet, *Le Peuple*, Part II, "De l'affranchissement par l'amour," develops this theme, as does his remarkable study of Joan of Arc: "cette folie heroïque est la sagesse même" (Michelet, *Jeanne d'Arc*, p. 74) and "la singulière originalité de cette fille, le bon sens dans l'exaltation," (ibid., p. 87); Naquet, *Religion*, p. 193.

106. Hippeau, *L'Instruction publique*, pp. 132–3.

107. Quoted by Sauvestre, *Sur les genoux*, p. 9.

108. Simon, *L'Ecole*, pp. 209–10.

109. Hippeau, *L'Instruction publique*, pp. 135–9.

110. *Archives départementales de l'Yonne*, 43 T 1, *Rapport sur l'organisation de l'enseignement primaire en Suisse*, presented to the General Council of the Yonne by M. Frontier, 1876.

111. Hippeau, *L'Instruction publique*, pp. 102-5. The girls sang the "Marseillaise" for him, too.
112. Dupanloup, *La Femme chrétienne*, p. 100,
113. As Michelet put it crudely, "Being what she is she must have a lover . . . How much better for all that she love her son." Michelet, *Du Prêtre*, p. 204.
    If Flaubert saw the tragedy as Emma's – and the destruction of a stupid, decent provincial doctor as secondary – other men were less imaginatively generous.
114. For unmarried girls and poor women, gainful employment in decent surroundings was, of course, considered essential. Duruy had buttressed his appeal for female secondary education with the prospect that it would assure women of honest employment, and therefore urged that fees be waived for poor girls. Maurain, *La politique écclésiastique*, p. 818. Simon, too, had argued against factory work for women and asked for training, principally in needlework, that was more compatible with their "social destiny." Nevertheless, no profession, save that of schoolmistress, was seriously suggested for young women.
    A similar limitation foresaw the moral presence of women in politics but excluded their active participation. Carnot, however, recommended that an exception be made for the governance of education. Speaking at a school *fête* on July 14, 1872, he recalled that the Convention had foreseen a civic role for women: As *mères de famille* they might serve on committees that chose teachers and supervised schools. (AF F[17] 12531). Jean Macé eventually proposed to the Senate that women shopkeepers be eligible to vote for the tribunals of commerce, but that proposal was received less enthusiastically than were his others. Edouard Petit, *Jean Macé*, p. 393.
115. Ange Guépin, *Projet du rituel d'initiation au second grade*, p. 2. Guépin's widow directed the Ecole Guépin, created at Nantes for the vocational education of girls with funds contributed for his candidacy in 1869 and, after his death, bequeathed to the city for its most urgent social need. The school was generously subsidized in the 1880s at the urging of the young deputy Georges Clemenceau – whose father, like Guépin, had practiced medicine in Nantes. *Archives de France*, F[17] 12540.
116. Ferry, "L'Egalité d'éducation," p. 10.
117. Michelet, *Le Peuple*, pp. 233-4. "Si seulement les deux enfants, le pauvre et le riche, avaient été assis aux bancs d'une même école, si, liés d'amitié, divisés de carrières . . . Ils conserveraient dans leur amitié désintéressée, innocente, le noeud sacré de la Cité." Earlier in the same work, however, in the autobiographical introduction dedicated to Quinet, he recalled his own experience as a scholarship student at the Collège de Charlemagne: "I began to appreciate one thing, that I was poor." Ibid., p. 67.
118. Hippeau, *L'Instruction publique*, p. 49. "Réunir dans les mêmes écoles, faire asseoir sur les mêmes bancs et participer à une éducation commune les enfants de toutes les conditions, est le moyen le plus assuré de conserver dans le nation cet esprit de'égalité qui est la loi suprême des institutions véritablement démocratiques."
119. Proudhon, *De la justice*, pp. 5-6.
120. Taine, *Notes sur l'Angleterre*, pp. 13-14, 212. Laboulaye, author of *L'Etat et ses limites* and *Le Parti libéral, son programme et son avenir*, shared with Tocqueville a fondness for the republican patriciate of New England. He hoped that

their "individual initiative" in the patronage of schools and institutions of benevolence would be emulated in France. In a copy of his translation of Channing, found in the municipal library at LeHavre, an exasperated reader had scrawled, "De l'audace, pauvre idiot!"

121. Quoted in M. Dommanget, *Blanqui et l'opposition révolutionnaire à la fin du Second Empire*, p. 63.

122. Jules Vallès, *L'Enfant*, p. 114.

123. Quinet, *Les Jésuites, Oeuvres complètes*, vol. 2, p. 173. Widener Library received in 1899 the undated thirty-volume complete works from Mme Quinet. The text of vol. 2 is taken from the tenth edition of *Les Jésuites* (1873).

124. "La force des choses provoque les révolutions. Par son perfectionnement moral et son action personelle l'homme seul crée, fonde, et organise les sociétés qui en sortent." Vacherot, *La Démocratie*, p. xiv.

2. Organizing the alternative society

1. AD Yonne III M^{1}233. "Their fractious ways" approximates *leur habitude frondeuse*, deplored in the subprefect's "Report on the political, moral, and material situation." Sens, the scene of religious violence in 1562, was represented in the Third Republic by the resourceful Mayor Guichard. AM Lyon I^2 46A, from a police report on the development of electoral committees into a standing central committee.

2. Macé recalled Bert's question in his own address to the general assembly of the Ligue de l'enseignement at Lille in 1885 which was printed in the *Bulletin de la Ligue française de l'enseignement*, p. 196.

3. "Je suis le fils d'un camionneur. Je suis un camionneur des idées." Edouard Petit, *Jean Macé, sa vie et son oeuvre*, p. 13. A "camionneur" was still a worker; Macé's adherents would be "commis-voyageurs," travelling salesmen.

4. Ibid., p. 15.

5. Jean Macé, *Histoire d'une bouchée de pain*, p. 62. The book is dedicated to Etienne Geoffroy Saint-Hilaire; Macé's science books for children reveal the author *au courant* and warmly partisan in nineteenth-century scientific debates.

6. Ibid., preface.

7. Jean Macé, *Les Origines*, p. 4.

8. Jean Macé, *L'Arc de Triomphe*, p. 2.

9. Jean Macé, *Le Petit Catéchisme Républicain*, p. 5.

10. Jean Macé, *Les Vertus d'un républicain*, p. 9. He opposed *la fierté républicaine* to *l'orgueil aristocratique* and pleaded, above all, for a "disinterested" support of the Republic, deploring that in the first twenty-four hours of the Second Republic, petitioners sought four thousand jobs in government. Ibid., pp. 43–5.

11. Ibid., pp. 27 – 8.

12. Jean Moreau (Macé), *Lettre d'un garde national à son voisin*, p. 3.

13. Macé, *Le Petit Catéchisme*, p. 15.

14. Jean Macé, *Une Profession de foi d'un communiste*, p. 2.

15. "Cette communion des intélligences par qui s'est fait le progrès de l'humanité, n'est-elle pas un bel example à donner à ceux qui ont tant de peine à comprendre la communion des intérêts." Ibid., dedication.

16. Ibid., pp. 5–7; Macé, *Les Origines*, p. 8; Macé, *Une profession de foi*, dedication: "prévoyante et bienveillante."

17. Macé, *Le Petit Catéchisme*, p. 23.

18. Macé, *Les Origines*, p. 12; Jean Macé, *Le Théâtre du Petit-Chateau*, p. 7.
19. Ibid., p. 5; Petit, *Jean Macé*, p. 211.
20. Macé, *Théâtre*, p. 9;.
21. Macé, *Bouchée*, p. 31.
22. Her age is never specified, but her heartbeat, ninety times a minute, would put her "anywhere in latency," according to S. Norman Sherry, M.D., Assistant Clinical Professor of Pediatrics, Harvard Medical School.
23. *Bouchée*, pp. 19–20.
24. Ibid., p. 65.
25. Ibid.
26. Ibid., p. 328.
27. "Il est dangereux de trop faire voir à l'homme combien il est égal aux bêtes, sans lui montrer sa grandeur. Il est encore dangereux de lui faire trop voir sa grandeur sans sa basesse." *Pensées*, chapter IV.
28. Ibid., p. 323.
29. Ibid., p. 303. "Le sang de notre globe, c'est l'eau qui contient tous les germes de fécondité." Edward K. Kaplan has written an enthralling book, *Michelet's Poetic Vision, A Romantic Theory of Nature, Men and Women*. He discusses Geoffroy Saint-Hilaire's theory of evolution and clarifies the notion of *ébauche* on pp. 13–15.
30. Macé, *Bouchée*, p. 337.
31. Ibid., p. 264.
32. Ibid.
33. Ibid., p. 61.
34. Ibid., pp. 323–4.
35. Macé, *Théâtre*, pp. 33–62. This is the burden of *A Brébis tondue Dieu mesure le vent*, a heartrending piece: The widow and daughters of a professor about whose pension there is some difficulty wait, without food or medicine, on Christmas Eve, to be paid for their embroideries. Hearing of their plight, wealthy women give them instantly as alms money that they actually owe the destitute family. There are *éclaircissements*, shame, reconciliations on the basis not of charity but respect, and the husband of one client is found to be a college classmate of the dilatory *fonctionnaire*.
36. Ibid., pp. 91–145.
37. Ibid., p. 158.
38. Macé, *Bouchée*, p. 174.
39. Ibid., p. 284.
40. The history of the publishing house of Hetzel deserves attention. It published Macé, Jules Verne, Erckmann-Chatrian, and a *Cours d'économie domestique* by Mme Hippeau, but it did not confine its sponsorship to the unexceptionable: Hetzel also printed Michelet's *La Sorcière*, which Hachette would not touch.
41. Alfred Darimon, *Histoire d'un parti*, pp. 66–7. The government was eager to make the oath a condition even of candidacy. The Cinq were Jules Favre, Emile Ollivier, Ernest Picard, Darimon, a follower of Proudhon, and Hénon, mayor of Lyon.

    Nefftzer, educated at Strasbourg in the Protestant Faculty of Theology, and described as "the most positivist of the metaphysicians" by André Lavertujon (*Gambetta inconnu*, p. 58), urged resumption of political activity and supported the Liberal Union of 1863. Others, like Edgar Quinet, refused to return to France under the general amnesty of 1859 and cautioned others

not to be deceived by the emperor's overtures. Madame Quinet, *Depuis l'exil,*
pp. 163 and 197.

42. Zeldin, *Political System,* pp. 28–65.
43. Maurice Reclus, *Jules Ferry,* p. 39.
44. Ibid., pp. 40–1.
45. The duc de Persigny, *Les Doctrines de L'Empire,* pp. 137–8.
46. Laboulaye, *Le Parti libéral,* p. 40. "Entre l'égoisme individuel et le despotisme de l'état (qui n'est qu'une autre forme d'égoisme), l'association place la foi, la science, la charité, l'intérêt commun, c'est-à-dire, tout ce qui rapproche les hommes et leur apprend à se supporter et à s'aimer mutuellement." As a professor of the Collège de France, he defended the autonomy of the institution and the rights, as members, of his incendiary colleagues Michelet and Quinet when their courses were suspended by the July Monarchy. Hazard, *Michelet,* p. 273.
47. Edouard Laboulaye, "La Liberté antique et la liberté moderne," *L'Etat et ses limites,* pp. 135–7.
48. For example, a circular from the Ministry of the Interior instructed prefects, in 1865, to tolerate strikes over "merely" economic grievances and to take no actions against workers unless their actions were manifestly antidynastic. (AD, *Bouches-du-Rhône,* M⁶ 88, June 12, 1865.)
49. Maurain, *La Politique ecclésiastique,* p. 683. Letter of October 1863. Cf. also Jean Rohr, *Victor Duruy,* p. 16.
    Duruy was an archetypal popular Bonapartist. His father had been a "worker" – that is, a Gobelin foreman of considerable expertise and authority – and an officer in the national guard. The family traced its origins to Flemish weavers brought to France by Colbert.
50. Duruy, *Notes et souvenirs,* vol. 1, pp. 210–11.
51. Ibid.
52. Among these, that mayors were forbidden to ask electors how they voted, to hand out ballots for any candidate, to open closed ballots, or to receive open ones; and that transcripts of the electoral committee's proceedings must include any protest presented to it. AD Yonne, IIM¹ 159.
53. AD Yonne, IIM¹ 159; "une instruction sérieuse pour tous"; "la propagation gratuite de l'instruction qui seule peut rendre les citoyens égaux."
54. AM Lyon, "Troubles," I² 43, Report of March, 1867.
55. Raymond Oberlé, *L'Enseignement en Mulhouse de 1789 à 1870,* pp. 51–2; Charles Moiset, "Notes sur l'Histoire de l'instruction primaire dans le département de l'Yonne depuis 1833," *Annuaire de l'Yonne,* pp. 64–5; Elwitt, *Making of the Third Republic,* p. 215.
56. AD Rhône T76 (ancien). Letter of November 7, 1852. (The archives of the department of the Rhône have undergone several reclassifications. Therefore, the code numbers are sometimes amplified by "ancien" and "nouveau," or by "rouge" and "noir."
57. See Rohr's *Victor Duruy.* I think that Rohr exaggerates Duruy's political incompetence. He may have been maladroit with the Chamber of Deputies, but his own writings suggest a sound, if optimistic, grasp of political possibilities.
58. AF F¹⁷ 12527, *L'Indépendant rémois,* October 29, 1868, reprinted from the *Gironde.*
59. Maurain, *La Politique ecclésiastique* p. 939. Indeed, I have found it difficult to share Theodore Zeldin's appreciation of the career of Emile Ollivier and the

"Liberal" Cabinet of 1869. Whatever the appointment of Ollivier may have meant to those who remembered his father and brother as republicans, the purging the same year of the cabinet member most associated with the *program* of the democratic opposition seems to me more significant. Furthermore, I would not attribute government losses in the elections of 1869, as Zeldin does, to the greater prosperity, and hence greater potential venality of opposition candidates. Cf. Theodore Zeldin, *Emile Ollivier and the Liberal Empire of Napoleon III* and, especially, his *Political System*, pp. 97–9.

60. AF F^{17} 12527, *Procès-verbaux de la Société industrielle de Rheims* in *L'Indépendant rémois*, November 24, 1868.

61. Jacques Ozouf, *Nous les maîtres d'école*, p. 134. In the 1890s a provincial schoolmaster felt himself to be between two classes, separated from the peasantry by his learning and mode of life and from the bourgeoisie by his poverty. This social exile was made bearable only by "a dream of mediation." Ibid.

62. "Parmi les hommes notoirement hostiles au gouvernement, qui décernent des médailles aux instituteurs que nous sommes obligés de révoquer en raison de l'exaltation de leurs opinions politiques et qui semblent se poser en protecteur de ceux qui font un mérite de leur insubordination." *Archives de France* F^{17} 12531, letter of the prefect of the Pas-de-Calais to the minister of public instruction, June 18, 1850. The prefect complained, too, of the group's patronage of a teacher, Philippe, who resigned in order to avoid being fired and took refuge in Paris, whence he was alleged to be continuing his correspondence with "socialist chiefs" in the arrondissement of Saint-Omer. Carnot's support was presented as further evidence of the society's character (prefect's letter of April 6, 1850). The SIE consistently disclaimed any attempt to redress professional grievances, which, it agreed, must be dealt with by the academic hierarchy, and it produced a letter from the comte Boulay de la Meurthe affirming its moderate disposition.

63. AF F^{17} 12531.

64. Ibid.

65. The SIE's contributors are listed in their *Journal d'Education Populaire*, 2, nos. 8–9 (August–September 1866): 334–42.

66. AF F^{17} 12531. The prefect of police in Paris assessed the group as "honorable" in 1863, but scarcely seven of the forty-five leaders were devoted to the government. In religion the "gallican principle" prevailed.

67. Ibid. Letter of Malapert to Duruy, August 25, 1863. Malapert was the president of the SIE and, in the absence of Boulay de la Meurthe, was simultaneously serving as secretary to the Association philotechnique.

68. Rohr, *Victor Duruy*, p. 45, describes Jules Simon as a friend and admirer of the minister. As spokesman and publicist of the opposition, however, Simon also emphasized the inadequacy of Duruy's programs.

69. This practice was adopted by the Ligue de l'enseignement in the late 1870s. The political coloration and mission of its *conferenciers ambulants* could scarcely be doubted.

70. AF F^{17} 12542. Letter of Victor Duruy to the minister of the interior. "Mais elle voudrait rayonner au dehors, envoyer de tous côtés des orateurs ambulants chargés de parler et d'enseigner en son nom."

71. AF F^{17} 12531.

72. AF F^{17} 12529.

73. To some extent, this split may have reflected tensions within the group

between alumni of the Ecole Polytechnique and men who were not "old boys." Before 1843, only former students of the school were admitted to the association; thereafter, others might join but not serve as officers. In 1848, instructors with no ties to the school had become more numerous than alumni and sought a more equal share in the group's direction. However, when the Association philotechnique was created, a polytechnician assumed the sensitive post of chairman for educational policy. This would suggest that genuine differences, not just school ties, prompted the division.

74. AF F¹⁷ 12532. M. Devinck, former president of the tribunal of commerce and a municipal councillor; the mayor of the Third Arrondissement, which already supported a cooperative library and soon, under the regime of September 4, would establish free secular schools enjoying illustrious patronage; Fould, "négociant" of Saint-Denis; Hachette, the publisher; Ménier, the *chocolatier* and radical philanthropist, donor of the controversial "Prix Ménier" and later a pillar of the league; Rataud, mayor of the Fifth; Salmon, former deputy of the Meuse; De Wendel, *maître des forges*, deputy for Moselle; Cadet, *docteur en droit*; Hébert, *docteur-médecin*; Delorme, former censor at Louis-le-grand.

75. AF F¹⁷ 12529.

76. AF F¹⁷ 12529. The association had enjoyed the patronage of François Guizot in the thirties, so one imagines it could have, if it had wished, struck a more conspicuously elevating tone (although Guizot himself was ambivalent about education and mobility. Perhaps ambivalence is the psychic root of moderation). In his *Mémoires*, Guizot wrote that of all the sentiments that might animate a people, the one most deplorable if absent, but the one which if present must never be flattered or excited, was ambition. He knew nothing more dangerous for society or for the people themselves than "nasty, little, vulgar learning." François Guizot, *Mémoires pour servir à l'histoire de mon temps*, vol. 3, p. 64–5.

77. AF F¹⁷ 12529, *Documents*, pp. 36 – 9.

78. Model statutes for a *société de secours mutuelle* called for a high ratio of "patrons" to members, guaranteeing a large non–working class presence in each group. Cf. Jean Bennet, *Quand Napoléon III nommait les présidents des sociétés de secours mutuelle.*

79. AF F¹⁷ 12542. Letters from a worried subordinate suggest that one of the greatest concerns was simply whom to make responsible for the actions of "succursales" – local agents or the central office.

80. AF F¹⁷ 12529. "Un oeuvre toute de conciliation; à nous n'appartons pas la lumière qui brûle, mais la lumière qui éclaire." There were 24,065 adult courses then taught in France: 1,300 for women and 22,765 for men. In Meurthe there were 799, 774 in l'Aisne, 617 in Vosges, 667 in Pas-de-Calais, 604 in Côte d'or.

81. Srétan Maritch, *Histoire du mouvement social sous le Second Empire à Lyon*, pp. 179 ff.

82. Ibid., 182.

83. AF F¹⁷ 12542.

84. AF F¹⁷ 12529. Proposed statutes, 1869. Membership included active and honorary members. The president and the administrative council and the "professeurs titulaires" (those who had taught under the society's auspices for a year) were "active members." A consultative committee of "patrons" included those able to contribute to the prosperity of the work with money

or *éclat – savants*, artists, "self-made men," especially those who were alumni of the society's courses.

85. In circulars issued in April 1864 and January 1865, Duruy emphasized that although he might approve lecture series and free courses (*cours gratuits*), he could not, without encroaching upon the powers of the minister of the interior (who guarded his considerable prerogatives jealously), grant permission for meetings not *exclusively* educational in character. (AF F^{17} 12531).

86. Dupanloup, *La femme chrêtienne*, p. 91.

87. Elwitt, *Making*, pp. 185–6.

88. Macé, *Les Origines*, p. 100.

89. AD Bouches-du-Rhône, M^6 163. "Autant il est convenable de seconder, de favoriser tout ce qui a pour but de moraliser et d'instruire le peuple, autant il est indispensable de la garantier des funestes effets que produiraient sur lui des doctrines antisociales et des fâcheuses lectures."

90. Ibid. "On devra en éliminer avec une juste sévérité les romans dont la lecture pourrait laisser une impression regrettable, on aura soin également d'exclure les livres de polémique sociale ou religieuse, et ceux qui, sous prétexte d'économie politique, pourraient servir à propager des théories dangereuses ou subversives."

91. AD Bouches-du-Rhône M^6 163. "Le Gouvernement . . . ne saurait admettre que les partis hostiles viennent recueillir le bénéfice de ses efforts, s'en attribuer le mérite apparent et y trouver un nouvel élément de force pour le combattre."

92. Oberlé, *L'Enseignement*, p. 126.

93. When Henri Tolain defended the use of the strike by the International before the National Assembly, alleging that the clergy themselves fomented strikes when it suited their purposes, the Alsatian Scheurer-Kestner (later as vice-president of the Senate a crucial early *dreyfusard*) supported his charges. Henri Tolain, *L'Internationale*, pp. 15–16.

94. Weill, *L'Idée laïque*, pp. 150–2.

95. Numa Denis Fustel de Coulanges, *The Ancient City*, p. 132.

96. Oberlé, *L'Enseignement*, pp. 41–2: "une fusion sociale sinon de croyance"; "L'enfant ne donne jamais de réponse qu'il n'en puisse rendre compte par le raisonnement."

97. Ibid., p. 69.

98. Ibid., p. 47.

99. Reprinted in Macé, *Les Origines*, p. 22 ff.

100. Ibid., p. 36.

101. Ibid., p. 37. "À ce signal beaucoup répondront, même parmi ceux qui vous pourriez considérer comme mal disposés pour vous. Ils y ont tous un trop grand intérêt . . . Voilà la véritable réconciliation entre les petits et les grands."

102. Macé, *Les Origines*, pp. 33–4.

103. Ibid., pp. 28–9. "On ne demande pas qu'on fasse des enlèvements d'enfants."

104. Macé, *Les Origines*, p. 101. "Projet d'Association pour la formation des bibliothèques communales dans le Haut-Rhin."

105. Ibid., p. 46.

106. Ibid., p. 72. "The society is forbidden any direct purchase or official designation of books"; ibid., pp. 104–5, "La direction venue d'en haut

n'est pas ce qui manque à nos communes."

107. Ibid., pp. 142–6; ibid., p. 318.
108. Charles Sauvestre, "Sociétés républicaines d'instruction," Bibliothèque Nationale 8 R Piece 2786, n.d. (I believe Sauvestre's talk was delivered in 1874.)
109. The Société des Bibliothèques communales du Haut-Rhin did eventually collect dues.
110. Macé, Les Origines, pp. 62–3. Reprinted from "L'Histoire d'une bibliothèque communale," Courrier du Bas Rhin, January 29, 1863, pp. 114 ff.
111. Ibid., pp. 369 ff.
112. Cordial contacts were maintained, nonetheless, with the Franklin Society. Jules Simon, the staunchly anti-Bonapartist vice-president of the group, spoke to the library society in Mulhouse in November of 1864. Macé shut no doors unnecessarily. (Les Origines, pp. 133 f.)
113. AF F17 12535. The Société, begun in 1862, offered a selection of books, "aucun qui puisse rien effaroucher," and included among its founders an aide-de-camp of the emperor, two members of the Academy, and an academic inspector-general. By 1874, it, too, was identified with the struggle for a secular republic; Macé, Les Origines, p. 82.
114. Ibid., p. 47.
115. Ibid., p. 53.
116. Macé, Les Origines, p. 203. Reprinted from L'Opinion Nationale, October 25, 1866.
117. Ibid., p. 215. "On prend son pays comme il est quand on veut travailler pour lui."
118. AF F17 12542.
119. André Guépin, Avis aux électeurs de la Loire-Inférieure; ibid., Royalistes et républicaines, pp. 1–2.
    Purged from the faculty of medicine in 1852, Guépin was reinstated by Jules Simon in 1870. In 1869, Guépin was elected deputy and he became, in September 1870, one of Gambetta's prefects. A freemason, he attributed the glory of his order to its understanding that the well-being of a people was always in direct proportion to the respect accorded labor: "We should hope to be a great mutual school . . . able to understand the duties, mission, and functions of humanity." Guépin, Esquisse, p. 5; Macé, Les Origines, p. 25.
120. Although calling for local initiative and a vigorous revival of provincial life, Macé refused to associate himself with conventional diatribes against the capital. "Paris leads us because she is France in microcosm," he wrote in the Revue d'Alsace in 1862. Reprinted in Macé, Les Origines, pp. 39–41.
121. Letter of January 3, 1867: ". . . au milieu d'un peuple qui a abdiqué et qui'il s'agit de faire rentrer en possession de lui-même sans rien casser." Cited by Petit, Jean Macé, p. 243.
122. "Toutes les énergies honnêtes et convaincues dont beaucoup se croient impuissantes parce qu'elles se sentent isolées." Macé, Les Origines, p. 318.
123. Ibid., pp. 286, 229. The bulletin of the league, number 2, listed nine of them: the Groupe spirite of St.-Aignan, Marseille, Angers, Chatellerault, and Montauban, the newspaper Le Spiritisme at Lyon, and three other societies – one at Rouen and two in Paris. Their adherence puzzled me. My learned friend Georgess MacHargue, whose book Facts, Frauds, and Phantasms deals with British and American nineteenth-century spiritualism,

thought that their interest might have something to do with their condemnation by the Vatican but probably was better explained by the eclectic nature of the avant-garde. Psychic research – like vegetarianism, temperance, or feminism – was sometimes an element in an audaciously utopian program, sometimes an expression of pious and respectable meliorism.

124. Cf. Jacob Katz, *Jews and Freemasons in Europe, 1723–1939*, pp. 7, 156–9; and Mildred J. Headings, *French Freemasonry under the Third Republic*, passim.

125. AD Bouches-du-Rhône, M⁶ 61. The report of the *Police politique* on masonic lodges, June 26, 1861, conveniently included a list of venerables dismissed elsewhere in France.

126. Headings, *French Freemasonry*, p. 39. "Atelier" (workshop) is the most inclusive term for masonic organizations, referring to "chapters" and "councils" as well as to lodges.

127. *Le Monde maçonnique*, February 1867, pp. 639–40; ibid., May 1867, pp. 56–57.

128. *L'Action maçonnique*, no. 1, December 1, 1867, p. 1. *L'Action maçonnique* of March 1868 told of "the war against ignorance" at Marseille (pp. 111–12) and included, too, Vacca's description of his work at Metz: "The Metz circle of the league proposes to propagate 1) instruction and education and 2) ideas about cooperation in its various forms, consumption, credit, and production" (pp. 140–4). The Bordeaux news, ibid., December 15, 1869, p. 11; February 1, 1868, p. 69. In the department of the Seine there were 1,268 members; 401 in the Haut-Rhin; 292 in the Vosges; 241 in the Lot-et-Garonne; 238 in the Marne; and 217 in the Seine-Inférieure. The rest were scattered throughout France.

129. Lefrançais, *Souvenirs d'un révolutionnaire*, p. 272; *L'Action maçonnique*, March 1, 1868; ibid., January 15, 1869. I noted also, in ibid., October 1, 1868, a feminist argument of Lefrançais, derived from his profound egalitarianism. He objected to psychological arguments against female emancipation, arguing that a hierarchy of "faculties" was itself illegitimate, that justice demands free exercise of the faculties of each individual, not the more or less perfectly constituted faculties. His *Souvenirs* judge feminism to be a just but peripheral cause.

130. AF F¹⁷ 12542; He relented somewhat in this severity, or at least was reported to have done so in the fall of 1867. A group headed by Emile Lebon in Dieppe, petitioning the prefect of the Seine-Inférieure to permit them to organize a circle of the league, noted in a postscript to their letter that the principal of the city's *collège* had just informed them that His Excellency had authorized him to put his professors at their disposal. AD Seine-Maritime, Série M. Letter of October 27, 1867. The departmental archives at Rouen were burned during the Second World War. This petition is one of the few pieces of evidence extant for the Seine-Inférieure, now the Seine-Maritime.

131. AF F¹⁷ 12542. The emphasis is added.

132. *Bulletin du mouvement d'enseignement*, February 1869, p. 41. Boivin, "Les Origines de la Ligue de l'enseignement," p. 210.

133. Rohr, *Victor Duruy*, pp. 173–4.

134. AF F¹⁷ 12542, letter registered January 31, 1868.

135. AF F¹⁷ 12542.

136. Ibid. "On a dû enlever avec éclat, au prix de débats irritants, le bénéfice d'une autorisation antérieure."

137. Ibid. Funds, the thwarted minister complained, were never lacking for the church schools, although his budget was always insufficient. Moreover, the clergy were paid by the state; he saw no need to enhance their position.
138. AF F¹⁷ 2682; "un résurrection effectuée en bloc." Chateauneuf's report to the rector of the academy of Rennes was included in the rector's report to the minister of public instruction, December 29, 1868.
139. AF F¹⁷ 2682, August 24, 1868. Maggiolo's report and later communication from Maggiolo.
140. Maggiolo undertook in 1877 a statistical study of illiteracy in France. His conclusions (and his figures were the ones relied upon by Ferdinand Buisson in the *Dictionnaire de pédagogie et d'instruction primaire*) supported the notion of an enlightened northeast and a region of "ténèbres" in the west and south. Cf. Michel Fleury and Pierre Valmary, "Le progrès d'instruction élémentaire de Louis XIV à Napoléon III après l'enquête de Louis Maggiolo, 1877-1879," pp. 71-92.
141. AD Gironde, Fonds du rectorat 51. In May 1871 rectors of the provincial academies were asked to find jobs for eighteen hundred Alsatian teachers, all possessed of the *brevet élémentaire* and most of them graduates of normal schools. Maggiolo appealed for them and spoke of their "incontestable superiority." M. Taillefert, an inspector of schools in the Basses-Pyrénées, said that he had hoped that Bayonne would establish a secular school that might hire Alsatian *laïcs*, but "unfortunately the last elections have destroyed that hope." He wanted very much to have eastern teachers – everyone acknowledged that their educational level was higher – and their love of France would have been exemplary.
142. Elwitt, *The Making*, p. 188. He asserts further, "The Ligue de l'enseignement suffered no interference from government before 1870."
143. AF F¹⁷ 12527, letter of the prefect of the Marne to the minister of public instruction, August 31, 1868. The Hôtel de Ville at Rheims was burned by retreating Germans in 1918, and the municipal archives were lost. The *cercle rémois* is traceable through national archives.
144. AF F¹⁷ 12527, prefect's letter of August 31, 1868. In 1871, when the application was favorably received, two of the petitioners had become deputies, six were municipal councillors, three were assistants to the mayor, and Jules Simon, whose writings had formed part of their polemic, was minister of public instruction.
145. *L'Indépendant rémois*, October 29, 1868.
146. Ibid.
147. AF F¹⁷ 12527, petition of November 1861.
148. Ibid.
149. *L'Indépendant rémois*, October 29, 1868.
150. AF F¹⁷ 12527; "Procès-verbaux de la Société industrielle de Rheims," *L'Indépendant rémois*, November 24, 1868. This forthright defense of the freedom of association appeared simultaneously with the society's statement opposing recent workers' congresses. Their propensity to violence was deplored, although some advantage was seen in having antagonisms frankly expressed.
151. AF F¹⁷ 12526, prefect's reply to circular of July 1877 (during the electoral campaign that followed *le 16 mai*) requesting information on the activities of educational groups: "Quand on étudie des sociétés diverses, ce qui

frappe le plus, c'est l'esprit de suite, à agir ou sous un nom ou sous un autre."

152. Rathier, speaking at Tonnere (May 20, 1863). AD Yonne, II M¹ 159.

153. Macé, *Les Origines*, p. 229.

154. Ibid., p. 551. Private schools, of course, frequently *remove* pressure from public ones by diverting the interest of the exigent parents, but Macé was a great believer in "emulation." The city of Algiers supported the league's school after *le 4 septembre*, but even then it was maintained as a separate establishment. Members correctly anticipated that the public subsidy would be short-lived.

155. Cf. the excellent discussion of the *fréquentation* problem in Prost, *L'Enseignement*, pp. 97–102. Nineteenth-century commentators often saw truancy as another expression of the "wicked inclinations" of the poor: Although a child would remain in school during the winter, "au premier rayon du soleil du printemps," the restless child rushed outside to enjoy his dissipations. Quoted from *La Providence* in Eugène Buret, *De La misère des classes laborieuses en France et en Angleterre*, vol. 2, p. 5.

156. Macé, *Les Origines*, p. 444.

157. Charles Robert, *De L'Instruction obligatoire*, p. 24. Robert cited Batbie's *Traité théorique et pratique de droit public* in defense of this interpretation.

158. Jean Macé, "La Délibération du groupe havrais," an extract from the league's fifth bulletin (February 1870).

159. Ibid. Macé quoted himself: "On peut, sans entrer dans l'école, s'occuper des enfants qui restent dehors, faire la chasse aux parents coupables d'oubli et d'exploitation prématurée . . . subventionner au besoin l'indigence . . . décréter en un mot l'instruction obligatoire autour de soi par décret privé, à défaut d'un décret publique." The issue of who might enter a school became a bitter one. Later, when citizens' surveillance committees were established, the right of their members to enter a school, unless so entitled by some other office, was contested.

160. This may have been intended as a rebuke to Siegfried, whose political career began in 1870 (when he became *premier adjoint* at Le Havre). He served as the city's mayor from 1878 until 1886. André Siegfried, *Mes Souvenirs de la Troisième République*, p. 66.

161. Macé, "La Délibération." I have supplied the emphasis.

162. *Bulletin du mouvement d'enseignement par l'initiative privée*, no. 1 (May 15, 1868): 7–8. The first and only number was published by the Ligue de l'enseignement at Beblenheim.

163. Taxile Delord, *Histoire du Second Empire*, vol. 5, pp. 178–83. Delord does not record the composition of the executive committee that took this vote, nor speculate on the identity of the four men who abstained.

164. Dupanloup's attack was quoted in *Le Monde maçonnique*, February 1869, p. 592.

165. "Cette ligue bigarée, composée des éléments les plus diverses, disparates, hostiles." *Le Monde maçonnique*, January 1869, pp. 569 ff. *Le Monde maçonnique* seemed eager in this period to polarize religious debate in France. It had attacked Renan for his "reticence and circumspection" in *Les Apôtres*: A century after Diderot, they complained, must these subjects be dealt with so gingerly? Interestingly, in the same review, the journal noted, apropos of the growth of Christianity within the Roman Empire, that "association outside the state without destroying the state is the capital question of the

future," *Le Monde maçonnique*, (May 1866–1867): pp. 66–74.

166. Of course, Dupanloup was by no means an ultra. He was one of the ablest French opponents of the declaration of infallibility, and his gallican principles undoubtedly cost him a cardinal's hat.

167. *Le Monde maçonnique*, 1869, pp. 589–90.

168. Ibid., p. 591.

169. AM Lyon I² 46B. *Le Progrès* of September 19, 1868; police report of December 27, 1868.

170. Ibid., *Le Progrès*, September 19, 1868.

171. Ibid. *Un travailleur synthétique* suggests a worker both comprehending and engaged and hints at the possibility of a new synthesis of art, science, and *métier*.

172. Anonymous, *Le catéchisme de la morale universelle destiné à le jeunesse de tous les pays par une mère*, pp. 57 ff., 77.

173. Ibid., p. 76. The curriculum set forth for the schools of the Commune of Lyon would describe moral education similarly. The committee (Rossigneux among them), which administered the municipal schools in 1870, declared them *laïques*: Dogmatic teaching would be left to families and to ministers of the various cults. "But its solicitude [the Commune's] shall be wholly given to education of effective morality, of a morality distinct from any preconceived or exclusive system, born of progressive experience and supported by universal assent . . . [It will awaken] the most exacting notions of the rights and duties of the individual, toward himself, toward his family, toward society." AD Rhône T 161 (rouge) [T 34 (noir)], *Le Conseil d'administration aux pères et mères de famille*).

174. Paul Gerbod, *La Condition universitaire en France au XIXᵉ siècle*, pp. 504–7. Official displeasure at their involvement probably accounted for this. The league, although invariably urging better pay and more consideration for teachers, was never principally a vehicle for professional grievances or advancement.

175. Macé, *Les Origines*, p. 252.

176. *Bulletin du mouvement d'enseignement*, pp. 39–42.

177. Macé, *Les Origines*, p. 454.

178. "Cette convenance, cette politesse . . . chez les gens bien-élevées." Ibid., p. 252.

179. Ibid., p. 265; Elwitt, *The Making*, pp. 210–12.

180. André Siegfried described his father as an exuberant embodiment of a picaresque capitalism for which Weber seemed to have so little feeling. The foundation of his large fortune was laid during the American Civil War: As a young man of twenty-four, making a grand tour of the United States, he presented his letter of introduction at the White House just as President Lincoln was about to review the Army of the Potomac. Lincoln offered him a horse, they rode off together, and the impression he gathered of MacClellan's army convinced him the war would be a long one. The next year he established himself in Bombay to supply Mulhouse with Indian cotton. Siegfried, *Mes Souvenirs*, pp. 14–19. (Jules Siegfried's brother Jacques explored during the same period the possibility of growing cotton in North Africa, "cette colonie si riche d'avenir." *Bulletin de la Société industrielle de Mulhouse*, 33 (1863): 6.) The son recalled, too, his father's militant domesticity: Happily married to the daughter of a Protestant pastor, he urged the joys of the hearth upon Gambetta, "Il faut vous marier surtout à

l'heure où vous allez accéder au pouvoir." Siegfried, *Mes Souvenirs*, p. 97.

181. Jules Siegfried, "Des Cercles ouvriers à propos des workingmen's clubs en Angleterre," p. 868. (The article entire, pp. 859–74.)

182. Jacques Dupin, *Le Mouvement ouvrier à Auxerre, 1870–1880* (deposited in the departmental archives of the Yonne), p. 10, estimates the working-class population of the city, apart from artisans "proud of their specialty" and indistinguishable from small entrepreneurs, at no more than 10 percent of the population.

183. AD Yonne, III M⁴ 16. A police report of 1880 noted that the group had never functioned, for lack of adherents.

184. Siegfried, "Des Cercles," pp. 873–4. "Ils sont tout disposés à entrer dans les vues de personnes qui, par leur éducation et leur instruction, en savent plus qu'eux, mais ils aiment à être traités avec considération, ils aiment à être consultés."

185. Ibid., pp. 868–9. Liquor was not permitted at all, and smoking only in designated rooms.

186. Ibid., pp. 873–4. Were Alsatian magnates already concerned about lassitude and dilettantism among their sons?

187. Macé, *Les Origines*, p. 544. Junker had been the secretary of a protectionist group in the Nord that emphasized sectoral and regional rather than class antagonism. In 1869 he was responsible for a protest couched in constitutional and parliamentary language: "The workers of Roubaix associate themselves with the general protests of industry. They refuse to recognize the competence of any commission, chosen outside a regular mandate, that is other than the deputies in the legislative body, to judge the important question of import tariffs and [deny] their right to determine the future of our industry and our laborers." Quoted by Charles Fohlen, *L'Industrie textile au temps du Second Empire*, p. 431.

188. Robert Talmy, *L'Association catholique des patrons du Nord, 1884–1895*, p. 103; ibid., pp. 109–10. Moreau, when elected to the municipal council, served on committees dealing with schools, public works, and charity.

189. *Bulletin du mouvement d'enseignement*, pp. 25 ff. "Parmi les hommes bons, honnêtes, instruits, beaucoup, il est vrai, sont d'une timidité singulaire; ils passent pour égoistes parce qu'ils vivent chez eux et qu'on les croit incapables de faire un pas pour le bien public."

190. Charles Delescluze, *Aux Habitants des campagnes*, pp. 1-2. He asked for liberty for all municipalities to elect their mayors and their schoolmasters.

191. The Parisian league members, who assumed greater importance in the direction of the group after the war, were in the main republicans and militant anticlericals. Cf. Paul Lachapelle, "Le cercle parisien," p. 85 ff. The patronage of Madame Thiers was perhaps an exception to this rule: other members were Henry Martin, later a revanchist deputy and supporter of Déroulède's Ligue des Patriots; Emile Brélay, Ernest Hendlé, Léon Richer; Emmanuel Vauchez; Charles Sauvestre and Adolphe Guéroult of the *Opinion Nationale*; Louis Jourdon and Eugène Ténot of the *Siècle*, and Havin, the paper's director. Ténot had published sensational accounts of repression after the coup and a critique of the infamous *loi de sûreté générale*. The *Siècle* was the first paper to call for abdication after Sedan and on September 4 reprinted the decree of August 10, 1792, italicizing its clause, "the chief of the executive power is provisionally suspended from his functions." Cf. J. P. T. Bury, *Gambetta and the National Defense*, p. 94 ff.

192. The petitions were "received" by radical deputies, members of the league: Carnot *père*, Leblond, Magnin, Martin, Brélay, Scherer, Joigneaux, Bamberger, de Lacretelle, Laurent-Pichat, and Taxile Delord. Petit, *Jean Macé*, pp. 355–7.
193. *Bulletin de la Ligue de l'enseignement* I, pp. 7–23.
194. *Bulletin*, 1873, pp. 10–35; *Bulletin de la Ligue de l'enseignement* I, pp. 7–23; *Bulletin de la Ligue de l'enseignement* II.
195. Daniel Halévy, *La Fin des notables*, pp. 370–1.
196. Lachapelle, "Le cercle parisien," p. 120. I remember how furious I was, and how affronted, to learn that these documents had been wantonly destroyed. M. Gautier, the director of the league's Office of Documentation, rebuked me with luminous dispassionateness: "Madame, ils ont brûlé plus que papiers."
197. Maître M. Boivin, who so graciously shared his immense knowledge of Normandy with me, agreed that when attempting to document the activities of the league, one was frequently confronted with only two pieces of evidence: a copy of the prefect's *arrêté* announcing the group's dissolution, and then, some months or years later, an announcement, frequently in a paper owned or edited (or both) by league members, that the circle, which had in no wise ever deviated from *son but primitif*, was at last vindicated and free to resume its disinterested struggle. Cf. also Marcel Boivin, "Les Origines de la Ligue de l'enseignement en Seine-Inférieure."
198. Elwitt, *The Making*, pp. 195–6.
199. Note the importance attached to preexisting "core of committed petty bourgeois" in the politics of the Côte d'or. Girard, *Les Elections de 1869*, pp. 163–84.
200. Indeed, a modern account of Jansenist Auxerre sounds Augustan rather than Augustinian: "The people were pious, the bourgeoisie cultivated and curious about religious questions, the clergy zealous and austere, the magistracy respected and diligent. The bishop was truly the *defensor Civitatis*." Pierre Ordioni, *La Survivance des idées gallicanes et jansénistes en Auxerre de 1760 à nos jours*, pp. 7–9; ibid., p. 214. M. de Caylus established free instruction at L'Ecole Saint-Charles; the description of the curriculum is from a later period, 1791 (ibid., p. 123). The society maintained a library and also a laboratory for scientific experimentation. Among its members was the director of the Post Lepère, perhaps an ancestor of Charles Lepère, a member of the SPIP, elected deputy in 1871 and named minister of the interior in 1880.
201. Ibid., pp. 9–12; Ordioni stressed that the department's proverbial impiety had its roots not in the progress of rationalism so much as in the deliberate destruction of a vigorous Jansenist community.
202. AD Yonne III M^1 126; cited by A. Lévy, "A propos du coup d'état de 1851 dans l'Yonne," p. 188.
203. Ibid., Lévy's description taken from AF BB^{30} 383. Perhaps here it is well to remember Patrice Higonnet's perceptive suggestion that rural "artisans" may be landless laborers forced to find nonagricultural work, not necessarily skilled craftsmen. Patrice L.-R. Higonnet, *Pont-de-Montvert*, pp. 59–60.
204. AD Yonne III M^4 8–9.
205. The deputies Marie and Coste came to the burial of the impious Dr. Grénet at Joigny.
206. AD Yonne III M^1 267.

207. AD Yonne III M¹ 270. The subprefect suggested that the circle be closed.
208. AD Yonne II M¹ 159.
209 L. M. Tisserand, *Léopold Javal.* The biography has the character of an official obituary: Tisserand was then chief of the bureau of beaux-arts and historical works at the prefecture of the Seine. Ibid., pp. 32–7.
210. AD Yonne II M¹ 159. Javal said the designation had been unsolicited: It was acceptable only because it had been "proclaimed by the administration as an act of deference to the electors." His electoral posters assured voters that he wished to owe the honor of reelection solely to "your free and independent will."
211. AD Yonne II M¹ 159. Charton had not been a firebrand himself. The *Magasin pittoresque* did not print news per se; it was, for a work of "vulgarization," written at a fairly high level, devoted to the lives of self-made men, health, temperance, travel, and extremely chaste serials. The only notice taken of the Revolution of 1848 was an article that appeared toward the end of that year on "Symbols of Public Authority," which noted with satisfaction that the device "Liberty, Equality, Fraternity" was again the national one. *Le Magasin pittoresque*, 1848, p. 351. In August, after the June Days, there had appeared an article on penal colonies from the travel diary of a Captain Rigodit, which might interest readers, "if only as a geographical study." Ibid., p. 266.

   Perhaps most bizarre of all, there came early in the authoritarian empire a long, stupefyingly detailed article on the Houses of Parliament in London, noting the regard of the British sovereign for "ancient traditions" (ibid., 1853, pp. 49 ff.) like representative government. The first issue of 1853 had included a warning taken from Malesherbe: "It calls for a fine, sharp eye to grasp the line between prudence and dissimulation" (ibid., p. 7). Not until the middle sixties did the magazine caution, "For nations as for men there is no true or solid grandeur . . . unless force is based on liberty." Ibid., 1866, pp. 63–4.
212. AD Yonne II M¹ 159.
213. AD Yonne 81 T4. Duruy's authorization (December 1865) for the next year covered Challe, Bert, Lepère, Ribière, and ten other speakers.
214. "Municipaliser la réforme," Duruy, *Notes et Souvenirs*, vol. 1, pp. 220–2. The law of April 10, 1867, left communes the right to decree free schooling; and in organizing secondary courses for young women, Duruy instructed rectors to endeavor to make the initiatives appear to emanate from municipal councils. Maurain, *La Politique ecclésiastique*, p. 840.
215. AD Yonne 32 T1. In the year of the law's passage, nine towns took advantage of its provisions; the next year, fourteen more towns voted free schooling. By 1870 there were sixty-five schools in the Yonne where attendance cost nothing whatsoever.
216. AD Yonne 78 T 5.
217. AD Yonne 78 T5.
218. AD Yonne 81 T 2. Auxerre prided itself on being the first city after Paris and Marseille to profit from the law of June 10, 1868. Cf. G. Rouillé, *Les Sociétés d'instruction populaire dans l'Yonne,"* p. 124.
219. Rouillé, *Les Sociétés*, p. 126.
220. AD Yonne 81 T 2. Letter of April 9, 1869. Was Robert warning them to make themselves acceptable to his successor?

221. AD Yonne 81 T 2. *Compte-rendu historique*, May 30, 1874, prepared for the SPIP by Charles Moiset.
222. AD Gironde I M 244.
223. Rouillé, *Les Sociétés*, p. 126. A twenty-one–member committee designated a governing bureau. Rouillé defended this feature as "democratic": It maintained equality among members because no one enjoyed the "preponderant role" conferred by direct election.
224. Abel Chatelain, "La Ligue de l'enseignement et l'éducation populaire en Bourgogne au début de la Troisième République," p. 106.
225. AD Yonne II M¹ 175. The minister of the interior informed the prefect of the Yonne (March 6, 1869) that the *Phare de la Loire*, one of the most important progressive provincial papers, noted action taken by the municipal council of Appoigny to prevent the distribution of official ballot papers. Electors voted by selecting among ballots printed with the names of the various candidates: They chose one of several ballots and "deposited it in the urn." They did not mark off the preferred name on a list of all candidates. Therefore, the *distribution* of ballot papers was of critical importance and, obviously, subject to manipulation.
226. Rouillé, *Les Sociétés*, pp. 126–7.
227. AD Yonne II M¹ 184. Eleven petitions are extant; Telegram to prefect, Sens, April 28, 1870.
228. Javal, like other members of the Consistoire, took a guarded and moderate position on religious issues. After the Mortara case the freemason Adolphe Crémieux, an early patron of Gambetta, organized the explicitly reformist Alliance israélite universelle (cf. Jacob Katz, *Jews and Freemasons*, pp. 154–6). Younger Jews like Ernest Hendlé and Alfred Naquet, best known for his support of a divorce bill, were characteristic of a later generation that worked confidently with skeptics of Christian upbringing. Cf. also AD Bouches-du-Rhône M⁶ 163, Gaston Crémieux's public praise of freemasonry for envisaging "the federation of peoples and universal fraternity."
229. AD Yonne F 173, Papiers Paul Bert, includes a clipping from *La Constitution*, August 26, 1880, in which Bert recounted the establishment of the prize.
230. AD Yonne 81 T 4.
231. The libraries were founded at Guerchy, Seignelay, Neuilly, Boilly, Villemer, Fleury, Moneteau, Brion, Toucy, Branches, Bussy, Epineau, Champvalle, and Germigny.
232. Chatelain, *La Ligue*, pp. 108–9. The circle at Semur had been authorized, for one year only, in December of 1871 and encountered difficulties in extending its legal life. Its first bulletin, the only one extant, appeared in January of 1873.
233. AD Yonne 81 T 4. Letter of December 30, 1872.
234. AD Yonne III M¹ 312. The conservative mayor of Sens, M. Provent, had already asked the support of the administration in his struggle with a radical municipal council.
235. AD Yonne 81 T 4. This warning came in a letter dated December 24, 1872, authorizing the son of a Dr. Toutée to speak for the liberation of the *patrie* at Saint Fargeau. The man could not be fairly refused, the minister acknowledged, "considering the reserve he has demonstrated." Revanchist talks were considered especially dangerous, however; the government did not wish to provoke the Germans, and thus forbade the professor of

German at the *lycée* of Sens from speaking on "Henri Heine: the Germans and the French judged by a German."

236. AD Yonne 81 T 4, Ribière's letters to the Ministry of the Interior.

237. AD Yonne 81 T 4, letter of December 13, 1872. "L'Eclairage au gaz ne semble devoir en aucune occurrence amener de perturbation dans le pays." Perhaps this was not the case in 1872, but a few years later such a topic might be forbidden as evocative of the dangerous antithesis between light and shadow.

238. Ibid., letter of March 20, 1873.

239. Chatelain, *La Ligue*, p. 107.

240. "La guardienne des moeurs, la sauvegarde des vertus," *Bulletin de la SPIP*, no. 4, pp. 23–5. Flandin, the previous years, had been deemed "bien jeune," and thus disqualified from presenting his views on American history.

241. AD Yonne 81 T 2.

242. *Bulletin de la SPIP*, no. 4, secretary's report, April 1874.

243. AD Yonne 81 T 2, *Compte-rendu historique*, presented May 30, 1874, by Charles Moiset.

244. AD Yonne III M¹ 312; Sens, reported April 1875.

245. In this period Macé seemed less averse to a centralized distribution of books and, with Emmanuel Vauchez of the Paris circle, worked to found regimental libraries. Alfaric, *Jean Macé*, pp. 82–3.

246. AD Yonne 78 T 6. Mme Robert Parly, a granddaughter of Maximilien Cornebise, one of the library's original members, and a woman of vigorous lucidity, told me that Cornebise had indeed been a gardener in the seventies and had bought the farm on which her family now lives from the church after disestablishment. She characterized her family as "moderates": "We always flew the tricolor," she said, "not the *drapeau rouge*. But others did."

247. AD Yonne 81 T 2, *Bulletin* (SPIP), November 1874.

248. Ibid.

249. AD Yonne III M¹ 312, April 25, 1875. Sixteenth century, Cervantes and selections from the letters of Henri IV; seventeenth century, Bossuet, Corneille, Racine, Molière; eighteenth century, Montesquieu, Voltaire; contemporary, Guizot, Thiers, and Michelet, among others.

250. AD Yonne 81 T 2. There are two trivially different copies of the subprefect's letter as well as the report of the director of the Sûreté-général.

251. Rouillé, *Les Sociétés*, p. 131.

252. AD Yonne 81 T 2, January 9, 1875.

253. AD Yonne III M¹ 312, curé's letter, May 18, 1875.

254. Ibid. A report of June 1875 noted his attack on infallibility and on the doctrine of the Immaculate Conception, on oral confessions and, interestingly, his recapitulation of Jansenist objections to the first communions of young children and a parallel attack on infant baptism as merely magical, involving neither comprehension nor conviction.

255. Ibid. Guichard had interceded.

256. AD Yonne 32 T 1.

257. *Bulletin de l'instruction primaire du département de l'Yonne*, no. 69, August 5, 1876.

258. AD Yonne 43 T 1. Frontier's report is in the records of the Conseil général.

259. AD Yonne 81 T 2, decree of November 1, 1875. The minister of the interior now shared the prefect's estimation of the group, at least insofar

as to add his finesse to their subduing: Copies of the decree, he recommended, must be addressed to each group; notifying only the parent group would confirm Ribière's representation of the group's character. Minister's letter of November 12, 1875.

260. AD Yonne 81 T 2; Letter of May 24, 1876: *la voie calme et laborieuse qu'elle s'est tracée*; letter of October 31, 1876, prefect to SPIP. He told them he had conferred with the minister of the interior and that this had been the minister's worry.

"Groups of a different nature" fared less well in the Yonne. A Catholic Workers' Circle was begun in 1874 by self-styled members of the "ruling classes": It had not caught on, but in 1877 there was an attempt to revive it. The mayor of Auxerre noted then recent attacks on the "principles of '89" by prominent Catholic laymen, notably de Mun, and predicted that "at a time when all true friends of order seek reconciliation," the recognition of such a group could only "accentuate more and more divisions already so regrettable" (AD Yonne III M⁴ 16). In 1880 the police reported that the group, established in 1877, had never functioned, "lacking members."

261. AD Yonne III M¹ 284.
262. AD Yonne III M¹ 284. Report of E. Crousse, subprefect at Sens.
263. Rouillé, *Les Sociétés*, p. 132.
264. AD Yonne 81 T 2.
265. A. Challe, "Histoire des guerres du calvinisme et de la Ligue," pp. 309–11. The incident at Vassy, March 1, 1562, was a serious one: Soldiers riding with the duc de Guise set upon a congregation of Protestants meeting in a barn and killed perhaps a hundred. The episode at Sens is described now only as a "riot." James Westfall Thompson, *The Wars of Religion in France, 1559–76*, pp. 133–5. AD Yonne 78 T 5; Challe served, for example, on the committee of the municipal library, itself a vestige of the Second Republic. Another member, M. Ducharme, had been the director of the Normal School of the Yonne. Ducharme resigned his directorship after the coup of 2 décembre. I have not been able to discover the reasons he gave for his resignation, but perhaps he associated himself with the general council's protest against attacks on provincial normal schools, the restriction of their curriculum, and the end to merit admissions.
266. In 1862, Berryer eloquently defended strikers charged with "coalition," illegal under the antiguild legislation of 1791: "If a worker wants to share his intelligence with a fellow, he commits a crime." Berryer offered the corporatist labor arrangements of Louis XVI as an alternative to laissez-faire. Lacombe, *Berryer*, pp. 389–93. In 1863, Parisian typographers struck again in a protest, which a Catholic conservative might have found congenial, over the employment of women compositors. On this issue Catholics and Proudhonians opposed political economists and Marxists. Corbon, *Le Secret*, pp. 152–60.
267. AD Bouches-du-Rhône (henceforth AD BR) Iᵗ 8/1.
268. AD BR M⁶ 163, M⁶ 950. Alexander Labadié's membership card, number 350, for the Workers' Atheneum, is the only one preserved in the departmental archives. I suspect he is the same as "Labadié, businessman," and deputy mayor in 1848, the protagonist in a sensational scandal two years before. In 1864, the vicar of a suburban parish, Saint-Barnabas, visited the Labadié summer house often, ostensibly to catechize their maid. The father of the family intercepted indecent (or so he said: The unfortunate

cleric may have copied out devotional passages of dubious imagery) letters addressed to his thirteen-year-old daughter. He shot the priest, at very close range but not fatally, and the police reported that public opinion intensely championed the outraged parent. The affair, they said, could only harm the "interests of order and religion." AD BR M⁶ 61.

269. AD BR, M⁶ 163.

270 *L'Action maçonnique*, pp. 111–12. Royannez is described by the Marseillais historian Olivesi as an "ardent Blanquist" and as head of the city's free-thinkers. Antoine Olivesi, *La Commune de 1871 à Marseille*.

271. Macé, *Les Origines*, p. 284, reprinted in the third Bulletin of the league, May 1867, "un point d'appui tout prêt dans le groupe compacte d'hommes de progrès."

272. AD BR, M⁶ 163, letters of August 17 and 27, 1868; new statutes approved September 4, 1868.

273. AD BR, M⁶ 163; courses described in a letter of de Pleuc to the prefect, September 28, 1868.

274. Macé, *Les Origines*, pp. 413 ff.

275. "Se mettre en rapport direct avec les auditeurs," *Bulletin du mouvement*, pp. 39–42. The article is unsigned, but if it is not the work of Macé, it can scarcely have been published in Beblenheim without his knowledge and consent.

276. Ibid.

277. AD BR, M⁶ 163. The sixteen included three lawyers, Crémieux, J. Maurel, and Boucher; two "proprietors," Guizou and Hoeffer; two "employees," Rouvier and Converset; two "workers," Biscarel and Roger; a tailor; a crammer (*répétiteur*); a merchant; an architect; a bookkeeper; and one self-described "man of letters." In comparison, of the twenty-five leading members of the Ligue marseillaise for whom there is occupational information, two are lawyers, two doctors, two engineers, one a captain in the army, and three businessmen – *commerçants, négociants* – and three others: one each, a bookkeeper, employee, or "commercial representative." The mason, carpenter, cabinetmaker, and dressmaker may be artisans or employers, because only one, a mechanic, specified that he was an "ouvrier-mécanicien," but the others gave only their specialty. One man, seemingly torn between the old regime and the new, described himself as an eldest son and a foreman.

278. AD BR, M⁶ 163. Police report of meeting of September 18, 1868.

279. AD BR, M⁶ 163. October 21, 1868.

280. AD BR, M⁶ 163. Their resignation is noted in a letter whose receipt was registered at the prefecture on September 24.

281. AD BR, M⁶ 163. Letter of November 8, 1868.

282. Ibid.

283. AD BR, M⁶ 90.

284. Ibid. Correspondence of December 1868.

285. AD BR, M⁶ 90. The existence of the committee and its composition were public knowledge; *Le Peuple* of February 14, 1869, listed Delpech, Maurel, Tardif, Brochier, Boucher, Rouvier, and Crémieux, and some others, "cobblers, painters, and accountants," as constituting the committee of the Phocéen Association to promote the candidacy of Léon Gambetta.

286. Barral, *Les Fondateurs*, pp. 66–9.

287. AM Lyon, I² 56 B, *Correspondence* Albert Richard, letter of February 24, 1869.

288. Ibid., May 22, 1869. A sum, not a synthesis; note Bastelica's use of positivist and practical (not Hegelian) language.
289. AD BR, M⁶ 163, Police report of meeting, November 20, 1869. The religious press was said to have argued that "man has no country but heaven and no mother but the Church."
290. Maurain, *La Politique écclésiastique*, pp. 533–40, remarked the increasing willingness of the government to bring criminal actions against ecclesiastics in the early 1860s. Michelet took approving notice of this in the preface to the second edition of *Du Prêtre*: "French justice, in its glorious reawakening, has taken to heart the defense of morality." Ibid, p. 536.
291. AD BR, M⁶ 163. Police report of meeting of November 20, 1869.
292. Bastelica, despite his reliance here on the imperative mandate, was not a democrat. He had written to Albert Richard, "I belong rationally to the minority. Am I not a republican? Scientifically I believe in the People no more than in God" (AM Lyon I² 56 B. October 6, 1869), barely a month before this meeting!
293. *L'Action maçonnique*, 1869. "Le niveau égalitaire ne s'établira qu'après qu'une saine morale et une solide instruction primaire auront élevé intellectuellement un peu plus ceux qui sont placés trop bas dans le catégorie sociale."
294. Ibid. "Intrusions donc et nous équilibrerons la société, qui ne risquera plus alors d'être un jour ébranlée sur sa base."
295. AD BR, M⁶ 309.
296. Ibid. The Fauchon letters, which are unfortunately undated, are found in the carton, "Republicans, 1869–71," of the departmental archives.
297. AD BR, M⁶ 163, November 20, 1869.
298. Ibid.
299. AD BR, M⁶ 309. "Prolonged and frenetic applause" was reported to have followed his address.
300. Olivesi, *La Commune*, makes excellent use of available material.
301. AD BR, M⁶ 90. Esquiros's *arrêté* cited the incompatibility of the Jesuits' expressed principles with the independence of all representative governments. Clipping from the *Journal de Marseille*, October 13, 1870.
302. AD BR, V M² 78. The *procès-verbaux* of the municipal council for the period March 23 to April 1, 1871, records these perplexities, including the ingenious proposal of "citizen Job" to fly both flags.
303. AD BR, O¹ *bis*, deliberations of the muncipal council, December 18, 1872.
304. AD BR, V M² 78.
305. AD BR, Iᵀ 8/2.
306. AD BR, O¹ *bis*. On May 7, 1872, Rech urged the *minimum* salary for clerical teachers. In 1872 and 1873 a large number of new lay schools were created in various quarters of the city and in the suburbs.
307. AD BR, V M² 78.
308. AD BR. Extract from *Régistres des délibérations du Conseil municipal de Marseille*, December 1, 1876.
309. AD BR, V M² 78. Gay, one of the *fougueux*, had been in the national guard in 1870.
310. AD BR, M⁶ 3403.
311. Ibid. Some police seemed to believe the receipt of mail from Geneva proof of complicity in the most satanic schemes.
312. AD BR, M⁶ 163. Brochier is listed among the fifty-four members.
313. AD BR V M² 78.

314. AD BR, M⁶ 163.
315. AD BR, M⁶ 2330. The topics were largely moral subjects such as the distinctions among *l'orgeuil, la vanité,* and *la fierté,* the role of married women in society, and the importance of masonic baptism.
316. AD BR M⁶ 950.

3. Establishing the republic

1. AF F¹⁷ 12448, trial of Lyonnais teachers before Departmental Council of the Rhône.
2. AF F¹⁷ 9173; AD Rhône T 529.
3. "Leur but de propager . . . les habitudes d'esprit et de vie publique des pays libres," quoted by Jean Macé, "A Cercles catholiques," pp. 35 ff.
4. Bury, *Gambetta,* p. 94 ff; P. Henry, *Histoire des préfets,* p. 199 ff.
5. Georges Duveau, *La Pensée Ouvrière sur l'éducation,* p. 42.
6. AD Rhône T 161. *Ecoles Primaires Municipales de Lyon, Le conseil d'administration aux Pères et Mères de Famille.*
7. Sometimes, a bust of the Republic in a phrygian cap replaced religious symbols. AF F¹⁷ 12529.
8. AD Rhône, T 161. "En reprenant possession des Ecoles primaires entre-tenues aux frais de la Commune de Lyon."
9. AF F¹⁷ 9173. *Les Règlements et programme des écoles primaires municipales de la ville de Lyon* (henceforth *Règlements*), introduction.
10. AD Rhône T 161, also found in AF F¹⁷ 12448.
11. *Règlements.*
12. Michelet, *Le Peuple,* p. 215. "Le moyen age est pour lui un terrible pédagogue; il lui propose le symbole le plus compliqué qu'on ait enseigné jamais, le plus inaccessible aux simples."
13. Program of the schools of the Third Arrondissement of Paris, reprinted in the Bulletin I, p. 141 ff.
14. Report of academic inspector at Marseille, AD BR, I^T 4/8. He regretted, too, that even in arithmetic children were not taught to reason and that experiences of ordinary life were seldom incorporated in their lessons.
15. *Bulletin* I, p. 141 ff.
16. AF F¹⁷ 12529.
17. *Bulletin* I, p. 141 ff.
18. AF F¹⁷ 12529. *Compte-rendu, Les écoles libres du 1ᵉʳ arrondissement, 1878–79.*
19. Ibid., p. 13. These celebrations were not usually despised by radicals, because of the opportunities for speech making and republican conviviality they afforded. Prize-giving ceremonies had long aroused the suspicious dread of the minister of the interior, who asked Duruy to localize by canton the distribution of prizes to teachers of adult courses. He wished to avoid ceremonies in the capital of each department; he especially did not want to gather together men involved with the education of adults – that is, voters. AF F¹⁷ 2682.
20. Ibid., pp. 14–16.
21. *Règlements,* article 62.
22. AF F¹⁷ 12448.
23. AF F¹⁷ 12526. The Municipal Archives of Bordeaux include references of the trials of their teachers.

24. *Règlements.*
25. AF F[17] 12448. Printed declaration of Conseil d'administration.
26. AF F[17] 9173. Aubin, the *inspecteur primaire* of the Academy of Lyon, to minister of public instruction, July 19, 1871; Mayor Hénon to minister of public instruction, August 26, 1871.
27. AF F[17] 9173. Letter of minister to prefect, July 1871.
28. *Règlements.*
29. AF F[17] 9173. LeRoyer to the minister of public instruction, April 16, 1871.
30. AF F[17] 9173. The report to the mayor, March 15, 1871, concerning liquidation of the society's schools, noted that Jews and Protestants had spontaneously offered their facilities to the city.
31. *Règlements.* Article 14 required that school materials be provided free, on the basis of "attestation de l'indigence."
32. AF F[17] 9173, August 25, 1871. The rector of the Academy of Lyon assured the minister that it had not been an "atheistical demonstration." Public celebrations had become matters of bitter controversy since the municipality forbade religious processions in public thoroughfares.

    Again in 1873 a throng of three thousand gathered on Arlès-Dufour's grounds for Prize Day. Deputy Ordinaire wrote, "They are establishing for all time the reign of liberty and social emancipation." Deputies Guyot and Barodet also sent letters. Dr. Guyot, who missed the celebration of La Muletière, for one, at Villefranche, exhorted parents that their duty was to resist the "invasion of clericals that menaces us." Langlade told the assembled children, "You will make efforts . . . to maintain and protect our young Republic and to defend its institutions." AF F[17] 12448; Edgar Quinet, *La République*, p. 113.
33. AF F[17] 9173, prefect's letter, August 21, 1871.
34. In 1874, under a different regime, the administration was less solicitous of the interests of this group. The society, dispensing municipal funds and enjoying a large autonomy, could be replaced by academic functionaries. Its "pure and simple reconstitution was in no way desirable." AF F[17] 12525. Report of the rector of the Academy of Lyon to the minister of public instruction, February 1874.
35. AF F[17] 9173, minister's letter, November 22, 1871; Garnier, in April 1872, seemed to be not at all embarrassed that he, editor of the great organ of provincial autonomy, was conspiring with the prefecture against the government of the city of Lyon.
36. AF F[17] 9173.
37. Ibid., prefect's letter, April 25, 1872. Pascal recalled, too, his "courageous defense" (with his pen) of the Christian Brothers at Toulouse "against the violences of M. Duportal." Armand Duportal, republican prefect of Haute-Garonne, supported the municipal council of Toulouse in the secularization of its schools, an act that Pascal felt deserved the disapprobation of all "true liberals."
38. AD Rhône T 161 *rouge* (T 34 *noir*). Barodet's letter of May 8, 1872.
39. AD Rhône T 161 *rouge. Rapport au conseil d'administration des écoles de la commission chargée étudier la loi de 1850.*
40. AF F[17] 9173. The numbers eventually decreed gave slight preponderance to secular schools; of seventy-four boys' schools, forty-one were to be lay and thirty clerical, with two Protestant and one Jewish school kept distinct.

Girls' schools were divided among thirty-five secular and thirty-one "religious," three Protestant, one Jewish school. Pascal's *arrêté* in AD Rhône T 161 *rouge*.

41. AD Rhône T 259. Loenger had managed in the spring of 1879 to unite metal workers in one association. AD Rhône 4M4 505.
42. AF F[17] 9173.
43. Bibliothèque Nationale NAF 16932 Archives Hetzel.
44. AM Lyon I[2] 44. The crowd that stormed into the prefecture on September 4 found this document, which conferred, as such lists must, great distinction. Andrieux seemed to be a voice for moderation. He cautioned Albert Richard in November of 1870 that any attempt against the new republic would produce a dangerous reaction. AM Lyon I[2] 56B.
45. AM Lyon I[2] 46 A.
46. Barodet, in his chagrin at being omitted from the enemies' list, insisted that the Cercle de la Ruche had been a formidable thorn in the side of the Second Empire. Désiré Barodet, *Eclaircissements historiques*, p. 10. I have seen no evidence of this, but at least the men were acquainted.
47. *Le Petit Lyonnais*, October 1, 1872.
48. AF F[17] 12448.
49. AD Rhône T 259. He said on the same occasion that clerical education left boys in ignorance and led girls to prostitution.
50. AF F[17] 9173; AD Rhône T 529, police report of ELL supporters in the Sixth identified them as weavers and *chefs d'atelier*. One woman, a glovemaker, was "hard-working, respectable, proud, and irreligious." Another couple, both weavers, went to freethinking meetings. The wife had learned to read in ELL adult courses.
51. AD Rhône 259. They reiterated its insistence upon secular schooling as the way to inspire children with love for their family and their country, with duty and respect for society.
52. AF F[17] 9173. On 21 March, 1873, the Conseil d'état upheld the decision of the prefect of the Rhône to require maintenance of some congregational schools and sustained, too, his inscription of expenditures for the salaries of the teaching brothers.
53. John Labusquière, *La Troisième République, 1871–1900*, pp. 96–97.
54. AD Rhône 4M4 505. Decree of June 19, 1873.
55. AD Rhône T 259.
56. AD Rhône T 260. Andrieux's own book, *La Commune*, is highly critical of the commune and curiously silent on the problem of the schools. Like LeRoyer, Andrieux opposed "extremism" but was inclined to support radical secularists on the general issues of public enlightenment and civil liberties.
57. AF F[17] 12448.
58. AD Rhône T 260; report of October 18, 1873.
59. AD Rhône T 259.
60. AD Rhône 4 M 826/2.
61. AD Rhône 4 M 826/4.
62. AD Rhône 4 M 4 505.
63. Jacques Gouault, *Comment la France est devenue républicaine*, p. 114. Gouault argued that the *communards* made the radicals seem moderate and plausible by contrast.
64. Elwitt dismisses this group as "representing the commercial and manufacturing entrepreneurs of central Paris." Elwitt, p. 49. He offers no evidence,

nor does he specify what sort of representation he implies: Agency, coincidence of immediate interests, or a more general correspondence of class position.

65. Floquet had not a good opinion of Thiers, who met their plea for cessation of the bombardment of Neuilly offhandedly: "C'est une assez mauvaise population." Archives de France, A. P. Floquet, Papiers Floquet, *Procès-verbaux de la Ligue républicaine pour les droits de Paris*, p. 86. See also Louis Morris Greenburg's *Sisters of Liberty*, which argues that this effort of conciliation was made plausible by the strong, traditional emphasis on municipal self-government that was part of the communes.

66. Jean Macé, *Les Idées de Jean-François*, pp. 53–6.

67. AF F¹⁷ 12529.

68. Duveau, *La Pensée*, p. 45.

69. AF F¹⁷ 12529. *Appel au commerçants.*

70. AF F¹⁷ 12529. Report of the prefect of police, 1874.

71. E. Spuller, "Discours prononcé à la distribution solennelle des prix aux élèves des deux sexes," August 18, 1878, pp. 13–14.

72. AD BR M⁶ 164. Report of Augustin Tardieu, March 19, 1866, and related correspondence.

73. AD BR I^T 8/1. Extract of proceedings of municipal council of Arles, February 16, 1871.

74. AD BR I^T 8/2.

75. AF F¹⁷ 12526. Prefect's *arrêté*, December 10, 1873.

76. AF F¹⁷ 9175.

77. AF F¹⁷ 12526. *Arrêté* of December 10, 1873.

78. Ibid.

79. Ibid., Mayor's letter, December 1871.

80. AF F¹⁷ 9175.

81. Ibid.

82. Ibid., Victor Duruy had, in some measure, aided the municipal council. In 1866 he had agreed to the closing of a Catholic school (the school of the rue de la Cloche d'or) and created a secular school to replace it. In 1867 M. Saint René-Taillandier headed a commission that urged an increase in the number of lay schools to two and reduction of Catholic schools to three. This was the *status quo ante* 1870. Even the voice of the minister of the interior had been raised against the congregations. When their defenders had argued that an attack on the teaching orders meant a diminution in number of absolutely free places, the minister of the interior urged the prefect to reassure the population that the two issues, secularization and free schooling, were entirely separate questions.

83. Ibid.

84. Ibid. Escarguel's letter, October 20, 1873, and subsequent prefect's report.

85. AF F¹⁷ 9174. Inadequate levels of school attendance and achievement were attributed partly to the indifference of families, but in large measure to the monopoly permitted religious orders. A report on primary education submitted to the municipal council of Vichy in March of 1871 complained further of "insalubrity" of religious establishments and also of "commercial ventures whose accounts were not made available to us." The enterprise to which the report referred was a private boarding school (*demi-pensionnat*) cited by the municipality in a legal maneuver to prevent reinstallation of religious teachers. In 1874 the city argued that ecclesiastics had forfeited

their title as public teachers in directing a private school and that this incompatibility was tantamount to resignation. The case went up to the Conseil d'état, but Vichy desisted before the decision was rendered, acquiescing, presumably, in the prefect's demand that it support schools of both characters.

86. Frédéric Morin's works, *La Séparation de l'Eglise et de l'état* and *La Confession*, had been published under the pseudonym Miron. G. Weill, *Histoire de l'Idée laique*, p. 243.

87. AF F¹⁷ 9174.

88. Bertholon's article quoted in AF F¹⁷ 9175.

89. Ferry's letter to the minister of public instruction, December 20, 1871, AF F¹⁷ 9174. The commune of Beauvoisin in the Gard had also asked for a breveted lay schoolmistress. The prefect regretted that it was precisely the most violent radicals who were elected to the municipal council and he rejected their request.

90. *Bulletin* I, 1872, pp. 10–11.

91. *Ibid*, Daughters of brigade members would be given preference, with daughters of league members, in admission to the school. Members of the ambulance corps might also be elected to the supervisory committee. A headmistress was found for the school – one personally recommended by Macé – and its patrons prided themselves on the rigor of the school's program. It was obviously a school for the daughters of the *gens éclairés* of the colony.

92. Ibid.

93. AF F¹⁷ 9174.

94. AF F¹⁷ 12531, *Projet, Société d'instruction élémentaire*, 1876, Article 111.

95. Cf. reports on the SIE AF F¹⁷ 12535, and on the Association philotechnique, AF F¹⁷ 12544. These fluctuations were also evident in the cabinet: There would be eighteen ministers of the interior between 1870 and 1877 and changes almost as frequent, and no less political in nature, in the Ministry of Public Education, Henry, *L'Histoire*, p. 213.

96. AF F¹⁷ 12525, F¹⁷ 12526, F¹⁷ 12527.

97. C3477. Thus, a defeated republican candidate, Barbadette, qualified actions taken in the Charente-Inférieure.

98. Macé, "A Cercles catholiques, pp. 18, 21–2. When Pope Pius IX warned Catholics in November 1873 against impious secret societies, Charles-Emile Freppel, bishop of Angers, used the publication of the encyclical as an occasion to denounce the Ligue de l'enseignement by name. The pope soon thereafter enjoined Freppel to continue his efforts to extirpate that evil, "cette déplorable plantation des enfants de ténèbres." Prosper Alfaric, *Jean Macé*, p. 81. De Mun would be defeated by a radical doctor in 1878, after his narrow victory the previous fall had been invalidated by the National Assembly. His opponent had complained that the clergy "abusively employed their moral authority" on de Mun's behalf. Archives de France, C3490.

99. Talmy, *L'Association catholique*, pp. 9–13.

100. Macé, *L'Ennemi*, pp. 5, 38 ff., 66.

101. Talmy, *L'Association catholique*, pp. 19–21. The appeal issued by Catholic employers at Lille describing the "religious and moral reorganization of the factory" spoke of reforms that could not have been unrelated to the achievement of greater productivity, insofar as they were not merely symbolic acts such as the placing of a crucifix or a religious picture in the

workrooms. The plea, which was intended to arouse the social conscience of Catholic employers and the enthusiasm of workers, dealt mainly with sex segregation in the factories, the provision of separate exits for men and women workers, surveillance of lavatories and "judicious choices of foremen." The Catholics were concerned, as secular supporters of professional education had been, with recruitment of skilled and dependable foremen. The appeal also suggested that almost-universal device to prevent rash spending of meager wages: Workers might be paid not in cash but with "payment vouchers." Presumably – although this is left unsaid – these would be current only at company or approved shops.

102. *Bulletin de la Ligue de l'enseignement*, II, p. 224.
103. Macé, *L'Ennemi*, pp. 34–5.
104. Macé, "A Cercles catholiques," pp. 23, 39. These words are capitalized in Macé's text.
105. Papers included the *Progrès du Côte d'or* at Dijon; *La Démocratie France-Comtoise* at Besançon; *L'Avenir* at Rennes; the *Patriote* and the *Travailleur* – under the eyes of Freppel at Angers; the *Gironde*, the *Courrier de l'Aisne*, and others in the Midi. "A Cercles catholiques," pp. 53–4, 62–3.
106. Jean Macé, "L'Instruction obligatoire," *Les Idées de Jean-François*, vol. 5, pp. 50–1, 56–7.
107. Jean Macé, "La Vérité sur le suffrage universel," *Les Idées de Jean-François*, vol. 4, pp. 34–5, 42. He insisted in another pamphlet of this period on a variation of Prévost-Paradol's suggestion in *La France Nouvelle* for three-member constituencies in which voters might concentrate or distribute three preferences. Macé went further than Prévost-Paradol and suggested that votes of deputies within the assembly be weighted in proportion to the popular votes that each had received.
108. Gouault, *Comment la France*, p. 160.
109. AF F[17] 12526.
110. Paul Lachapelle, "Le Cercle parisien et la Ligue française de l'enseignement," p. 95.
111. *Bulletin* I, pp. 185–6.
112. Ibid., pp. 10–11.
113. Ibid., p. 187.
114. Ibid., p. 208.
115. Ibid., pp. 190–9.
116. Ibid., pp. 178, 219; *Bulletin* II, p. 196.
117. *Bulletin* II, *Compte rendu*, 1879, p. 3.
118. AF F[17] 2655, Académie de Lyon, June 1872.
119. Cited by Prost, *l'Enseignement*, p. 213; *Sénat* 4/6/81, pp. 780f.
120. AF F[17] 12527. Jules Simon, then minister of public instruction, declined to endorse the competition. He felt that during parliamentary debate on a new law governing primary education, he could "order nothing that would appear to put into execution its provisions." Marginalia, perhaps by Simon, added "order nothing *for the moment*." Underlined in manuscript.
121. Elwitt hints that Ménier's "vast" cocoa plantations in Nicaragua could have done with some reforming, too, but presents no evidence. Elwitt, *The Making*, p. 247.
122. Edith Thomas, *The Women Incendiaries*, pp. 112 ff.
123. AF F[17] 12526.
124. In the late 1860s a concern for professionalism and an awareness that

215

overt pressure could be counterproductive militated against the crasser forms of electioneering. Eugène Spuller had defended the schoolmasters of Dijon who refused to campaign for the official candidate and against Joseph Magnin, a member of the League. The case was decided against the plaintiffs, with costs, but the rector of the academy of Dijon advised Duruy that teachers should not be made to canvass. In rural areas, especially, schoolmasters should be available at home: Their advice then would have the opposite effect to that which it would produce unsolicited. "The peasant is made that way." In by-elections in the Seine in 1864, the Interior Ministry asked that teachers be given only verbal instructions and those "with the reserve that the exceptional situation calls for." AF F[17] 2682.

125. AF F[17] 12526.
126. Ibid. He had authorized the group in October of 1873, rather a late date for such a group to win a prefect's approbation, so his insistence upon the group's honorable character may be in large measure an attempt to justify his action.
127. AF F[17] 12526.
128. Ibid.
129. Ibid.
130. AF F[17] 12525.
131. AF F[17] 12527. The prefect of the Ardennes, noting the "inexperience" of local league representatives in matters of education, judged "the movement is good but the administration must direct it."
132. Ibid.
133. AF F[17] 12526 and F[17] 12527.
134. AF F[17] 12526.
135. Ibid. The terms of their authorization did not require such consultation, but it had been customary.
136. AF F[17] 12526.
137. AF F[17] 12526. Goblet, protesting the dissolution before the National Assembly, insisted on the books' moderate tenor: One, he said, proved Rousseau to have been not an atheist but a deist; another had characterized Robespierre as a man of "large and strong faith."
138. AF F[17] 12527.
139. AF F[17] 12526.
140. Ibid.
141. Ibid.
142. Reclus, Le Seize Mai, pp. 48–50.
143. Ibid., pp. 55–6.
144. AF C3477.
145. Reclus, Le Seize Mai, pp. 50, 71.
146. Ibid., and Henry, L'Histoire, p. 218.
147. Reclus, Le Seize Mai, p. 50.
148. Ibid., pp. 50–1; Jules Ferry, "Discours Prononcé à la Réunion à la gauche républicaine," p. 5; Bulletin, 1877, president's report, p. 20.
149. Ibid., p. 21.
150. AF F[17] 12682.
151. AF F[17] 12538, July 28, 1877. In the Aisne and the Ardennes, Henri Martin and several other deputies were forbidden to speak at academic ceremonies. Bulletin, "Comptes-rendus des cercles," December 31, 1871, p. 175.
152. AF C3477, Barbadette's protest.

153. AF F¹⁷ 12527, July 1877.
154. AF C3477.
155. AF C3490.
156. AF F¹⁷ 12527.
157. *Bulletin*, "Comptes-rendus des cercles," 1877, p. 177.
158. AF F¹⁷ 12527.
159. AF F¹⁷ 12527. Report of the prefect of the Marne, 1877; *Bulletin*, "Comptes-rendus," 1877, pp. 21–2, 200–1.
160. AF F¹⁷ 12527. Prefect of the Yonne, July 1877.
161. *Bulletin*, "Comptes-rendus," 1877, pp. 222–3.
162. AF F¹⁷ 12527. Report of the prefect of the Seine-Inférieure, July 1877.
163. AF BB¹⁸ 1793.
164. Reclus, *Le Seize Mai*, p. 102.
165. *Bulletin*, president's report, 1877.

Conclusion

1. Péguy, pp. 30–4; Durkheim, p. 470.
2. Prosper Alfaric, *Jean Macé*, p. 102; Bert, "Rapport sur l'obligation," pp. 3–4.
3. Ibid., p. 12.
4. Loi du 30 octobre 1886, Article 7, *Règlements organiques de l'enseignement primaire, décembre 1886–janvier 1887*.
5. Text of *la loi du 28 mars 1882 établissant l'obligation et la laïcité de l'enseignement primaire*, cited in E. Benoit-Lévy and F.-B. Bocande, *Manuel pratique pour l'application de la loi sur l'instruction primaire*, p. 11.
6. Ibid., pp. 29–30.
7. Mace, *L'Ennemi*, pp. 85–6.
8. Jean Macé, "Conférence sur les sociétés républicaines d'instruction," pp. 4, 31–2.
9. AF F¹⁷ 12531.
10. AF F¹⁷ 12533.
11. AF F¹⁷ 12526.
12. Ibid.
13. *Bulletin*, 1881 p. 341.
14. *Bulletin*, 1881, pp. 442–3.
15. *Bulletin* II, pp. 250–1.
16. Ibid. Some of the lecturers: Zopff (ibid., p. 599), Mayor Kuss's assistant, now vice-president of the Orphélinat de la Seine; Emile Lefevre (ibid., p. 601), who had left the wool trade to become a "travelling salesman of instruction"; Joseph Vinot, who had joined the *Association philotechnique* in 1849 and who had begun, under the auspices of the SIE normal courses for young women in 1864 (pp. 125–6).
17. Ibid., p. 248.
18. Ibid., pp. 249 ff.
19. *Bulletin*, 1882, pp. 108–9. In 1882 the region of the North, including the departments of the Aisne, Nord, Oise, Pas-de-Calais, and the Somme, sent delegates from sixty-one local groups. The Northeast (the Ardennes, the Aube, the Marne, Haute-Marne, Meurthe-et-Moselle, Meuse, and the Vosges) accounted for forty-seven member societies. The Northwest (Calvados, Eure, Eure-et-Loire, the Manche, Orne, Sarthe, and the Seine-Inférieure), thirty-one; the West, ten only. The East (the Côte d'or, the Ain,

Doubs, Jura, Haute-Saone, Saône-et-Loire, the Yonne, and the territory of Belfort) was perhaps the best-organized area and sent representatives from forty-seven groups. (The Jura and the Vosges were areas of intense activity: There had been meetings of the *Sociétés républicaines de l'Est* since 1879. Macé, "Conférence," p. 4.) There were thirteen circles in the Southeast and Algiers; eighteen in the Aude, the Bouches-du-Rhône, Gard, Hérault, and Var; and seven in the Ardèche, Loire, Rhône; six in the Southwest; thirty-three in the Gironde and its neighboring departments, six in the Midi, nineteen in the Center, and forty-three in the Seine-et-Marne and Seine-et-Oise.

20. *Bulletin*, 1885, p. 250 ff. In his eulogy for Engel-Dollfus, buried in Mulhouse, Macé said, "Six feet beneath the earth, Engel-Dollfus is in France" (Jean Macé, "Discours de clôture," p. 8.)
21. Alfaric, *Jean Macé*, pp. 125–7.
22. AF F[17] 12527. Henri Brissac, in *Le Citoyen*, asked what more could one expect from a group that had just listened spellbound to Gambetta, "the chief of opportunism himself."
23. Jean Jaurès, "Le Bilan social du XIXe siècle," p. 309.
24. Jean Jaurès, "Le Socialisme et le radicalisme en 1885," pp. 6–7.
25. *Bulletin*, 1885, p. 198. Macé often expressed his purpose in these terms: "de chauffer les coeurs tièdes, d'éclairer les esprits sans lumières. Après quarante ans passés, j'en suis encore au même point." Macé, *Les Origines*, p. 7.
26. Michelet, *Le Peuple*, p. 165.
27. D. R. Watson, "The Politics of Educational Reform in France during the Third Republic, 1900–1940," p. 85, and John E. Talbott, *The Politics of Educational Reform in France, 1918–1940*, pp. 23–4. Watson and Talbott engaged in *Past and Present* in a debate about the degree of class bias of the Radical program.
28. These teacher-training schools supported model primary schools, probably the best free elementary education available in France: Charles Péguy attended one such. According to Talbott, of 1,000 scholarships given in 1900 for *lycée* or *collège*, only 275 were awarded to graduates of the primary school system, and 707 went to children from the "elementary classes of secondary institutions." It is possible that these figures confound the free public model schools attached to provincial normal schools with the private classes. John E. Talbott, *The Politics of Educational Reform in France 1918–1940*, p. 19.
29. Edmond Goblot, *La Barrière et le niveau, étude sociologique sur la bourgeoisie française moderne*, 1925; Pierre Bourdieu and J. C. Passeron, *Les Héritiers, les étudiants et la culture*; Talbott, *Politics*, pp. 29–32; ibid, pp. 18–19, draws on Goblot's suggestive work.
30. As Eugen Weber has shown in his splendid book, *Peasants into Frenchmen*.
31. Antoine Prost, *L'Enseignement*, p. 380.
32. Michelet, *Le Peuple*, p. 151.
33. Georges Duveau, *La vie ouvrière*, p. 269. For the indiscipline of French workers and the corresponding abundance of foremen, as contrasted with the self-discipline of British hands, Duveau relied upon the observations of the contemporary economist and novelist Louis Reybaud, ibid., p. 255.
34. Albert O. Hirschman, "The Changing Tolerance for Income Inequality in the Course of Economic Development," pp. 553–6.
35. Taxile Delord, *Histoire du Second Empire*, vol. 5, p. 176.

36. Gambetta, quoted by Barral, *Les Fondateurs*, pp 228–31.
37. Marx, *The Eighteenth Brumaire*, p. 54.
38. Marx, *Capital*, vol. 3, p. 863. Cf. also ibid., vol. 1. The infamous Dr. Andrew Ure is quoted as a supporter of machine production, but there were others, notably a Dr. Farre, who argued for legislation on the grounds that the common law, which calls for action to prevent premature death, can control the factory system, the cruellest means by which such deaths are brought about. Ibid., vol. 1, p. 280.
39. Jules Ferry used this formulation, "la société qui procède de la Révolution française" – the society that "follows," logically as well as historically, from the Revolution – in his discussion of educational equality before the SIE at the Salle Molière, April 10, 1870. Ferry, "L'Egalité d'education," pp. 28–9.
40. Bourgeois, who popularized the term, recalled that the committee organized by the "democratic party" in 1849, on which Macé served as secretary, had called itself *La Solidarité républicaine*. Léon Bourgeois, *La Solidarité*, Armand Colin, Paris, 1903.
41. Woloch, *The Jacobin Legacy*, p. 173.
42. Léon Bourgeois, *La Solidarité*, p. 21.
43. Stephen Lukes has remarked upon the similarity between the *Ecole normale supérieure*, where both Durkheim and Jaurès were educated, and Jowett's Balliol, where the first generation of the administrative civil service was formed under the influence of T. H. Green (Stephen Lukes, *Emile Durkheim*, p. 45). Cf. also Melvin Richter, *The Politics of Conscience*, p. 283 ff. Fritz Ringer described the contempt of German intellectuals for Manchesterite ideas in *Max Weber and the Decline of the German Mandarins*.
44. Darlu also wrote "Solidarité et Morale Personelle" for a collection, by Léon Bourgeois and Alfred Croiset, *Essai d'une Philosophie de la Solidarité*. "Solidarité" appears on pp. 121–61 of that work.
45. Durkheim, *Division*, pp. 10ff. In 1898 legislation was extended to *sociétés de secours mutuelles* the organizing rights granted trade unions in 1884. Zeldin, *France 1848–1945*, vol. 1, p. 661.
46. Ibid., p. 671. I doubt whether the solidarists had drastic change in mind: They believed themselves to be advancing unexceptionable improvements, not revolutionizing society. It should be said, however, in praise of Zeldin, that in noting their achievements at all, he takes them more seriously than most commentators have been inclined to do.
47. In the party designation *Radical socialiste*, "socialist" qualifies "radical," not the reverse, as the conventional English translation would suggest. The process by which prewar solidarists became "socialist radicals" was not unlike the metamorphosis undergone in Britain by left Liberals who turned Labourite, convinced of the increasing salience of economic barriers to equality among citizens.
48. Durkheim, *Elementary Forms*, p. 478.
49. Emile Durkheim, "The Determination of Moral Facts," *Sociology and Philosophy*, p. 52. Here again I take issue with Zeldin, who has written that the radicals differed from traditionalists only on the "metaphysical" (and therefore empty?) question of the origin of morality. The content of their ethics he finds essentially similar. It is true that neither advocated murder, thievery, or the breaking of promises; but was it trivial that *laïcs* held moral codes to be human creations, and thus fallible and corrigible? Furthermore, the "metaphysical" differences are accepted as trivial only in the radicals' formu-

lation. Catholics would not have been ready to include revelation among the *adiaphora*.

50. In this spirit he noted with approval the much-derided Jacobin attempts to establish a cycle of revolutionary holidays: "Everything leads us to believe that [the work] will be taken up again sooner or later." He was unembarrassed, too, by the letter of the law and suspicious of moralities of intention. Indeed, his most fundamental anthropological insight – that the categories of sacred and profane are the first classification because they preserve the integrity of the social group (Durkheim, *Elementary Forms*, pp. 52–63) cannot but evoke the *Havdalah* ceremony at the end of the Sabbath. *Havdalah* means separation or division. The prayer recites the antithesis between holy things and all others (here, as for Durkheim, the profane is a residual category), between the Sabbath and the days of the week, between light and darkness, between Israel and other peoples.

51. Emile Durkheim, "Address to the Lycéens of Sens," *Emile Durkheim on Morality and Society*, p. 28.

52. Ibid., p. xvii, in the fine introduction by Robert Bellah, editor of the volume.

53. Durkheim emphasized in *The Division of Labor* that society was attractive as well as coercive (Durkheim, *Division*, p. 15) and in "The Determination of Moral Facts" that "duty does not exhaust the concept of morality. . . . For us to become the agents of an act it must interest our sensibility to a certain extent and appear to us as, in some way, *desirable*" (Durkheim, *Sociology*, p. 36).

54. Ibid., *Division*, p. 32. In *Suicide* Durkheim persisted, "Only the enemies of reason could rejoice . . . if this segment of reality [society] which alone has so far denied or defied [the human mind] should escape it even temporarily." Emile Durkheim, *Suicide*, p. 36.

55. Steven Lukes, *Emile Durkheim*, p. 75.

56. Durkheim, *Division*, pp. 36 and 52. As he refused to admit that a distinction between facts and values prevents science from informing choice, so he exploded the means–ends dichotomy invoked to limit scientific advice to exclusively technical questions. "Every means is from another point of view, an end. . . . There are always several routes that lead to a given goal, a choice must therefore be made between them. If science cannot indicate the best goal to us, how can it inform us about the best means to reach it? Why should it recommend the most rapid in preference to the most economical, the surest rather than the simplest, or vice versa? If science cannot guide us in the determination of ultimate ends, it is equally powerless in the case of those secondary and subordinate ends called means." Emile Durkheim, *The Rules of Sociological Method*, p. 48.

57. Ibid., *Professional Ethics and Civic Morals*, p. 11.

58. He saw no need to deny that "ethics may have some transcendental basis beyond experience" (Durkheim, *The Division of Labor*, p. 33). That question he willingly consigned to "metaphysicians." He held, with all secular democrats, that revelation, however precious to the individual or sect vouchsafed it, could not claim public authority.

59. Ibid., *Division*, p. 33.

60. Ibid., p. 35.

61. Ibid., p. 34; ibid.; *The Elementary Forms*, p. 470.

62. Ibid., pp. 26–9.

63. Talcott Parsons has noted that the idea of introjection or internalization

was also common to both men. (Talcott Parsons, *The Structure of Social Action*, Vol. I, pp. 386–8.) In reply to early criticism of the "collective conscience," Durkheim made plain, "we of course do not at all intend to hypostasize the collective conscience. We do not recognize any more substantial a soul in society than we do in the individual." Durkheim, *Suicide*, p. 51.

64. Ibid., *Division*, pp. 100–1.
65. Ibid., "Individual and Collective Representations," *Sociology and Philosophy*, p. 34.
66. Ibid., *The Elementary Forms*, p. 240; "Determination," p. 59.
67. This term, which strikes some as infelicitously sociological, has fine revolutionary roots. Restif de la Bretonne accounted thus for the flight of the first émigrés, "On craint l'effervescence." Restif de la Bretonne, *Les Nuits revolutionnaires*, p. 74.
68. Ibid., *The Elementary Forms*, p. 471.
69. Ibid., p. 241.
70. Ibid., p. 246.
71. Ibid., *Professional Ethics*, pp. 211–13.
72. Ibid., p. 69.
73. Durkheim, unlike Mussolini, assumed that labor and capital would have conflicting interests and proposed, accordingly, separate institutions for each, rather than one vertically integrated body for each industry or sector. Ibid., *Division*, p. 6.
74. There follows a remarkable elaboration of the relations between the conscious and unconscious mind that is reminiscent of Freud's injunction, "Where Id was, Ego shall be": "In the centre of our consciousness there is an inner circle upon which we attempt to concentrate light." Ibid., *Professional Ethics*, p. 65; pp. 80–1.
75. Ibid., p. 220.
76. Ibid., p. 68.
77. Georges Sorel, *Reflections on Violence*, p. 32.
78. Matthew Arnold, "The Popular Education of France," *Democratic Education*, p. 11.
79. Ibid., pp. 9–10.

Bibliography

Books, articles, and speeches

Acomb, Evelyn Martha, *The French Laic Laws - 1879-1889*, Columbia University Press, New York, 1941.

Agulhon, Maurice, *Le Cercle dans la France bourgeoise, 1810-1848, Etude d'une mutation de sociabilité*, Librairie Armand Colin, Paris, 1977.

Alain (pseudonym of Emile Chartier), *Eléments d'une doctrine radicale*, Gallimard, Paris, 1923.

Alfaric, Prosper, *Jean Macé, fondateur de la Ligue française de l'enseignement*, Le Cercle parisien de la Ligue française de l'enseignement, Paris, 1955.

Andrieux, Louis, *La Commune à Lyon en 1870 et 1871*, Perrin et Cie, Paris, 1906.

Anonymous, *Le Catéchisme de la morale universelle destiné à la jeunesse de tous les pays par une mère*, Au bureau de la morale indépendante, Bibliothèque Nationale R43221, Paris, 1868.

Arnold, Matthew, "The Popular Education of France," *Democratic Education, The Complete Prose Works of Matthew Arnold*, vol. 2, R.H. Super (ed.), The University of Michigan Press, Ann Arbor, 1962, pp. 3-165.

Balzac, Honoré de, *Lost Illusions*, Ellen Manning (trans.), Dana Estes and Company, Boston, 1901.

Le Médecin de campagne, Garnier-Flammarion, Paris, 1965.

Barodet, Désiré, *Eclaircissements historiques* (privately printed? Lyon?), 1898.

Barral, Pierre, *Les Fondateurs de la Troisième République*, Collections U, Armand Colin, Paris, 1968.

Bennet, Jean. *Quand Napoléon III nommait les présidents des sociétés de secours mutuelles*, Société régionale d'imprimerie et de publicité, Estampes, 1959.

Benoit-Lévy, E., and F.-B. Bocande, *Manuel pratique pour l'application de la loi sur l'instruction obligatoire*, Cerf, Paris, 1882.

Bert, Paul, *L'Enseignement laïque*, Bibliothèque pédagogique, Paris, 1880.

L'enseignement secondaire des jeunes filles, Chambre des Députés, Deuxième législature, vol. 15, no. 1036, 1878-1879.

Rapport sur la gratuité, Chambre des Députés, vol. 38, no. 2605, 1880.

Rapport sur l'obligation, Chambre des Députés, vol. 38, no. 2606, 1880.

Bigot, Charles, *Les Classes dirigeantes*, G. Charpentier, Paris, second ed., 1881.

Bloch, Marc, *Feudal Society*, L. A. Manyon (trans.), Phoenix Books, University of Chicago Press, Chicago, 1964.

Boivin, Marcel, "Les Origines de la Ligue de l'enseignement en Seine-Inférieure, 1866-1871," *Revue d'histoire économique et sociale*, 46, no. 2, 1968, 203-31.

Bourdieu, Pierre, and J. C. Passeron, *Les Héritiers, les étudiants et la culture*, Editions de minuit, Paris, 1964.

Bourgeois, Léon, and Alfred Croiset, *Essai d'une philosophie de la Solidarité*, Félix Alcan, Paris, second ed., 1907.

La Solidarité, Librarie Armand Colin, Paris, third ed., 1902.

Briggs, Asa, *The Making of Modern England, 1783-1867*, Harper Torchbooks, New York, 1959.

Bibliography

Brogan, Denis W., *The Development of Modern France*, Hamish Hamilton, London, 1940.

Buret, Eugène, *De la misère des classes laborieuses en France et en Angleterre*, Paulin, Paris, 1840.

Burke, Edmund, *Reflections on the Revolution in France*, J. M. Dent Sons, Ltd., London, 1969.

Bury, J. B., *History of the Papacy in the Nineteenth Century*, Schocken Books, New York, 1963.

Bury, J. P. T., *Gambetta and the National defence: A Republican Dictatorship*, Longmans, Green and Co., New York, 1936.

Challe, A., "L'Histoire des guerres du calvinisme et de la Ligue," *Bulletin de la Société des sciences d. l'Yonne* (called also *Bulletin des sciences historiques et naturelles de l'Yonne*), 1864.

Chatelain, Abel, "La Ligue de l'enseignement et l'éducation populaire en Bourgogne au début de la Troisième République," *Annales de Bourgogne*, vol. 27, 1955, pp. 104–14.

Clamageran, J.-J., *La France républicaine*, Librairie Germer Baillière, Paris, 1873.

Clemenceau, Georges, *American Reconstruction, 1865–1870*, Fernand Baldensperger (coll. and ed.), The Dial Press, 1928.

Cobb, Richard, *A Second Identity, Essays on France and French History*, Oxford University Press, New York, 1969.

Commissaire, Sébastien, *Mémoires et souvenirs*, Garcet et Nisius, Paris, 1888.

Compayre, Gabriel, *Jean Macé et l'instruction obligatoire*, Librairie Paul Delaplane, Paris, n.d.

Condorcet, *Rapport et projet du décret sur l'organisation générale de l'instruction publique*, L'Imprimerie nationale, Paris, 1792.

Corbon, Anthime, *Le Secret du peuple de Paris*, Pagnerre, Paris, 1863.

Darimon, Alfred, *L'Histoire d'un parti, Le Cinq sous l'Empire*, E. Dentu, Paris, 1885.

Delescluze, Charles, *Aux Habitants des campagnes*, Association typographique, Lyon, 1870.

Delord, Taxile, *Histoire du Second Empire*, Germer Baillière, Libraire-Editeur, Paris, 1869–75.

Deraismes, Maria, *Une lettre au clergé français*, E. Dentu, Paris, 1879.

Dessoye, A., *Jean Macé et la fondation de la ligue de l'enseignement*, C. Marpon et E. Flammarion, Paris, 1883.

Dolléans Edouard, *L'Histoire du mouvement ouvrier 1830–1871*, Librairie Armand Colin, Paris, 1953.

Dommanget, Maurice, *Blanqui et l'opposition révolutionnaire à la fin du Second Empire*, Librairie Armand Colin, Paris, 1960.

Dunham, Arthur Louis, *The Anglo-French Treaty of Commerce of 1860 and the Progress of the Industrial Revolution in France*, University of Michigan Press, Ann Arbor, 1930.

Dupanloup, Félix, *L'Athéisme et le péril social*, Claude Douniol, Paris, 1866.
  La Femme chrétienne et française, Claude Douniol, Paris, 1868.

Dupin, Jacques, "Le Mouvement ouvrier à Auxerre, 1870–1880," manuscript in the Archives départementales de l'Yonne.

Durkheim, Emile, *The Division of Labor in Society*, George Simpson (trans.), Free Press of Glencoe, Glencoe, Ill., 1933.
  The Elementary Forms of Religious Life, Joseph Ward Swain (trans.), The Free Press, New York, 1965.

Bibliography

Emile Durkheim on Morality and Society, Robert Bellah (ed.), The University of Chicago Press, Chicago, 1973.

Moral Education, E. K. Wilson and H. Schnurer (trans.), The Free Press, New York, 1961.

Professional Ethics and Civic Morals, Cornelia Brookfield (trans.), Routledge & Kegan Paul, London, 1957.

The Rules of Sociological Method, George E. G. Catlin (ed.), The Free Press, New York, 1938.

Sociology and Philosophy, D. F. Pocock (trans.), Cohen and West, Ltd., London, 1953.

Suicide, George Simpson (ed.), The Free Press, New York, 1951.

Duruy, Victor, *L'Administration de l'Instruction Publique de 1863 à 1869*, Imprimerie de Jules Delalain, Paris, n.d.

Notes et souvenirs, 1811–1894, 2 vols., Librairie Hachette, Paris, 1901.

Duveau, Georges, *Les Instituteurs*, Editions de Seuil, Paris, 1957.

La Pensée ouvrière sur l'éducation pendant la Seconde République et le Second Empire, Domat, Paris, 1948.

La Vie ouvrière en France sous le Second Empire, Gallimard, Paris, 1946.

Eisenstein, Elizabeth, "The Evolution of the Jacobin Tradition in France: The Survival and Revival of the Ethos of 1793 under the Bourbon and Orleanist Regimes." Unpublished doctoral dissertation, Radcliffe College, 1952.

Elwitt, Sanford J., *The Making of the Third Republic, Class and Politics in France, 1868–1884*, University of Louisiana Press, Baton Rouge, 1975.

Erckmann-Chatrian (Emile Erckmann and Alexandre Chatrian), *Contes et romans nationaux*, Jean-Jacques Pauvert et la Librairie Hachette, Paris, 1962.

Ferry, Jules, *Les Comptes fantaisiques (sic) de Haussmann*, Armand LeChevalier, Paris, 1868.

Discours et opinions de Jules Ferry, Paul Robiquet (ed.), Armand Colin, Paris, 1893.

"Discours prononcé à la Réunion de la gauche républicaine" (March 19, 1876), Imprimerie de Debuisson et Cie, Paris, 1876.

"L'Egalite d'éducation," Salle Molière, April 10, 1870. Reprinted by the Société pour l'instruction élémentaire, Paris, n.d.

Les Luttes électorales en 1863, E. Dentu, Paris, 1863.

Flaubert, Gustave, *Oeuvres*, 2 vols., Bibliothèque de la Pléiade, Gallimard, Paris, 1951-2.

Fleury, Michel, and Pierre Valmary, "Le progrès d'instruction élémentaire de Louis XIV à Napoléon III après l'enquête de Louis Maggiolo, 1877-9," *Population* 12, no. 1 (January–March 1957): 71–92.

Fohlen, Charles, *L'Industrie textile au temps du Second Empire*, Librairie Plon, Paris, 1956.

Foner, Eric. *Free Soil, Free Labor, Free Men: The Ideology of the Republican Party before the Civil War*, Oxford University Press, New York, 1970.

Fustel de Coulanges, Numa Denis, *The Ancient City*, Doubleday Anchor Books, Garden City, N.Y., 1956.

Gerbod, Paul, *La Condition universitaire en France au XIXᵉ siècle*, Presses Universitaires de France, Paris, 1965.

Girard, Louis, with Antoine Prost and R. Gossez, *Les Conseilleurs-Généraux en 1870*, Presses Universitaires de France, Paris, 1967.

Les Elections de 1869, Marcel Rivière et Cie, Paris, 1960.

Goblot, Edmond, *La Barrière et le niveau: étude sociologique sur la bourgeoisie française moderne*, Félix Alcan, Paris, 1925.

Gouault, Jacques, *Comment la France est devenue républicaine, Cahiers de la Fondation nationale de sciences politiques*, vol. 62, Librairie Armand Colin, Paris, 1954.

Greenberg, Louis Morris, *Sisters of Liberty, Marseille, Lyon, Paris and the Reaction to a Centralized State, 1868–1871*, Harvard University Press, Cambridge, Mass., 1971.

Guépin, Ange, *Avis aux électeurs de la Loire-Inférieure*, Imprimerie de L. Guérard, Nantes, n.d., c. 1848.

   Esquisse d'une philosophie maçonnique, Imprimerie de L. Toinon et Cie, Paris, 1868.

   Evénéments de Nantes, Imprimerie de Burolleau et Cie, Nantes, n.d., c. 1830.

   Philosophie du XIXe siècle, Gustave Sandré, Paris, 1854.

   Philosophie du socialisme, ou Etudes sur les transformations dans le monde et l'humanité, Gustave Sandré, Paris, 1850.

   Projet de rituel d'initiation au second grade, Imprimerie de (sic) Eliambre et Plédran, Nantes, 1869.

   Royalistes et républicains, Imprimerie de L. Guérard, Nantes, n.d., c. 1848.

   Traité d'économie sociale, Bibliothèque populaire, Paris, 1833.

Guizot, François, *Mémoires pour servir à l'histoire de mon temps*, vol. 3, Michel Lévy Frères, Paris, 1860.

Halévy, Daniel, *La Fin des Notables*, Bernard Grasset, Paris, 1930.

   La République des ducs, Bernard Grasset, Paris, 1937.

Halévy, Elie, *Thomas Hodgskin*, Société nouvelle de libraire et d'edition, Paris, 1903.

Hazard, Paul, *Michelet, Quinet, et Mickiewicz et la vie intérieure du Collège de France de 1838 à 1852*, Presses Universitaires de France, Paris, 1938.

Headings, Mildred J., *French Freemasonry under the Third Republic*, Johns Hopkins University Studies in Historical and Political Science, Series 66, no. 1, 1949.

Henry, Pierre, *Histoire des préfets*, Nouvelles Editions Latines, Paris, 1950.

Higonnet, Patrice L.-R., *Pont-de-Montvert*, Harvard University Press, Cambridge, Mass., 1971.

Hippeau, Célestin, *L'Instruction publique aux Etats-Unis, Rapport adressé au Ministre de l'Instruction Publique*, Didier et Cie, Paris, 1872.

Hirschman, Albert O., "The Changing Tolerance for Income Inequality in the Course of Economic Development," *The Quarterly Journal of Economics*, 87 (November 1973).

Hobsbawm, Eric J., *Primitive Rebels*, W. W. Norton and Company, Inc., New York, 1959.

Jaurès, Jean, "Le Bilan sociale du XIXe siècle," introduction to *La Troisième République*, Jules Rouff et Cie, Paris, 1908?

   "Le Socialisme et le radicalisme en 1885," introduction to *Discours parlementaires*, vol. 1, Edouard Cornély et Cie, Paris, 1904.

Jourdain, Charles, *Le Budget des cultes*, Librairie Hachette, Paris, 1859.

Kaplan, Edward K., *Michelet's Poetic Vision, A Romantic Theory of Nature, Men and Women*, University of Massachusetts Press, Amherst, 1977.

Katz, Jacob, *Jews and Freemasons in Europe, 1723–1939*, Harvard University Press, Cambridge, Mass., 1970.

Kayser, Jacques, *Les Grandes Batailles du radicalisme*, Marcel Rivière et Cie, Paris, 1962.

Laboulaye, Edouard, *L'Etat et ses limites*, Charpentier, Libraire-Editeur, Paris, 1863.

225

Le Parti libéral, son programme et son avenir, Charpentier, Libraire-Editeur, Paris, 1863.

Labusquière, John, *La Troisième République, 1871–1900, Histoire Socialiste,* Jean Jaurès (ed.), Jules Rouff et Cie, Paris, 1908?

Lacombe, Charles de, *Berryer sous la République et le Second Empire, Vie de Berryer,* vol. 3, Librairie Firman-Didot et Cie., Paris, 1895.

Lachapelle, Paul, "Le Cercle parisien et la Ligue française de l'enseignement," *Cahiers laïques,* nos. 4–48 (1958). 81–128.

Lavertujon, André, *Gambetta inconnu,* Gounouilhou, Bordeaux, 1905.

Lefebvre, Georges, *The Coming of the French Revolution,* R. R. Palmer (trans.), Princeton University Press, Princeton, 1947.

Lefrançais, Gustave, *Souvenirs d'un révolutionnaire,* Imprimerie Charles Hautstont, Brussels, 1902.

Legrand, Louis, *L'Influence du positivisme dans l'oeuvre scolaire de Jules Ferry,* Marcel Rivière et Cie, Paris, 1961.

Legrand, Louis-Désiré, *Le Mariage et les Moeurs en France,* Librairie Hachette, Paris, 1879.

Lévy, A., "A propos du coup d'état de 1851 dans l'Yonne," *Annales de Bourgogne,* 25 (1953): 185–93.

Lhomme, Jean, *La Grande bourgeoisie au pouvoir, 1830–1880,* Presses Universitaires de France, Paris, 1960.

Littré, Emile, *Par quelle conduite la République française peut-elle consolider le succès qu'elle a obtenu?,* third ed., Charavay Frères, Paris, 1879.

Lovett, Clara, *Giuseppe Ferrari and the Italian Revolution,* University of North Carolina Press, Chapel Hill, 1979.

Lukes, Steven, *Emile Durkheim,* Allen Lane, London, 1973.

Macé, Jean, *L'Arc de triomphe,* Imprimerie de A. René, Paris, 1848.

L'Arithmétique du Grand-papa, Histoire de deux petits marchands de pommes, fifteenth ed., Bibliothèque d'éducation et de récréation, J. Hetzel et Cie, Paris, n.d.

"A cercles catholiques, les sociétés républicaines," *Les Idées de Jean François,* vol. 8, Imprimerie H. LeVasseur, Laon, 1874. Reprinted by Bibliothèque démocratique, Paris, 1877.

"Conférence sur les sociétiés républicaines d'instruction, faite à Pontivy," December 19, 1878, Librairie centrale des publications populaires, Paris, 1879.

"La Délibération au groupe havrais," February 1870, extrait du cinquième bulletin en préparation, reprinted by Imprimerie de Dubusson, Paris, 1876.

L'Ennemi, Bibliothèque républicaine, Paris, 1880.

L'Histoire d'une bouchée de pain, forty-sixth ed., Hetzel et Cie, Paris, n.d. (first published by E. Dentu, Paris, 1861).

Les Idées de Jean-François, vols. 1–8, "Bibliothèque à trois sous," E. Vauchez, Librairie de la Bibliothèque démocratique, Paris, 1872–6.

Lettre d'un garde national à a son voisin par Jean Moreau, Imprimerie LeNormant, Paris, 1848.

La Morale en action, Le mouvement de propagande intellectuelle en Alsace, J. Hetzel, Paris, 1865.

Les Origines de la Ligue de l'enseignement, 1861–1870, G. Charpentier and E. Fasquelles, Paris, 1891. Also published by Charpentier as *La Ligue de l'enseignement à Beblenheim* in 1900.

Bibliography

Le Petit catéchisme républicain, Garnier Frères, Paris, 1848.

Une Profession de foi d'un communiste, Imprimerie de A. Lacour, Paris, 1848.

Séance de clôture du 4ᵉ congrès de la Ligue de l'enseignement, Imprimerie de Chaix, Paris, 1884.

Théâtre du Petit-Chateau, fourth ed., Hetzel, Paris, 1865.

Les Vertus du Républicain, Furne, Libraire-Editeur, Paris, 1848.

MacHargue, Georgess, *Facts, Frauds, and Phantasms*, Doubleday and Company, Garden City, N.Y. 1972.

Marcilhacy, Christianne, *Le Diocèse d'Orléans sous l'épiscopat de Mgr. Dupanloup*, Henri Plon, Paris, 1962.

Maritch, Sretan, *Histoire du mouvement social sous le Second Empire à Lyon*, Librairie Arthur Rousseau et Cie, Paris, 1930.

Martin du Gard, Roger, *Jean Barois*, Gallimard, Paris, 1921.

Marx, Karl, *Capital*, Foreign Languages Publishing House, Moscow, 1961.

Early Writings, Vintage Books, New York, 1975.

The Eighteenth Brumaire of Louis Napoleon, International Publishers, New York, 1963.

Mathiez, Albert, *La Révolution et l'église; études critiques et documentaires*, Librairie Armand Colin, Paris, 1910.

Maurain, Jean, *La Politique écclésiastique du Second Empire, 1852–1869*, Félix Alcan, Paris, 1930.

Michelet, Jules, *The History of the French Revolution*, Gordon Wright (ed.), University of Chicago Press, Chicago, 1967.

Jeanne d'Arc, Editions Gallimard, Paris, 1974.

Nos Fils, sixth ed., A. LaCroix et Cie, Librairie Internationale, Paris, 1877.

Le Peuple, Julliard, Paris, 1965.

Du Prêtre, de la femme, de la famille, Hachette/Paulin, Paris, 1845.

Mill, J. S., *On the Subjection of Women*, MIT Press. Cambridge, Mass., 1970.

Mismer, Charles, "La Fondation de la Ligue de l'enseignement, Jean Macé et son oeuvre," *Revue bleue*, March 1895.

Moiset, Charles, "Notes sur l'histoire de l'instruction primaire dans le département de l'Yonne depuis 1833," *Annuaire de l'Yonne*, G. Rouillé, Auxerre, 188-.

Montesquieu, Charles Secondat, baron de, *Considerations on the Causes of the Greatness of the Romans and Their Decline*, David Lowenthal (trans.), The Free Press, New York, 1965.

Mun, le comte Albert de, *Le Législation sociale et le régime corporatif, Oeuvre des cercles catholiques des ouvriers* (discours, 7 juin, 1884) T. Levé, Paris, 1884.

Naquet, Alfred, *Religion, Propriété, Famille*, Poupart-Duval, Paris, 1869.

Oberlé, Raymond, *L'Enseignement à Mulhouse de 1789 à 1870*, Publications de la Faculté des Lettres de l'Université de Strasbourg, Paris, 1961.

Olivesi, Antoine, *La Commune de 1871 à Marseilles*, Librairie Marcel Rivière et Cie, Paris, 1950.

Ollé-Laprune, Léon, *Etienne Vacherot 1809–1898*, Perrin et Cie, Paris, 1898.

Ordioni, Pierre, *La Survivance des idées gallicanes et jansénistes en Auxerre de 1760 à nos jours*, Imprimerie moderne, Auxerre, 1933.

Ozouf, Jacques, *Nous les maîtres d'école*, Collections Archives, Julliard, Paris, 1967.

Parsons, Talcott, *The Structure of Social Action*, The Free Press, New York, 1968.

Péguy, Charles, *Notre jeunesse*, Gallimard, Paris, 1957.

Perroux, François, *Prises de vues sur la croissance de l'économie française, 1780–1950*, Income and Wealth, series 5, Bowes and Bowes, London, 1955.

Persigny, Victor Fialan, duc de, *Doctrines de l'Empire*, Henri Plon, Paris, 1865.

Petit, Edouard, *Jean Macé, sa vie et son oeuvre*, Librairie Aristide Quillet, Paris, n.d. (after 1914).

Poisson de la Chabaussière, Auguste-Etienne-Xavier, *Le Catéchisme français*, Puynesge (printers to the department of the Gironde), Bordeaux, An V (1797–1798).

Pommier, J., "Les Idées de Michelet et de Renan sur la confession," *Journal de Psychologie normale et pathologique*, 33rd year nos. 7-8, 15 July-15 October 1936, Félix Alcan, Paris, pp. 514–44.

Popper, Karl, *The Open Society and Its Enemies*, Princeton University Press, Princeton, N.J., 1950.

Prévost-Paradol (Lucien Anatole Prévost called), *La France nouvelle*, Michel Lévy Frères, Librairies-Editeurs, Paris, 1865.

Prost, Antoine, *L'Enseignement en France, 1800–1967*, Collections U, Armand Colin, Paris, 1968.

Proudhon, Pierre-Joseph, *De la Justice dans la révolution et l'église*, Garnier Frères, Paris, 1858.

Quinet, Edgar, *L'Enseignement du peuple, Oeuvres politiques avant l'exil, Oeuvres complètes*, vol. 14, Hachette, Paris, n.d. (first published, 1850).

Les Jésuites, Oeuvres complètes, vol. 2 Hachette, Paris, n.d. (first published, 1843).

La République, les conditions de la régénération de la France, Oeuvres complètes, vol. 26, Hachette, Paris, n.d. (first published by Dentu, Paris, 1872).

Quinet, Mme Edgar (née Hermione Asaki), *Edgar Quinet, Avant l'exil*, Calmann-Levy, Paris, 1888.

Edgar Quinet, Depuis l'exil, Calmann-Levy, Paris, 1889.

Reclus, Maurice, *Jules Ferry*, Flammarion, Paris, 1947.

Le Seize Mai, Librairie-Hachette, Paris, 1931.

Reinach, Joseph, *La Politique opportuniste*, Bibliothèque Charpentier, Paris, 1890.

Rémond, René, *The Right Wing in France from 1815 to de Gaulle*, J. M. Laux (trans.), University of Pennsylvania Press, Philadelphia, 1966.

Renan, Ernest, *La Réforme intellectuelle et morale*, third ed., Michel Lévy Frères, Paris, 1872.

Souvenirs d'enfance et de jeunesse, Calmann-Levy, Paris, 1883.

Restif de la Bretonne, Nicolas-Edmé, *Les Nuits révolutionnaires*, Le Livre de poche, Paris, 1978.

Richter, Melvin, *The Politics of Conscience, T. H. Green and His Age*, Harvard University Press, Cambridge, Mass., 1964.

Ringer, Fritz, *Max Weber and the Decline of the German Mandarins*, Harvard University Press, Cambridge, Mass., 1969.

Robert, Adolphe, *Statistique pour servir à l'histoire du 2 décembre 1851*, Librairie de la Renaissance, Paris, 1869.

Robert, Charles, *Les Améliorations sociales du Second Empire*, vols. 1 and 2, Librairie Hachette, Paris, 1865.

De l'Ignorance, Librairie Hachette, Paris, 1867.

"Les Institutions créées par les chefs d'industrie en faveur de leurs ouvriers," Imprimerie impériale, Paris, 1866.

De l'Instruction obligatoire, Librairie Hachette, Paris, 1871.

Robertson, Priscilla, *Revolutions of 1848*, Harper Torchbooks, New York, 1952.

Rohr, Jean, *Victor Duruy, Ministre de Napoléon III*, Bibliothèque constitutionelle et de science politique, R. Pichon et R. Durard-Auzias, Paris, 1967.

Bibliography

Rothney, John, *Bonapartism after Sedan*, Cornell University Press, Ithaca, N.Y., 1969.

Rouillé, G., "Les Sociétés d'instruction populaire dans l'Yonne," *Annuaire de l'Yonne*, 1880.

Sauvestre, Charles, *Monita secreta societatis Jesu, Instructions secrètes des jesuites*, fourth ed., Dentu, Paris, 1865.

Société républicaine d'instruction d'Issoudun, L'enseignement civique (lecture), Imprimerie de Motte et Gousty, Issoudun, 1880.

Sur les genoux de l'église, Dentu, Paris, 1868.

Sauvestre, Mme Charles, *Guide pratique pour les écoles professionelles des jeunes filles*, Librairie Hachette, Paris, 1868.

Schapiro, Meyer, "Courbet and Popular Imagery: An Essay in Realism and Naïveté," *The Journal of the Warburg and Courtauld Institute*, 4, nos. 3–4 (April–July 1941): 164–91.

Scheurer-Kestner, Auguste, *Souvenirs de jeunesse*, Charpentier, Paris, 1905.

Screech, Michael Andrew, *The Rabelaisian Marriage: Aspects of Rabelais' Religion, Ethics and Comic Philosophy*, Arnold, London, 1958.

Seignobos, Charles, *Le Declin de l'Empire et l'établissement de la Troisième République, Histoire de France Contemporaine*, Ernest Lavisse (ed.), Librairie Hachette, Coulommiers, 1921.

Siegfried, André, *Mes Souvenirs de la Troisième République: Mon père et son temps, Jules Siegfried, 1836–1922*, Editions du Grand Siècle, Paris, 1946.

Siegfried, Jules, "Des Cercles ouvriers à propos des workingmen's clubs en Angleterre," *Bulletin de la Société Industrielle de Mulhouse*, 38 (November 1868).

Simon, Brian, *Studies in the History of Education, 1780–1870*, Lawrence and Wishart, London, 1960.

Simon, Jules, *L'Ecole*, Librairie Internationale, Paris, 1865.

L'Ouvrière, sixth ed., Librairie Hachette, Paris, 1867.

La Politique radicale, third ed., Librairie Internationale, Paris, 1868.

Sorel, Georges, *Reflections on Violence*, T. E. Hulme (trans.), Collier Books, New York, 1950.

Sorlin, Pierre, *Waldeck-Rousseau*, Armand Colin, Paris, 1966.

Spuller, Eugene, "Discours prononcé à la distribution solennelle des prix aux élèves des deux sexes," August 18, 1878, *Ecoles libres, laïques, gratuites du IIIe arrondissement*, Paris.

Figures disparues, Félix Alcan, Paris, 1886.

Stearns, Peter, *Paths to Authority, The Middle Class and Industrial Labor Force, 1820–1848*, University of Illinois, Chicago, 1978.

Stendhal, *Lucien Leuwen*, Editions de la revue blanche, Paris, 1901.

Sutherland, Gillian, *Policy-Making in Elementary Education, 1870–1895*, Oxford University Press, 1973.

Taine, Hippolyte, *Notes sur l'Angleterre*, Librairie Hachette, Paris, 1872.

Talbott, John E., *The Politics of Educational Reform in France, 1918 – 1940*, Princeton University Press, Princeton, 1969.

Talmon, Jacob Leib, *The Origins of Totalitarian Democracy*, Secker and Warburg, London, 1952.

Talmy, Robert, *L'Association catholique des patrons du Nord, 1884–1895*, Imprimerie Morel et Condurant, Lille, 1959.

Tchernoff, I., "Les candidatures ouvrières," *La Revue socialiste*, Paris, 1906.

Bibliography

"L'Extrême gauche socialiste-révolutionnaire en 1870–1871," Bureau de l'Action nationale, Paris, 1918.

Le Parti républicain au coup d'état et sous le Second Empire, A. Pedone, Paris, 1906.

Ténot, Eugène, *Paris en décembre 1851*, Armand Le Chevalier, Paris, 1868.

La Province en décembre 1851, Armand LeChevalier, Paris, 1868.

Ténot, Eugène, and Antonin Dubost, *Des Suspectes en 1858, étude historique sur l'application de la loi de sûreté générale*, Armand LeChevalier, Paris, 1869.

Thomas, Albert, *Le Second Empire, Histoire Socialiste*, Jean Jaurès (ed.), Jules Rouff et Cie, Paris, 1908.

Thomas, Edith, *The Women Incendiaries*, James and Starr Atkinson (trans.), George Braziller, New York, 1966.

Thompson, James Westfall, *The Wars of Religion in France, 1559–76*, Frederick Ungar Publishing Company, New York, 1909.

Tisserand, L. M., *Léopold Javal, Député de l'Yonne, 1804–72*, Imprimerie Gustave Perriquet, Auxerre, 1873.

Tocqueville, Alexis de, *Democracy in America*, Vintage Books, New York, 1945.

The Old Regime and The French Revolution, Doubleday Anchor Books, Garden City, N.Y., 1955.

Souvenirs, Oeuvres complètes, vol. 12, Gallimard, Paris, 1964.

Tolain, Henri, *L'Internationale*, Dentu, Paris, 1872.

Trotabas, J.-B., *La Notion de laïcité dans le droit de l'Eglise catholique et de l'Etat républicain*, La Pensée universitaire, Aix-en-Provence, 1959.

Ullman, Joan Connelly, *The Tragic Week, A Study of Anticlericalism in Spain 1875–1912*, Harvard University Press, Cambridge, Mass., 1969.

Vacherot, Etienne, *La Démocratie*, F. Chamerot, Paris, 1860.

Vallès, Jules, *L'Enfant*, Garnier-Flammarion, Paris, 1968.

Vauchez, Emmanuel, *L'Education morale*, Ancienne imprimerie Veuve-Enard, Saint-Claude, 1895.

Manuel d'instruction nationale, Librairie Hachette, Paris, 1885.

Messieurs de Loyola, Ancienne imprimerie Veuve-Enard, Saint-Claude, 1895.

Vermorel, Auguste, *Les Hommes de 1848*, Décembre-Allonier, Paris, 1869.

Wahl, Nicholas, "The French Political System," in Samuel Beer and Adam Ulam (eds.), *Patterns of Government*, Random House, New York, 1958.

Walras, Leon, *Les Associations populaires de consommation, de production, et de crédit*, Dentu, Paris, 1865.

L'Economie politique et la justice, Librairie de Gillaumin et Cie, Paris, 1860.

Watson, D. R., "The Politics of Educational Reform in France during the Third Republic, 1900–1940," *Past and Present*, no. 34 (July 1966): 79–99.

Weber, Eugen, *Peasants into Frenchmen*, Stanford University Press, Stanford, 1976.

Weber, Max, "The Social Psychology of the World Religions," in *From Max Weber: Essays in Sociology*, H. H. Gerth and C. Wright Mills (eds.), Oxford University Press, Oxford, 1946, pp. 267–301.

Weill, Georges, *Histoire du catholicisme libéral en France, 1828–1908*, Félix Alcan, Paris, 1909.

Histoire de l'idée laïque en France au XIXe siècle, Félix Alcan, Paris, 1929.

Histoire du parti républicain en France, 1814–1870, Félix Alcan, Paris, 1900.

Woloch, Isser, *The Jacobin Legacy, the Democratic Movement under the Directory*, Princeton University Press, Princeton, 1970.

Zeldin, Theodore, *Conflicts in French Society; Anticlericalism, Education and Morals in the Nineteenth Century*, Allen and Unwin, London, 1970.

Bibliography

Emile Ollivier and the Liberal Empire of Napoléon III, Clarendon Press, Oxford, 1963.

France 1848–1945, vol. 1, *Ambition, Love and Politics*, and vol. 2, *Intellect, Taste and Anxiety*, Clarendon Press, Oxford, 1973–1977.

The Political System of Napoleon III, Macmillan, London, 1958.

Periodicals

L'Action maçonnique, Paris, 1867–9

Bulletin de l'Instruction primaire au département de l'Yonne, Auxerre.

Bulletin de la Ligue de l'enseignement, I, *Comptes-rendus, travaux du cercle parisien*, Imprimerie Nouvelle, Paris, 1868–77. (In 1881, the *Comptes-rendus* of the Cercle parisien were transformed into the *Bulletin de la Ligue française de l'enseignement.*)

Bulletin de la Ligue de l'enseignement, II, *Comptes-rendus du Cercle parisien*, A. Chaix et Cie, Paris, 1878–80.

Bulletin de la Ligue française de l'enseignement, vol. I, Aux bureau de la ligue française de l'enseignement, Paris, 1881–5.

Bulletin du mouvement d'enseignement par l'initiative privee, no. 1, Beblenheim (Haut-Rhin), May 15, 1868.

Bulletin de la Société Industrielle de Mulhouse, Mulhouse, 1826–70.

Bulletin de la Société pour la propagation de l'instruction populaire, Auxerre.

Journal d'Education populaire, Société d'instruction élémentaire, Paris.

Le Magasin pittoresque, Paris, 1833–70.

Le Monde maçonnique, Paris, 1867–69.

Archives

NATIONAL ARCHIVES

Series AP: Private papers
    49AP. Papiers Charles Floquet
Series BB^{18}: General correspondence of the Ministry of Justice, criminal division
    BB^{18} 1788. Dijon-Lyon, concerning legislative elections of 1869
    BB^{18} 1793. Riom-Toulouse, elections of 1869
Series C; *Procès-verbaux* of National Assemblies
    C 3448. Elections 1871–6, A–Bouches-du-Rhône
    C 3449. Elections 1871–6, Charente-Inférieure
    C 3451. Elections 1871–6, Gironde-Loire
    C 3455. Elections 1871–6, Seine-Seine-Inférieure
    C 3476. Elections 1877, Aude-Calvados (Series C 3474–3500, 1877)
    C 3477. Elections 1877, Cantal-Charente-Inférieure
    C 3478. Elections 1877, Côte d'or
    C 3490. Elections 1877, Morbihan
    C 3497. Elections 1877, Seine-Inférieure
Series F^{1C} III: "Esprit Public et élections"
    F^{1C} III. Aisne 7
    F^{1C} III. Seine-Inférieure 6
Series F^7: *Police générale*, from the Archives of the Ministry of the Interior
    F^7 12682 to F^7 12684 "16 mai"

Series F[17]: Archives of the Ministry of Public Instruction

F[17] 2655. Options of *conseils généraux, conseils d'arrondissements,* 1871–2

F[17] 2676. The Ligue de l'enseignement, press clippings

F[17] 2677. *Conseil supérieur et commissions,* late 1860s

F[17] 2682. *Diverses,* elections 1861–9

F[17] 9173. Laicizations, brought before the *conseil d'état,* Lyon

F[17] 9174. Laicizations, Toulouse and others

F[17] 9175. Laicizations, Toulon, Perpignan, and others

F[17] 12448. "Affaires contentieuses"

F[17] 12525. Rectors' replies to the circular of December 24, 1873.

F[17] 12526. Prefects' reports to the circular of December 24, 1873, *très confidentielle;* and "tentatives diverses."

F[17] 12527. "Tentatives diverses en faveur de l'instruction primaire," dossier of the Ligue de l'enseignement

F[17] 12528. "Tentatives diverses," Paris

F[17] 12529. "Tentatives diverses," Third Arrondissement, Paris

F[17] 12530. "Tentatives diverses," Paris

F[17] 12531. "Tentatives diverses, *Société d'instruction élémentaire*

F[17] 12532. "Tentatives diverses," Paris

F[17] 12533. "Tentatives diverses," *Oeuvres des apprentis et des jeunes ouvriers*

F[17] 12534. "Tentatives diverses," *Société Fénélon, Oeuvres des Faubourgs*

F[17] 12335. "Tentatives diverses," Paris

F[17] 12536–12537. "Tentatives diverses," Paris

F[17] 12538. *Des initiatives diverses en faveur de l'instruction primaire* (departments) A –

F[17] 12539. *Des initiatives diverses,* Gironde

F[17] 12540 – 12544. *Des initiatives diverses,* departments

Series F[19]: Archives of the Administration of Cults

F[19] 5606. *Agissements cléricaux,* 1860–9.

F[19] 5610. *Agissements cléricaux,* enquête of 1888 on the episcopacy

NATIONAL LIBRARY

Nouvelles Acquisitions Françaises 16932 (archives of the publishing house of Hetzel)

DEPARTMENTAL ARCHIVES

Bouches-du-Rhône

Series I[T]: Public instruction

I[T] 4/8. Statistics 1868

I[T] 8/1. Laicizations

I[T] 8/2. Laicizations

Series M[6]: Political police

M[6] 61. Reports of freemasons, cooperatives 1853–66

M[6] 88. Charitable associations

M[6] 90. *L'Association phocéenne* 1867–71

M[6] 163. Meetings, popular libraries, 1869

M[6] 164. Internationale, Tardieu on public education

M[6] 309. Secret societies

M⁶ 950–61. Reports (1850–1900) on associations deemed political (in alphabetical order)

M⁶ 2330. Freemasons

M⁶ 3403. Freethinkers 1873–1912

Series O¹ *bis:* Deliberations of the Municipal Council of Marseille

Series V M² 78: *Procès-verbaux*, Municipal Council of Marseille

"Republicans 1869–1871," unclassified carton

Gironde

Fonds du rectorat 51, Academic administration

Series IM: Police reports

    I M 344. Republican and anticlerical demonstrations, 1868

    I M 360. Meetings and demonstrations, 1870–6

Rhône (the archives of the department of the Rhône have been classified and reclassified; cartons may be identified by old or new or red or black code numbers)

Series 4 M: Police

    4M 826/2, 826/4. Various reports, associations, meetings, disturbances

    4M4 505. "Events of 1870–71," by quarter of the city of Lyon

Series T: Public instruction

    T 76^ancien. Society for Primary Education

    T ¹⁶¹ ʳᵒᵘᵍᵉ (T³⁴ ⁿᵒⁱʳ). Report on the administrative council of the "Pères et Mères de Famille"

    T²⁵⁹. Education

    T²⁶⁰. Education

Seine-Maritime (old Seine-Inférieure)

Series M: Police reports

Yonne

    F 173. Papiers Paul Bert

Series II M¹: Elections

    II M¹ 159. General elections, 1863

    II M¹ 175. "Incidents," 1869

    II M¹ 184. Meetings concerning plebiscite, 1870

Series III M¹: Administrative police

    III M¹ 16

    III M¹ 126

    III M¹ 233

    III M¹ 267. Closing of Protestant school

    III M¹ 270. "Marianne," cercle du Commerce

    III M¹ 284. Events following May 16, 1877

    III M¹ 312. Public meetings

Series III M⁴: Associations

    III M⁴ 8–9. Masonic lodges, 1852–61

    III M⁴ 16. Society for Popular Instruction

    III M⁴ 17. Lectures, freethinkers

Series T: Public instruction

    32 T¹. "Gratuité," free public education

    43 T¹. Report on Swiss schools

    78 T⁵⁻⁶. Popular libraries

    81 T². Society for the Propagation of Popular Instruction

    81 T⁴. Courses and lecture series, 1864–76

MUNICIPAL ARCHIVES

Lyon
Series I²: Police, general and political
   I² 43. Political Associations and electoral committees, 1864–8
   I² 44. Plebiscite, 1870
   I² 46 A and B. Clubs and societies, 1849–70; individual dossiers
   I² 56 B. Correspondence of Albert Richard
   I² 61. Newspapers, including *L'Excommunié*

Index

Index

Index

Prévost-Paradol, 12–13, 21, 23–4
Protestant Reformation, 22–3, 27, 95, 112
Protestants, 24, 31, 46–7, 54, 72, 96, 108–9, 128, 159
Proudhon, Pierre-Joseph, 23, 30, 46, 167
public assistance, 25, 121, 134, 146

Quinet, Edgar
on Catholicism, 26–7, 30, 38
on education, 128, 137
events of 1848, 15, 19
social thought, 21, 31, 47
on women, 39, 40–1

rationalism, 5, 35, 37–8, 73, 124–5, 171–3
Renan, Ernest, 31
Renouvier, Charles, 15, 21, 36
Rheims (Marne), 63, 82–3, 149, 159
Ribière, Hippolyte, 98–112, 159, 161
Richard, Albert, 116, 130, 212n44

Sauvestre, Charles, 22, 27, 75, 88, 150
school boards, 64–5, 66, 124, 129–30
Semur (Saône-et-Loire), 103, 142, 154–5, 160
Sens (Yonne), 49, 60, 96, 101, 103–6, 107–8, 111, 117
Siegfried, Jules, 86, 90–2, 159
Simon, Jules
and educational societies, 66–7, 197n112
as minister of public instruction, 64, 87, 127–9, 148, 159, 199n144
politics, 57, 62, 83, 155
writings, 39, 41, 108
sociability, 6, 7, 17, 46, 92, 114, 169
see also, association, voluntary; solidarism
socialism, 10–11, 18, 26, 35, 51, 79, 165, 168
see also, Internationale; workers
Société pour les écoles libres et laïques, 131–4
Société industrielle de Mulhouse, 72–4, 86, 90
Société industrielle de Rheims, 83–4, 159
Société pour l'instruction élémentaire, 43, 63, 64–7, 106, 123, 135, 153, 164

Société d'instruction primaire du Rhône, 61–2, 66, 127–30, 164
Société Saint-Vincent-de-Paul, 58–9, 81
solidarism, 168–70, 174–6
solidarity, 4, 12, 28
Somme, 3, 153–4
strike, right to, 10, 113, 196n93, 207n266
Syllabus of Errors, 18, 54, 154

Taine, Hippolyte, 41, 46–7, 156
teachers
certification of, 16, 66, 120, 127, 139 (see also normal schools)
politicization of, 64, 145, 150–2, 154, 163
social position of, 67, 76, 90, 166–7
trials of, 123, 133–4
Thiers, Adolphe, 2, 9, 24, 58, 103–4, 111, 189n102, 213n65
Tocqueville, Alexis de, 1, 4, 8, 12–3, 23–4, 28–9, 63, 169
toleration, 74, 76, 83, 87, 117, 125, 145
Toulon (Var), 139–40, 149
Toulouse (Haute-Garonne), 143

Vacherot, Etienne, 21–2, 34, 38, 41, 47, 57, 87
Vauchez, Emmanuel, 147–8, 165
Veuillot, Louis, 26
Vichy (Allier), 141–2
Vichy government, 32, 93

Women, 3, 6, 18, 38–46, 67, 91
see also education, of women
Workers
associations of, 59, 75, 88–92, 112, 155
education of 67–8, 71, 72–4
factory labor, 5, 20–1, 32
politics, 3, 11, 14, 18, 20, 31, 35–7, 64, 167–9
see also Internationale; socialism; solidarism; strike

Yonne, 45, 61, 95–112, 159

Zeldin,Theodore, 1, 7–10, 43–4, 57, 169–70
Zola, Emile, 18